Rivalry and the Disruption of Order in Molière's Theater

Rivalry and the Disruption of Order in Molière's Theater

Michael S. Koppisch

Madison • Teaneck
Fairleigh Dickinson University Press

Associated University Presses
2010 Eastpark Boulevard
Cranbury, NJ 08512

The paper used in this publication meets the requirements of the American National Standard for Permanence of Paper for Printed Library Materials Z39.48-1984.

Cataloging-in-Publication Data
is on file with the Library of Congress.

For Paula

Contents

Acknowledgments

I AM GRATEFUL TO MY TEACHERS RENÉ GIRARD, LIONEL GOSSMAN, AND the late Nathan Edelman for all they did to set me on the path I have followed since my years in school. Each in his own way taught me invaluable lessons that have remained with me throughout my career.

It has been important for me to know that I could always rely upon my friends A. C. Goodson, Louise Horowitz, and David Rubin for their conversation and good counsel. I owe a special debt to Frieda S. Brown. Since we became colleagues in 1970, she has supported me, encouraged me, and, above all, led me to do better. Her friendship has extended to reading and editing much of what I have written, including the present volume. Whatever merit my work may have is due in large part to her efforts. Its flaws, of course, are all mine.

I have benefited greatly from the good work of Dawn Martin, who prepared the index, and the kindness and professionalism of the entire staff of Associated University Presses.

I dedicate this book to Paula. Her love sustains me.

I acknowledge with thanks permission to include here material, in modified form, from the following of my essays on Molière:

"'Partout la jalousie est un monstre odieux': Love and Jealousy in *Dom Garcie de Navarre*." *Papers on French Seventeenth Century Literature* 12 (1985): 461–79.

"Dom Juan's Equal Opportunity Rivalry." *Papers on French Seventeenth Century Literature* 53 (2000): 385–92.

"The World Turned Upside Down: Desire and Rivalry in *Amphitryon*." In *Homage to Paul Bénichou*, edited by Sylvie Romanowski and Monique Bilezikian, 175–95. Birmingham, Ala.: Summa Publications, Inc., 1994.

"Désordre et sacrifice dans *George Dandin*." *Travaux de Littérature* 9 (1996): 75–86.

"'Til Death Do Them Part: Love, Greed, and Rivalry in Molière's *L'Avare*." *L'Esprit Créateur* 36 (1996): 32–49.

"'Bonne Soupe' or 'Beau Langage': Difference and Sameness in *Les Femmes savantes*." *Stanford French Review* 10 (1986): 281–97.

"Molière et le problème de l'ordre." In *Création et recréation: un dialogue entre littérature et histoire. Mélanges offerts à Marie-Odile Sweetser*, edited by Claire Gaudiani, 135–50. Tübingen: Gunter Narr Verlag, 1993.

Excerpt from AMPHITRYON by Jean Baptiste Poquelin De Molière, translation copyright © 1995, 1994, 1993 by Richard P. Wilbur. Caution: Professionals and amateurs are hereby warned that these translations, being fully protected under the copyright laws of the United States of America, the British Empire, including the Dominion of Canada, and all other countries which are signatories to the Universal Copyright Convention and the International Copyright Union, are subject to royalty. All rights, including professional, amateur, motion picture, recitation, lecturing, public reading, radio broadcasting, and television, are strictly reserved. Particular emphasis is laid on the question of readings, permission for which must be secured from the author's agent in writing. Inquiries on professional rights (except for amateur rights) for AMPHITRYON should be addressed to Mr. Gilbert Parker, William Morris Agency, 1350 Avenue of the Americas, New York, NY 10019. Inquiries on translation rights should be addressed to Harcourt, Inc., Permissions Department, 6277 Sea Harbor Drive, Orlando, FL 32887-6777. The amateur acting rights of this translation are controlled exclusively by The Dramatists Play Service, Inc., 440 Park Avenue South, New York, NY 10016. No amateur performance of the play may be given without obtaining in advance the written permission of the Dramatists Play Service, Inc., and paying the requisite fee.

"Don Juan," "School for Husbands," from *Tartuffe and Other Plays* by Molière, translated by Donald M. Frame, copyright © 1967 by Donald M. Frame. Used by permission of Dutton Signet, a division of Penguin Group (USA) Inc.

"Imaginary Invalid" by Molière, "The Would-Be Gentleman" by Molière, "Miser" by Molière, translated by Donald M. Frame, from *The Misanthrope & Other Plays* by Molière, translated by Donald M. Frame, copyright © 1968 by Donald M. Frame. Used by permission of Dutton Signet, a division of Penguin Group (USA) Inc.

Rivalry and the Disruption of Order in Molière's Theater

Introduction

As I WAS WRITING THE ESSAYS ON MOLIÈRE'S MAJOR PLAYS THAT WOULD become chapters in this book, I always had in the back of my mind Paul Hazard's contrasting portraits of the great seventeenth-century preacher, defender of the faith, and staunch apologist for the monarchy, Jacques-Bénigne Bossuet. On one hand, the bishop of Meaux represents the classical ideal of order in all its splendor. He possesses with absolute certainty the truth on which that order lies and proclaims the "nécessité primordiale de l'ordre"[1] [primordial necessity of order]. Everything about Bossuet attests to his belief in a well-ordered universe:

> On ne voit Bossuet que dans sa majesté souveraine, et tel qu'il apparaît sur la toile de Rigaud. Si c'est une banalité que de rappeler ce portrait somptueux, elle s'excuse parce qu'elle est pour ainsi dire nécessaire: son style, sa pompe, son éclat, ont pour toujours rempli nos yeux. Ou bien nous imaginons l'orateur en train de prononcer quelque discours funèbre: dès les premiers accords, nous nous sentons emportés dans les régions du sublime . . . nous croyons avoir entendu quelque prophète de Dieu, qui n'a jamais vécu que dans le surhumain.[2]

> [Whenever we think of Bossuet, we always behold him in his sovereign majesty, as Rigaud depicted him in his famous portrait. It may be a commonplace to bring in a reference to that magnificent work of art; if so, it is an excusable commonplace, for the simple reason that it is unavoidable. The manner of the thing, its pomp and splendour, once seen, never fade from the recollection. Or again, we may behold the great orator delivering one of his famous funeral panegyrics. From the very opening sentences, we feel as though borne aloft into the realms of the ineffable . . . it is as though we had been listening to some prophet of God, some dweller in a region more than human.]

Seen, however, more toward the end of his career and in the context of a growing number of challenges to established orthodoxy, Bossuet appears in a quite different, less resplendent light. This Bossuet, "humilié, douloureux"[3] [humbled and plunged deep in sorrow], no longer grandly intones and vigorously imposes the truth so much as he guards it and frantically tries to protect it against the onslaught of new ways of thinking. To Paul Hazard, this is the truer image of Bossuet: "il n'est pas le bâtisseur paisible d'une somptueuse cathédrale, bâtie tout entière dans le style Louis XIV: mais, bien plutôt, l'ouvrier qui court, affairé, pressé, pour réparer des brèches chaque jour plus menaçantes"[4] [No imperturbable, untroubled builder, he, of some splendid cathedral in the sumptuous Louis XIV style; no, not that, but much rather a harassed workman, hurrying away, without a moment to lose, to patch up cracks in the edifice that everyday grow more and more alarming]. By fending off threats to the good order of God's universe, Bossuet vindicates his unshakable faith in Him.

Now Molière and Bossuet are hardly kindred spirits. In the *Maximes et réflexions sur la comédie*, Bossuet imagines the comic poet before the gates of heaven hearing the words from St. Luke's version of the Sermon on the Mount: "Malheur à vous qui riez, car vous pleurerez"[5] [Woe betide you who laugh, for you shall cry]. Nonetheless, the religious writer and the comic do share a preoccupation with order that marks seventeenth-century thought, politics, and society. Richelieu, Mazarin, and Louis XIV attempted to unify France under a centralized government that would control every aspect of French life, and to a remarkable extent, they succeeded. Descartes's belief that by properly ordering the powers of the intellect, one can discover the truth and even dominate forces of nature represents a prevalent mode of thought in the Classical period. For religious writers like Bossuet, order has its origin in God rather than human thought or the monarchy, but it manifests itself in a way similar to that foreseen by the authorities of this world, that is, in a society founded on the belief in God, beholden to the monarch for its well-being, and organized around well-ordered families that constitute it. In this paradigm, disturbance at the local level of the family can ripple upward to disrupt the whole social order.

Larry Riggs, among others, argues cogently that Molière's theater subverts what he calls the "imperialistic universalism" of French culture during the reign of Louis XIV.[6] *Les Femmes savantes* and *Le Tartuffe*, for example, "direct critical attention at the two major universalizing movements in the French culture of Molière's time: rationalism, which had recently been updated and energized by Descartes, and aggressive Christian moralism."[7] By having his learned ladies adopt "a discourse of mastery" obviously borrowed from the dominant society of their day, Molière mocks and undermines the hegemonic impulse that produces such "authoritarian discourses."[8] Likewise, the ambition of the old miser Harpagon in

L'Avare to control everyone becomes, in its relentlessness, self-de-structive and, as Riggs sees it, implies that Molière understands the weakness inherent in the will to absolute power of an individual or, more importantly, a society. In the end, a social order with that will to power at its root undoes itself.[9]

Whether or not Molière's plays actually influence the ultimate downfall of the monarchy and its all-encompassing discourse of power, they do lay bare serious defects in the political, social, and philosophical systems of their moment in history. In this sense, they have about them a certain subversive cast. However, the late Paul Bénichou reminds his readers that Molière wrote for the court and owed his fame to it.[10] As Bénichou asserts, "il ne fut rien moins que fermé à l'idéal aristocratique de son temps"[11] [he was nothing less than closed to the aristocratic ideal of his day]. Despite the imperfections of the social order, which he never forgot and often made fun of, Molière understood its utility, indeed its neces-sity.

He also saw the chinks in the armor of both those on the side of the prevailing order and those who would thwart its exigencies. His father figures, natural defenders of family order, become ob-jects of ridicule when they demand absolute obedience from their offspring. The children and their lovers, though, in their some-times exaggerated resistance to paternal authority, breach stan-dards of behavior no less than the obsessive parents. Thinking of the inheritance that he and his sister will eventually reap from their greedy father, Harpagon's son, Cléante, wonders what good it will do them if it comes only after they are beyond the age at which they can enjoy it (1.2). This implies that the sooner the old man dies the better and reflects an utter lack of respect for Harpa-gon as father. Similarly, in relations between husbands and wives, both often behave badly. The eponymous protagonist in *George Dandin* has married in order to acquire noble rank, thereby trans-gressing the bounds of the social hierarchy and calling down on himself the wrath of his wife and her parents, but they, by their doings, deny to George the dignity and obeisance appropriate to the role of husband. Over and over in Molière's plays, characters whose single-minded pursuit of some goal endangers the order of their world are countered by opponents who seem more reason-able but, when examined closely, speak and act just as harmfully as those whom they view, often rightly, as their oppressors.

In other words, both its protectors and their challengers jeopar-dize good order, and Molière's comedies show why. As Lionel Gossman demonstrates in *Men and Masks*, a seminal book on Molière and one on which I have relied greatly, desire of a quite particular kind almost invariably drives his characters. Whatever specific objective their desire fixes on, they also want others to recognize their success in achieving their end. In fact, without such affirmation by others, they have no sense of accomplishment. Monsieur Jourdain, the *bourgeois gentilhomme*, would not only attain the status of *gentilhomme* but also wants others to accept him as one. This means that he must capture the attention of others and their assent to what he wants. They must conform to his will, he must exercise power over them. The almost inevitable clash of wills resulting from such power plays creates circumstances in which rivalry among characters proliferates. That rivalry, more than any word or gesture of an individual character, poses the greatest threat to order.

While order, for Bossuet, holds the place of a high moral value, in Molière's theater it plays a more functional, if equally important role. It permits the kinds of distinctions—between good and evil, right and wrong, legal and illegal—that make it possible for society to function smoothly. Rivalry develops as those differences become deeper and increasingly dramatic, and it pits seeming opposites against each other. But repeatedly in Molière's plays, the difference between rivals is diluted as they spar with each other. Similarities in thought, word, and deed come to predominate and chaos, in which good and bad, right and wrong can no longer be so easily told apart, looms. This structural characteristic of rivalry and its workings, richly illuminated in the writings of René Girard, provides the basis for my reading of major comedies of Molière.

The centrality of *Le Misanthrope*, with which I begin, stems from its way of portraying rivalry as a dynamic force that determines how characters relate to one another, rather than a defining trait that delimits the behavior of an individual character, as in Molière's earlier, unsuccessful *Dom Garcie de Navarre*. Strikingly, the later masterpiece looks back insistently to the earlier work, which turns uniquely on its protagonist's perverse, self-defeating feelings of rivalry. A comparison of the distinct treatments of rivalry in these two works brings to light a radical shift in Molière's comedies toward making rivalry a mode of behavior that structures much of the action in his plays. The workings of rivalry in *Le Misanthrope* offer a model for reading others of Molière's works.

A commonplace in writing about comedy emphasizes its quest for an order disturbed by the machinations of absurd or baneful characters. Molière's comedies bear out this widely held notion. Although the situations in which they find themselves and the object

of their overwhelming desire vary tremendously, Molière's characters fall into patterns of comportment that repeat themselves from
play to play. Their desire for power and its accompanying need
to control others regularly make them each other's rivals, and the
mechanisms of rivalry, once put in motion, endanger good order.
Molière always finds a way to restore order, but a troubling suggestion that it cannot endure invariably hangs over the conclusions of
his plays. A denouement that eventuates in order definitively established evades Molière just as it had Bossuet.

References in my text to the works of Molière, unless otherwise
indicated, come from the Georges Couton edition. I have listed all
editions of Molière from which I have quoted material under the
name of Molière in Works Cited.

The sources of translations of passages from Molière's plays are
given in the notes. Translations of lines from *Dom Garcie de Navarre*
and *George Dandin* are my own. In a few cases, I have also used my
own translations of passages from other plays. When this occurs, it
is indicated in the text. Translations of texts from works not by Molière are my own, unless their source is given in the notes.

1

Love and Rivalry: The Ties That Bind

WHEN HE CREATED *LE MISANTHROPE*, MOLIÈRE HAD ALREADY PRO-
duced *Les Précieuses ridicules*, *L'Ecole des femmes*, *Le Tartuffe*, and *Dom
Juan*, all of which have long since entered the canon of French classical comedy. Yet, while writing his greatest play, he harked back
repeatedly to *Dom Garcie de Navarre ou le prince jaloux*, a work that
had been a hopeless failure. Neither *Dom Garcie de Navarre* nor *Le
Misanthrope* is truly funny. Both plays are about jealous lovers who
see rivals everywhere.[1] Dom Garcie's rivals are mostly imaginary,
Alceste's quite real. The objects of their desire, Done Elvire and
Célimène, do little to allay their lovers' jealousy; indeed, they often
stir it up. Dom Garcie and Alceste are so similarly convinced of
their lovers' treachery that lines about it from the earlier play slip
seamlessly into *Le Misanthrope*.[2] Confronting Done Elvire and Célimène with "proof" of their supposed infidelity, the two protagonists justify their jealousy in the same words: "Voilà ce que
marquaient les troubles de mon âme: / Ce n'était pas en vain que
s'alarmait ma flamme" (*Dom Garcie* 4.8.1276–77; *Le Misanthrope*
4.3.1289–90) [I was uneasy, and I knew that things weren't
right—/ I felt this coming, that's why I was in a fright].[3]

Despite such obvious similarities between the two works and Molière's persistent attachment to one of his least successful efforts,
Dom Garcie de Navarre and *Le Misanthrope* represent radically different ways of portraying characters and their desires. Dom Garcie is
a Cartesian figure, complete with an inner self, a "moi" [self] that
can be defined and, ideally, brought under control by an exercise
of will. Garcie fails at this. Not by chance do all of his imagined
rivals become no rivals at all. That Dom Sylve, the only real threat
to Dom Garcie, turns out to be Elvire's brother eliminates even
him as a potential contender for her love. "Et dans votre rival elle
trouve son frère," Done Ignès tells the jealous lover (5.6.1841)
[And in your rival she finds her brother].[4] Garcie's obsession with
rivals is a simple, albeit dominant, character flaw, an illness of un-

known origin. His jealousy is an innate trait, a defining characteristic that determines the prince's personality and behavior. One easily imagines how La Bruyère would conclude a portrait of Dom Garcie ranting against Done Elvire and all those whom, he assumes, she favors with her attentions: "Il est jaloux" [He is jealous].

In *Le Misanthrope*, Molière departs from this view of human nature and provides a key to a reading of his other great comedies. Unlike Dom Garcie, Alceste has true rivals, even though none of them stands a chance of being loved by Célimène, and his jealousy differs fundamentally from that of his predecessor. Its roots are not buried deep in his own character; rather, as a function of his will to power over others, it depends as much upon them as upon Alceste himself.[5] His preoccupation with rivals derives from his encounters with other characters and the dynamics of his attempts to control this them. Rivalry in *Le Misanthrope* is not, then, what Done Elvire sees as the result of a "maladie . . . digne de pitié" (5.6.1867) [sickness . . . worthy of pity].

Shortly after admitting to his friend, Philinte, his weakness for Célimène despite her evident faults (1.1.225–34), Alceste divulges the most important aspect of the rivalry he feels with her other suitors. Although he believes that Célimène loves him, Alceste perceives all of her admirers as rivals. But if Célimène loves you, Philinte wonders, why worry about rivals?

> C'est qu'un coeur bien atteint veut qu'on soit tout à lui,
> Et je ne viens ici qu'à dessein de lui dire
> Tout ce que là-dessus ma passion m'inspire.
>
> (1.1.240–42)

> [You know that when a man's in love, he'll much prefer
> To keep his mistress to himself. Right now, I plan
> To tell her what I think, persuade her, if I can.]

Love, like jealousy, in this formulation, originates in a need to dominate others. Alceste's love expresses itself as a desire—his heart "veut"—for Célimène's total devotion.[6] He has come precisely in order to explain this to her. She must attend to him alone. In this, he remains as consistent as he is exacting. At the end of the play, after Célimène refuses to go off with him to "mon désert" (5.4.1763) [some deserted spot], Alceste rejects her in words that recall what he had said to Philinte:

> Non: mon coeur à présent vous déteste,
> Et ce refus lui seul fait plus que tout le reste,

> Puisque vous n'êtes point, en des liens si doux,
> Pour trouver tout en moi, comme moi tout en vous,
> Allez, je vous refuse. . . .
>
> (5.4.1779–83)[7]

> [No. That's it now. I detest
> You—now you've turned me down, you can forget the rest.
> Since you're not ready to give up the things you do,
> And come away with me, as I would do for you,
> You'd better go. I feel disgusted. . . .]

Loving Célimène sounds very much like conquering her, like making her utterly dependent upon her lover, who can accept nothing less than her desiring him as fully as he claims to desire her. "Vos désirs avec moi ne sont-ils pas contents?" he asks (5.4.1773) [If we're together, surely you'll be satisfied?].

Célimène had already detected a certain aberrance in Alceste's love when he attacked her for having written the letter he had obtained from Arsinoé. She admits that the letter is in her hand but suggests that it was addressed to a female friend, not one of Alceste's rivals. Alceste refuses to believe this, calls Célimène a traitor, and, as he had earlier, refers to his own love for her as a weakness: "Ah! traîtresse, mon faible est étrange pour vous" (4.3.1415) [I've such a passion for you that it's quite absurd]. Strange indeed, for as Alceste goes on to explain, he loves Célimène so much that he wishes her ill:

> Oui, je voudrais qu'aucun ne vous trouvât aimable,
> Que vous fussiez réduite en un sort misérable,
> Que le Ciel, en naissant, ne vous eût donné rien,
> Que vous n'eussiez ni rang, ni naissance, ni bien.
>
> (4.3.1425–28)

> [I wish people would tell you you were hideous,
> I wish that you'd become degraded, piteous;
> I wish that you'd been born a beggar girl, or worse,
> No pedigree, no home, no money in your purse.]

Reduced to this deplorable state, Célimène would be saved by Alceste and owe him everything: "tenir tout des mains de mon amour" (4.3.1432) [owing all your wealth and happiness to me]. Just beneath the surface of this passionate love lurks an intense struggle for power in which Célimène becomes as much his rival as the object of his love.[8] She ironically agrees about the strangeness of her lover's feelings for her: "C'est me vouloir du bien d'une étrange manière" (4.3.1433) [I must say, that's the oddest way to wish me well!]. Who will dominate at each step along the way assumes greater importance than love.

Epistolary misadventures also plague the jealous lover in *Dom Garcie de Navarre*. During his first conversation with Done Elvire, as she admonishes him against jealousy, "ce monstre affreux" (1.3.257) [this dreadful monster], and encourages him to rise above it, a letter for her arrives. Sensing, rightly enough, Garcie's apprehension that the letter comes from a rival, Done Elvire has him read it to her. The letter has been sent by Done Ignès, and in it, she laments that the tyrant, Mauregat, continues to pursue her. Chagrined, Dom Garcie promises to show his love for Elvire by restraining his jealousy. A short time later, however, Dom Lope, one of his confidants, gives Garcie part of a letter in Elvire's hand, torn from its matching half. The letter's first line begins "Quoique votre rival" (2.4.494) [although your rival]. Garcie hotly confronts Elvire with this incriminating evidence, only to discover, when she shows him the other half of the letter, that it was intended for him.

In the letter, Elvire tells Dom Garcie that his jealousy stands in the way of their love. He should be more afraid of himself than of any rival, for despite the valor with which he saved her from her enemies, his jealousy makes him "odieux" (2.6.621) [odious]. Garcie must not persist in seeing all other men as rivals. The time has come for him to change his character by destroying in himself the obstacle that separates him from Done Elvire. That obstacle is internal, "en vous" (2.6.616) [in you]. Garcie should rein in his jealousy and find happiness with her. Elvire's advice corresponds to that she had given a jealous Dom Garcie when the letter from Done Ignès was delivered: "Ah! prince faible! Hé bien! par cet écrit / Guérissez-le, ce mal: il n'est que dans l'esprit" (1.3.341–42) [Oh, weak prince! Now by this letter / Cure your sickness: it is only in your mind]. Jealousy, coupled as it generally is with rivalry, has the features of an illness susceptible to a cure. This malady, like a physical ailment, exists inside the character, who has both the responsibility and the capacity to treat it. Done Elvire will love and accept Garcie when "vous bannirez enfin ce monstre affreux" (1.3.257) [you finally banish this dreadful monster].

Love and jealousy, in Elvire's Cartesian thinking, are separate and mutually exclusive.[9] Both originate in the lover, who alone controls them. Elvire wants Dom Garcie's love to be "de la bonne sorte" [of the right kind] and threatens not to return his affection until "vous saurez m'aimer comme il faut que l'on aime" (1.3.248)[10] [you know how to love me as one ought to love]. She firmly believes in the power of self-control to correct a defective character trait. Garcie's putative rival, Dom Sylve, had abandoned Done Ignès for Elvire, who now rejects him, she claims, to avoid complicity in his unfaithfulness (3.2.906–11). His protestation of "tous les maux . . . que mon amour me donne" (3.2.961) [all the pain . . . that my love gives me] leaves Elvire unmoved. She encourages Dom Sylve to return to Ignès:

> Vous n'avez que les maux que vous voulez avoir,
> Et toujours notre coeur est en notre pouvoir:
> Il peut bien quelquefois montrer quelque faiblesse;
> Mais enfin sur nos sens, la raison, la maîtresse. . . .
>
> (3.2.962–65)

> [You have only the pain that you want to have,
> And we always have power over our own heart.
> It can at times show some weakness,
> But in the end, over our senses, reason, the mistress . . .]

If passions cannot be completely purged, will power can overwhelm and suppress them. Individuals take command of themselves by the effective use of reason, "la maîtresse." The heart may be fickle, but it is, nonetheless, always subservient to individual will. Dom Garcie agrees with this Cartesian perspective. He wants Elvire to declare her love for him but recognizes ultimately that "Mon plus grand ennemi se rencontre en moi-même" (4.9.1485) [I am my own greatest enemy]. Jealousy has its seat within him; only he can root it out—"Ce qui peut me rester dans mon malheur extrême, / C'est de chercher alors mon remède en moi-même" (5.3.1632–33) [What then remains for me to do in my great unhappiness / Is to seek my cure in myself]—though that may require his suicide, which Dom Garcie contemplates in the next lines (5.3.1634–35). Individual responsibility implies individual autonomy, the capacity to act without concern for, or even in spite of, the behavior of others.

In *Le Misanthrope*, Molière abandons individual autonomy as a principle on which to construct characters. For all of Alceste's insistence on his high-mindedness, honesty, and candor in dealing with others, he demonstrates that what matters most to him is having others recognize his superiority. Who he is counts less than what he wants others to see him as. "Je veux qu'on me distingue" (1.1.63) [I want to be distinguished from the rest], he tells Philinte, and to meet this goal, Alceste often subordinates his own desires to those of his rivals. Dom Garcie's strictly personal problem is replaced here with a profoundly interpersonal dilemma. Everyone, including the prince himself, would have Dom Garcie overcome his feelings of rivalry with others by inner fortitude and a supreme act of will. But rivalries in *Le Misanthrope* increase dependence upon others. Whatever personal strength the characters might as individuals be able to summon, they cannot liberate themselves from others' influence. Alceste has no self-contained inner sanctum upon which to settle his whole character, no essence that is his and his alone. To call Dom Garcie "le prince jaloux" [the jealous prince], as Molière does in the play's subtitle, defines the character. Alceste too is a "jaloux," but jealousy in his case can only be understood in relation to his encounters with other characters. As René Girard suggests, "the comic is rooted in the ultimate failure of all individualism."[11]

With the exception of the friendship of Philinte and Eliante, rivalry marks all significant human relationships in *Le Misanthrope*. Alceste and Philinte are at odds over how people ought to behave toward one another and are equally unyielding in their opposing positions. In addition to courting the same women, Alceste and Oronte clash over the quality of the latter's sonnet. The spat between Célimène and Arsinoé, as it degenerates into a characteristic kind of stichomythia, is emblematic of Molière's portrayal of rivalry in *Le Misanthrope* and in many of his other plays. In her coquettishness, Célimène vies with all other women for the attention of men. Her dispute with Arsinoé demonstrates how she does this and where it leads. Although lovers, Alceste and Célimène face each other as enemies. Lionel Gossman has shown that at issue between them is Célimène's freedom.[12] Will she determine her destiny or will he? Molière highlights rivalry in his greatest play by making even the minor characters, like the marquesses, Acaste and Clitandre, rivals for Célimène's love. Rivalry is everywhere in *Le Misanthrope*. And it is always the same in its form and consequences.

Erupting at approximately the midpoint of the play, the vicious—and brilliant—sparring of Célimène and Arsinoé draws attention to rivalry at its most raw, most blatant, most brutal. In his "Lettre sur la comédie du *Misanthrope*," Donneau de Visé speaks of this "scène entre deux femmes, que l'on trouve d'autant plus belle que leurs caractères sont tout à fait opposés et se font ainsi paraître l'un l'autre" (*OC* 2:136) [scene between two women that we find all the more fine because their characters are utterly opposed and thus bring each other out]. He calls Célimène "la jeune veuve aussi coquette que médisante" [the young widow as coquettish as she is backbiting] and her rival "une femme qui veut passer pour prude, et qui, dans l'âme, n'est pas moins du monde que la coquette" (OC 2:136) [a woman who would pass herself off as a prude, and who, in her heart, is no less worldly than the coquette]. In their battle of words, Molière accentuates the radical difference that separates them as well as the similarities, beyond the fact that both have their eye on Alceste, that ultimately close the gap between them. Young, beautiful, and witty, Célimène recognizes her attractiveness to men and plays to perfection the role of coquette. Arsinoé, by contrast, is a nasty prude, overly critical of all women more appealing than she. The prude and the coquette seem to have little in common. Their instinctive antipathy toward one another comes as no surprise. Their rivalry over Alceste could be expected to underscore the differences between them.

As they lay into each other, what becomes evident, however, is their similarity. By conveying others' negative comments about her rival, each insists she wants only to helpful. Their poisonous critiques have about them a cloying politeness that leaves intact the refinement of honnête discourse while casting the most offensive personal aspersions.[13] Having listened quietly to Arsinoé's scathing attack on her coquetry, Célimène tells her rival that she intends to respond in kind: "Je veux suivre, à mon tour, un exemple si doux, / En vous avertissant de ce qu'on dit de vous" (3.4.919–20) [You set a good example, but it's my turn now / To tell you how you strike your friends, if you'll allow]. Célimène's retort then takes the same form as Arsinoé's reproaches.[14] Molière further emphasizes the resemblance between Célimène and Arsinoé by having them employ the very same words to conclude their critiques:

> Madame, je vous crois l'âme trop raisonnable,
> Pour ne pas prendre bien cet avis profitable,
> Et pour l'attribuer qu'aux mouvements secrets
> D'un zèle qui m'attache à tous vos intérêts.
>
> (3.4.909–12)[15]

> [Madame, you're very reasonable, you'll receive
> My warning in good part, and heed it, I believe.
> I know you understand my motives, and I feel
> A keen desire to serve you, with devoted zeal.]

Both later claim not to understand why the other treats her so badly (3.4.989–92).

In this epic struggle between the prude and the coquette, each knows the truth about the other, which is not far from her own, and at the same time reveals her own nature.[16] Although Célimène carries the day, her words and behavior demonstrate how similar she is to her rival. As she said she would (3.4.919), Célimène imitates Arsinoé. They both want the same thing—Alceste—but each also wants the other to recognize her superiority, which will be proved by winning Alceste. On one level, Célimène lords it over her rival when she points to the difference in their ages, but she goes on to suggest that flirting with men and chastising one's neighbors, however contrary, have their seasons:

> Madame, on peut, je crois, louer et blâmer tout,
> Et chacun a raison suivant l'âge ou le goût.
> Il est une saison pour la galanterie;
> Il en est une aussi propre à la pruderie.
>
> (3.4.975–78)

> [Things can look good or bad, Madame, it all depends.
> An action sometimes seems quite right, sometimes offends.
> It's fine to flirt a bit, as long as you're still young;
> But when you're older, you'd much better hold your tongue.]

The opposition between "galanterie" and "pruderie" does not preclude the same person's indulging in both. Today's blameworthy behavior may become tomorrow's praiseworthy behavior, today's coquette tomorrow's prude: "Je ne dis pas qu'un jour je ne suive vos traces: / L'âge amènera tout, et ce n'est pas le temps, / Madame, comme on sait, d'être prude à vingt ans" (3.4.982–84) [I may decide to do the same as you one day; / But now, while I respect your prudent attitude, / At twenty, I've no need, Madame, to be a prude]. With Célimène's taunts, Molière shows that rivalry extenuates the difference between the two women as they battle for superiority. Both want the attention of others; they have simply chosen different ways of attracting it. Jealousy in *Dom Garcie de Navarre* distinguishes the prince from other men; rivalry in *Le Misanthrope* does just the opposite.

Many critics have attributed the theatrical perfection of the scene of Célimène and Arsinoé's quarrel to Molière's understanding of women, especially feuding women of a mind to act like shrews. René Jasinski, for example, claims that "Jamais le génie dramatique n'est allé plus loin. Molière met en scène l'éternel féminin, mais cette fois tel qu'il s'apparaît à lui-même, dépouillé de toute illusion masculine"[17] [Never has dramatic genius gone further. Molière puts on stage the eternal feminine, but now as it appears to itself, stripped of all masculine illusion]. However, rivalry between men in *Le Misanthrope* is identical in substance, if not in tone, to the competitiveness of Célimène and Arsinoé. The play opens on a dispute between Alceste and Philinte in which the two take opposite positions on the issue of the proper relationship of the individual to the social order. This debate, of course, is as old as humankind. Philinte advises compliance with the reigning mores of the time and avoidance of extreme positions, even virtu-ous ones: "La parfaite raison fuit toute extrémité, / Et veut que l'on soit sage avec sobriété" (1.1.151–52) [A reasonable man shouldn't go to extremes: / Be sensible, and don't indulge your crazy dreams]. To exercise good judgment requires flexibility of mind rather than rigorous conformity to principled positions: "Il faut fléchir au temps sans obstination" (1.1.156) [We try to fit in, and be worthy of respect]. Alceste, on the other hand, dedicates himself to the very "grande roideur des vertus des vieux âges" (1.1.153) [The stuffy moral code our ancestors display] that his friend con-demns.

Readers and audiences will almost inevitably take sides in this debate. In perhaps the most famous critique of *Le Misanthrope*, Jean-Jacques Rousseau defends Alceste against a Molière who, pandering to public taste, portrayed his protagonist as ridiculous.[18] Rousseau objects to Molière's undercutting what Philinte calls Al-ceste's "austère honneur" (75) [austere honor]. Jean-Jacques's vi-tuperative description of Philinte places Alceste's friend squarely in the opposing court:

> Ce Philinte est le Sage de la Pièce; un de ces honnêtes gens du grand monde, dont les maximes ressemblent beaucoup à celles des fripons; de ces gens . . . qui sont toujours contens de tout le monde, parce qu'ils ne se soucient de personne; qui, autour d'une bonne table, soutiennent qu'il n'est pas vrai que le peuple ait faim; . . . qui, de leur maison bien fermée, verroient voler, piller, égorger, massacrer tout le genre hu-main sans se plaindre. (51–52)

> [Philinte is the play's sage, one of those upstanding people of good so-ciety whose maxims so greatly resemble those of rogues; one of those people . . . who are always satisfied with everyone because they do not care about anyone; who, seated around a table filled with food, assert that it is not true that the people are hungry . . . who, looking on from their well-protected house, would, without complaining, watch all hu-mankind be robbed, plundered, butchered, massacred.]

If only because it is Rousseau's, this reading ought not be dis-missed lightly, though it is difficult, in the twenty-first century, to assent to the main line of its argument. Rousseau puts into stark relief the radical polarity of the couple Alceste-Philinte. This is structurally faithful to Molière's intention as he expresses it by having Philinte compare Alceste and himself to "Ces deux frères que peint *L'Ecole des maris*" (1.1.100)[19] [The brothers in the *School for Husbands*, Molière's play]. Like Ariste and Sganarelle, Alceste and Philinte are enemy brothers. Rousseau's critique rivets his readers' attention on their status as enemies. Molière knows that they are also brothers.

In defense of the values he upholds, Alceste displays a peevishness and unwillingness to compromise that, when juxtaposed against Philinte's supple worldliness, appear more misanthropic than virtuous. Marie-Odile Sweetser speaks of Alceste's "exigence d'absolu" [demand for absoluteness] and aptly ties it to the character's will to assert himself.[20] Alceste's imperious manner betrays the champion of high moral rectitude and reveals him as a petty tyrant who seeks both power over others and their explicit acquiescence to that power. To the extent that the targets of his aggression preserve their freedom by resisting him, Alceste modifies his own conduct, which eventually is dictated by theirs. What Alceste most wants, namely, recognition of his own superiority, must always take precedence over what they want, even if that forces him to act against his own interest or desires.

Since his presence at the gathering in her salon of Célimène's admirers, whom he considers rivals, would be painful, Alceste refuses to stay for it. Célimène insists: "Je le veux / . . . Je le veux, je le veux" (2.3.554, 557) [I want you to . . . I want you to, I want you to]. Alceste's repeated "je veux" in the play's first act becomes Célimène's as the two engage in a battle of wills. The lovers are now rivals and establish their authority by opposing each other. Seeing that Alceste will not heed an order to remain, Célimène tells him to go: "Hé bien! allez, sortez"(2.3.558) [All right, then, go]. Needless to say, he stays put. Alceste certainly does not obey Célimène, but he is not for that any the less subject to her command. Whether he does what she orders or what she forbids, it is she who plays the tune to which he dances. Alceste is linked to Célimène just as she is to him and to the other admirers whose attention she seeks.[21]

With his reasonableness and understanding of human feelings, no one, it would seem, could be further than Philinte from the loss of independence implied in such rivalry. And yet, in more ways than one, Philinte resembles his less rational, more choleric friend. In the famous sonnet scene (1.2), where the rivalry between Alceste and Oronte turns on whose poetry is better, Philinte too is implicated. He counters Alceste's reservations about Oronte's sonnet with warm praise for the poem. From simple advocacy of a more yielding, pliant attitude toward others, Philinte moves to acting on his principles and thus explicitly places himself in competition with Alceste. Once Oronte has left the stage, Philinte remonstrates with his friend: "Hé bien! vous le voyez: pour être trop sincère, / Vous voilà sur les bras une fâcheuse affaire" (1.3.439–40) [Look, can't you see you've been a good deal too sincere? / You've made things very awkward for yourself, I fear]. Philinte refuses, however, to abandon Alceste, who tells him bluntly, "ne suivez point mes pas" (1.3.445) [Don't follow me]. "Vous vous moquez de moi," Philinte responds, "je ne vous quitte pas" (1.3.446) [I'm coming too. You can't just go off in a huff]. How to explain the supposedly philosophical Philinte's persistence? Is he a disinterested proponent of a certain approach to human relations or is he not rather, like Alceste, reliant upon others to maintain his own commitment to what he believes is right?

Citing the passages in which Alceste denounces "l'ami du genre humain" (1.1.64) [the friend of all humanity] and declares to Philinte that "je hais tous les hommes" (1.1.118) [I hate all men], Pierre Force draws a significant parallel between the two:

> La position d'Alceste est à bien des égards symétrique de celle de Philinte (celle de Philinte telle qu'elle est décrite par Alceste). De même que Philinte enveloppe le genre humain, sans aucune exception, dans une espèce d'amitié fade, de même Alceste refuse d'épargner qui que ce soit dans la haine universelle qu'il porte aux hommes. On peut donc s'interroger sur le contenu de cette haine: n'est-elle pas comme l'amitié de Philinte, dévaluée?[22]

> [The position of Alceste is in many respects in symmetry with that of Philinte (as Alceste describes Philinte's position). Just as Philinte wraps all humanity, without exception, in a kind of insipid friendship, so Alceste, in the universal hatred he feels toward all men, refuses to spare anyone at all. We can, therefore, question the contents of this hatred: is it not, like Philinte's friendship, devalued?]

The very different principles that Alceste and Philinte prize and defend are indeed devalued. Alceste cheapens his call for sincerity by using it to control others. Philinte seems to recognize that authoritarianism like his friend's will not work, but this knowledge does not liberate him from a need for others similar to Alceste's. Philinte fully accepts his friend's pessimistic evaluation of human nature. He is no more surprised by human deceitfulness and

treachery than by the sight of "des vautours affamés de carnage, /
Des singes malfaisants, et des loups pleins de rage" (1.1.177–78) [a
flock of vultures, beaks agape, / A pack of angry wolves, or an aggressive ape]. When Alceste loses his case in court, Philinte agrees
that the decision was not made on the merits: "Non, je tombe d'accord de tout ce qu'il vous plaît: / Tout marche par cabale et par pur
intérêt" (5.1.1555–56) [Oh, no. You're right to feel a sense of
injury. / The world's run by a selfish, greedy coterie]. For Philinte,
as for Alceste, human iniquity is universal, but this is not a good
reason to abandon the human race. On the contrary:

> Tous ces défauts humains nous donnent dans la vie
> Des moyens d'exercer notre philosophie:
> C'est le plus bel emploi que trouve la vertu;
> Et si de probité tout était revêtu,
> Si tous les coeurs étaient francs, justes et dociles,
> La plupart des vertus seraient inutiles
> Puisqu'on en met usage à pouvoir sans ennui
> Supporter dans nos droits, l'injustice d'autrui.
>
> (5.1.1561–68)

> [Humanity's a mess, but let's be practical,
> And make sure our approach is philosophical.
> That's the best way to demonstrate we're really good;
> For if we tried to be as honest as we could,
> And everyone was decent, fair, and virtuous,
> Most of *our* virtues would become superfluous,
> Since what we use them for is helping us to bear
> Our grievances, when other people are unfair.]

No more than Alceste's misanthropy, Philinte's "philosophie"
cannot be understood without reference to others, since it too depends for its definition on them. Both Alceste's hatred of humankind and Philinte's affable accommodation of its foibles are
ultimately directed toward exerting influence over others. Philinte
recommends Alceste be more tractable so as not to set others
against him. Alceste should think more of how he might bring his
enemies around or, failing that, beat them in court: "Contre votre
partie éclatez un peu moins, / Et donner au procès une part de
vos soins" (1.1.183–84) [And don't keep ranting that the fellow's a
disgrace, / But pay attention to preparing your court case]. Alceste
prefers to prove his superiority by losing his case: "Je voudrais,
m'en coûtât-il grand-chose / Pour la beauté du fait avoir perdu ma
cause" (1.1.201–2) [I say, forget about the cost. / I want the truth.

No matter, if my case is lost]. This will, once and for all, establish society's corruption and, by contrast, his greater worth. Philinte would have him do much the same thing by another means. Were Alceste to follow his friend's good counsel, he would give evidence that Philinte's way is preferable and, at the same time, bow to his predominance. Philinte's desire to win is less forbidding than Alceste's, but he must convince Alceste in order to put his "philosophie" into practice. His later effort to dissuade Alceste from returning to his "désert" (5.4.1763) [deserted spot] again exposes the tenacity with which he remains attached to a friend so unlike himself. At play's end, when Eliante has agreed to marry him and by this gesture bestowed on him an honor that is "toute mon envie" (5.4.1799) [nothing I want more], Philinte's first thoughts are for Alceste, not for his bride-to-be: "Allons, Madame, allons employer toute chose, / Pour rompre le dessein que son coeur se propose" (5.4.1807–8) [Let's follow him, Madame, and let's do all we can / To try to change his mind, and make him drop his plan]. By ending the play with these lines, Molière underscores Philinte's need for others without whom he would lose the identity he so desires for himself.

Philinte does not, therefore, stand apart from all the other characters. He holds no privileged position and represents no personal or social ideal. That his modus operandi has clear advantages over Alceste's for the social order helps explain why many critics have seen him as the play's *raisonneur*, the character who has right on his side and speaks for the author. Just as Dom Garcie de Navarre is wrong to be jealous, so Philinte, read in this way, is right to urge upon Alceste a more conciliatory disposition toward his fellow human beings. In *Le Misanthrope*, however, Molière portrays the impossibility of immunity from the effects of rivalry. As much as rivals oppose each other, to the extent that they define themselves by that opposition, they rely upon each other for their self-definition. Rivalry, in Molière's great plays, eventuates in the weakening of the differences that separate the rivals and in the threat of personal defeat along with, at times, social chaos. For all his good sense and moderation, Philinte cannot completely escape the snare set by Alceste's rivalry with him and his own, though less intense, competition with his friend.

Unlike Philinte, Oronte, by loving Célimène, threatens Alceste in a way that makes their rivalry inevitable. In the second scene of the play, the two characters stake out opposing positions as Alceste criticizes Oronte's sonnet and proposes his "vieille chanson" (1.2.392) [old-fashioned song] as an antidote to "le méchant goût du siècle" (1.2.389) [our literary scene . . . thoroughly debased]. The relative worth of the two poems has generated much scholarly discussion but is really beside the point. The argument between Alceste and Oronte becomes so heated that Philinte, to maintain order, separates them. Rivalry has taken its normal course, delineating the differences between the rivals. Were it not for Philinte's intervention, a brawl might well ensue. When, however, it comes to Célimène, the real bone of contention between these rivals, they band together with one voice to compel her to choose between them. Oronte makes the demand, Alceste confirms it: "Oui, Monsieur a raison: Madame, il faut choisir, / Et sa demande ici s'accorde à mon désir" (5.2.1603–4) [Yes, Monsieur's right, Madame—I see I share his views, / And I agree the time has come for you to choose]. Alceste and Oronte are suddenly of one mind, and their language conspicuously proclaims their unity:

> ORONTE. Je ne veux point, Monsieur, d'une flamme importune
>   Troubler aucunement votre bonne fortune.
> ALCESTE. Je ne veux point, Monsieur, jaloux ou non jaloux
>   Partager de son coeur rien du tout avec vous.
> ORONTE. Si votre amour au mien lui semble préférable . . .
> ALCESTE. Si du moindre penchant elle est pour vous capable . . .
> ORONTE. Je jure de n'y rien prétendre désormais.
> ALCESTE. Je jure hautement de ne la voir jamais.
> ORONTE. Madame, c'est à vous de parler sans contrainte.
> ALCESTE. Madame, vous pouvez vous expliquer sans crainte.
> ORONTE. Vous n'avez qu'à nous dire où s'attachent vos voeux.
> ALCESTE. Vous n'avez qu'à trancher, et choisir de nous deux.
> ORONTE. Quoi? sur un pareil choix vous semblez être en peine!
> ALCESTE. Quoi? votre âme balance et paraît incertaine!
>
>   (5.2.1609–22)

[ORONTE. If you're the lucky one, I want to know today,
    Monsieur, I wouldn't dream of standing in your way.
ALCESTE. Monsieur, although my jealousy may drive me spare,
    I will have all her love or none, and I won't share.
ORONTE. If she finds your love more acceptable than mine . . .
ALCESTE. If she says what she feels, or gives the smallest sign . . .
ORONTE. I swear I'll go away from here: I know what's right.
ALCESTE. I swear I'll leave at once: I won't put up a fight.
ORONTE. Madame, it's your turn now. Don't be afraid to speak.
ALCESTE. Madame, explain yourself—and no more hide-and-seek.
ORONTE. All you need do is give your answer—that's the deal.
ALCESTE. All you need do is say exactly how you feel.
ORONTE. What's this? Your find it hard, do you? So we're unkind?
ALCESTE. What? Are you at a loss? Can't you make up your mind?]

By having his rivals mouth each other's words, Molière illuminates the paradoxical truth about rivalry. Its real danger lies less in the discord it sows than in its bringing to the fore the hidden identity between the rivals.[23] If Oronte and Alceste are truly alike, how is Célimène to choose? In the sonnet scene, Philinte prevents violence without deciding the question that separates Alceste and Oronte. Célimène, like Dom Juan faced with Charlotte and Mathurine, dodges the issue.[24]

Had the three of them not been interrupted by Arsinoé's arrival, Célimène would have had to evade Acaste and Clitandre in a similar way. These "petits marquis" also love Célimène and want her to decide which of them she will have, agreeing that the one not favored will withdraw "Et le [the other] délivrera d'un rival assidu" (3.1.844) [Not stay to cramp his rival's style]. It is Acaste and Clitandre who, at the end of the play, read in public Célimène's letters to them in which she has something negative to say about everyone. The rivalry between Acaste and Clitandre can be resolved only by Célimène's doing what for her would be inconceivable, settling on one lover over all the rest. Besides, in this instance, she loves neither of the two suitors. In any case, it would be hard to say what distinguishes Acaste from Clitandre, despite the intensity of their rivalry. They are more similar than dissimilar; they agree rather than disagree. In the play's last scene, the social milieu in which Alceste, Célimène, and her many admirers circulate plunges into turmoil because of the decision of Acaste and Clitandre to act in unison. As if to emphasize the absence of difference between them, Acaste reads aloud the letter Célimène has written to Clitandre, who, in turn, reads his rival's. The delicate social balance that Célimène has preserved by playing rival against rival breaks down. Oronte, Acaste, and Clitandre abandon her. Arsinoé withdraws, happy at her rival's downfall although infuriated at Alceste's rejection. Alceste and Célimène are left to restore harmony to a personal and social world that has collapsed around them.

They are, in large measure, responsible for what has happened and will pay the price for it, Alceste by having to withdraw from society and Célimène by losing her control over it. Alceste portrays Célimène as his moral opposite, sees her every flaw, and claims to love her in spite of her worldliness: "J'ai beau voir ses défauts, et j'ai beau l'en blâmer, / En dépit qu'on en ait, elle se fait aimer" (1.1.231–32) [I'm weak as water with her. All that I can do, / Is go on loving her. I'm sorry, but it's true]. The truth is quite another story. Lionel Gossman goes to the core of the relationship between the two:

It is precisely because Célimène is the most sought after and *worldly* of women (to all *appearances* the most unsuitable for Alceste) that he falls in love with her. It is not Célimène that Alceste loves or desires. She is irrelevant *as a person* to his "love." It is the world that he seeks to reach and possess through her. To have at his feet this woman whom all the world admires and courts would be to win the recognition of the world for himself. Alceste's love is entirely mediated by those very "gens à la mode" for whom he so loudly protests his contempt. He "loves" Célimène because she has what he wants—the admiration of the world— and cannot admit he wants, without at the same time admitting that he is not the free, frank, and independent person he wants to be admired as. The object of his desire is thus also his unavowed rival, and this *for the very same reason* that she is the object of his desire.[25]

Célimène's strategy differs from Alceste's but her objective is the same. She wants the same recognition from the very same people. By cleverly playing them off against each other, she keeps all their attention focused on herself.

As with many of Molière's couples, their understanding of each other far exceeds their self-awareness. What they see least of all is how alike they are and how their competing for attention intensifies that likeness. Célimène meets Alceste's complaint that she encourages Clitandre's advances with a barbed reply that in one line captures Alceste's truth: "Mais de tout l'univers vous devenez jaloux" (2.1.495) [You're growing jealous of the entire universe]. He perceives everyone, including Célimène herself, as a rival. Her resistance to him turns Célimène into a rival he must overcome, while at the same time she is the prize he must win. Although his retort shows no cognizance of the accuracy of Célimène's insight, it is as telling as hers: "C'est que tout l'univers est bien reçu de vous" (2.1.496). [The universe pays court to you, it's too perverse]. Alceste and Célimène are identical in their overwhelming preoccupation with "tout l'univers." They reflect each other, seeing in each other's eyes not a lover but themselves.[26] Gazing out at the world, they see everyone in the same light. Alceste's need for distinction and Célimène's for admiration lead each of them to deny the individuality of all others.

The champion of truth and the coquette are not two different souls who have fallen in love and seek common ground on which their affection might grow. On the contrary, they emerge as so much alike that their world collapses around them. It has been said that Molière's monomaniacal characters never change, and nowhere is this truer than in *Le Misanthrope*. Prepared though she is to marry Alceste, Célimène cannot leave society, she cannot aban-

don her coquetry. Nor can Alceste accept a life with her unless she
bestows upon him her unmitigated love and attention. They cannot form a union in which they will accommodate each other's differences and contribute to society's carrying on as it ought. For this
to happen, Molière seems to say, radical characters like Alceste and
Célimène must be neutralized or eliminated, and this is, in fact, the
path that comedy generally takes to restore good order.

With Célimène discredited by the airing of her letters to Acaste
and Clitandre, and Alceste on the verge of his definitive departure,
Eliante and Philinte step forward as the ideal couple whose betrothal concludes the play happily and holds out the model by
which society can regain its equilibrium. Or does it? With the last
two lines of *Le Misanthrope*, Molière recognizes that this restoration
of order, so appropriate to comedy, is at best temporary. The rivalry that has exposed the sameness underlying the characters' differences has been momentarily deactivated, not eradicated. In a
rich variety of guises, it recurs in all of Molière's great plays. He
engages it directly each time, reaches a happy conclusion—and
moves on in his next play to face it once again.

2
Power and Identity: The Method in Arnolphe's Madness

JEAN DONNEAU DE VISÉ IS NOT A WRITER TO WHOM ONE WOULD IN-stinctively turn for telling commentary on the work of Molière.[1] In the first chapter of his *Caractères*, La Bruyère calls the *Mercure galant*, which Donneau de Visé founded and edited, "immédiatement au-dessous de rien"[2] [distinctly less than nothing]. Donneau de Visé was also a minor playwright and the author of three volumes of *Nouvelles nouvelles* in which appeared the first published attack against *L'Ecole des femmes*. This blast he followed with three more assaults on the play—in *Zélinde ou la véritable critique de* L'Ecole des femmes *ou la critique de* La Critique, the *Réponse à* L'Impromptu de Versailles *ou la vengeance des marquis*, and, finally, his *Lettre sur les affaires du théâtre*—and he prided himself on being the author of a shabby ditty aimed at Molière, the "Chanson de la coquille." Boursault inserted this lewd piece into his *Portrait du peintre ou la contre-critique de* L'Ecole des femmes but dared not include it in the play's published version.[3] What La Bruyère says about the *Mercure galant* applies as well to Donneau de Visé's little song, which most literary historians have discreetly passed over (*OC* 1:1385).

The reason given in the *Nouvelles nouvelles* for Molière's preoccupation with cuckolds and jealous men is, quite simply, that he was himself "du nombre de ces derniers" (*OC* 1:1022) [one of their number]. Molière's comic genius cannot be completely denied, but *L'Ecole des femmes* is little more than "un monstre qui a de belles parties" (*OC* 1:1021) [a monstrosity that has some beautiful parts]. Yet in the midst of ad hominem barbs and a generally unenlightening critique of the play, Donneau de Visé poses some valid questions about the work. Why, for example, one of the characters in *Zélinde* wonders, does Molière have Arnolphe invite Chrysalde to join him for dinner with Agnès: "Il n'est pas vraisemblable qu'un homme qui craint si fort d'être cocu prie à souper avec sa maî-

35

tresse, sans aucune nécessité, un railleur qui semble lui prédire que, s'il se marie, son front ne sera pas exempt de porter ce qu'il craint" (*OC* 1:1027) [It is hardly credible that a man so fearful of being cuckolded would unnecessarily invite to join his mistress and him for supper a scoffer who seems to predict that if the host marries, he'll soon find on his forehead exactly what he most fears]. Molière, it is decided, uses the invitation as a ploy to indicate "la durée de sa pièce" [the duration of his play] and provide Chrysalde, "un personnage entièrement inutile" [a completely useless character], with a reason to reappear in the fourth act (*OC* 1:1027). But how superfluous is Chrysalde, and does Molière really have Arnolphe give the lie to his true character in the first act of the play? Seen from today's point of view, which recognizes Molière as one of the world's great comic writers, these responses to the question about Arnolphe's invitation to his antagonistic friend seem lame. The question itself, however, remains a provocative one.

The invitation to Chrysalde is not the only aspect of Arnolphe's behavior scrutinized by the characters in *Zélinde*. That Arnolphe would, on the basis of a letter from a friend whom he has not seen in four years, turn over to Horace one hundred *pistoles* strikes Argimont as incongruous (*OC* 1:1027–28). Arnolphe's largesse is all the more improbable, since immediately upon receiving the money, Horace tells his benefactor that it will be used to seduce Agnès: this surely "devrait aussitôt faire connaître à Arnolphe qu'il a mal donné son argent, et que son ami ne lui en emprunterait pas pour servir aux débauches de son fils" (*OC* 1:1028) [ought immediately let Arnolphe know that he was wrong to give away his money and that his friend would not borrow from him to pay for the debauchery of the friend's son]. Nor can Argimont fathom why Arnolphe insists on making Agnès read the famous *maximes du mariage*: "N'est-ce pas lui vouloir faire connaître, en un quart d'heure, ce qu'il a, pendant plusieurs années, pris soin de lui faire cacher, et lui enseigner les moyens de le faire cocu, en lui apprenant comment se gouvernent les femmes coquettes?" (*OC* 1:1030) [Isn't this like showing her in fifteen minutes what for several years he took care to keep hidden from her and teaching her the ways of making him a cuckold, by showing her how coquettish women behave?]. Horace, too, according to Argimont, behaves improbably. It makes no sense for him to persist in recounting to Arnolphe every detail of his eventful courting of Agnès, especially given the increasingly cold reception he receives from his jealous interlocutor. The initial "démangeaison de découvrir sa bonne fortune" (*OC* 1:1028) [itch to disclose his good fortune] is not enough to explain Horace's un-remitting urge to tell all.[4]

The criticism that Donneau de Visé levels against *L'Ecole des femmes* comes down, in large measure, to the claim that much of the play's action is unreasonable. In addition, Arnolphe and Horace are not always true to themselves, and Agnès is a witty but simpleminded girl, at one minute behaving so stupidly that Arnolphe's plan to "la rendre idiote autant qu'il se pourrait" (1.1.138) [bring her up as ignorant as possible][5] seems to have worked, and at the next, acting like a clever young woman (*OC* 1:1043). Zélinde thinks it preposterous that Horace gives Agnès to Arnolphe for safekeeping in the fifth act of the play. Molière, she suggests, would probably explain this gesture by saying that his young lover is an "étourdi" [scatterbrain], but "ce n'est pas une raison, et pour excuser ses fautes, il n'aurait qu'à dire que tous ses personnages sont fous; mais s'il est ainsi, il devait appeler sa pièce *L'Hôpital de fous*, et faire paraître les petites maisons sur le théâtre, comme a fait autrefois Beys" (*OC* 1:1044) [this is not a reason, and to make an excuse for Horace's mistakes, all he'd have to say is that all his characters are crazy; but if this is true, he should have called the play *The Mad House* and put the "petites maisons" on stage as Beys did before him]. This, of course, implies that they are not all completely mad, and it is, therefore, legitimate to expect from them a modicum of consistent, sane behavior. Despite Donneau de Visé's nasty tone and often superficial critique, the seemingly con-tradictory behavior on which he focuses attention calls for an ex-planation. After all, who would disagree with him when, in his *Lettre sur les affaires du théâtre*, he writes that "quoique nous voyons bien des jaloux, nous en voyons peu qui ressemblent à Arnolphe" (*OC* 1:1111) [although we see lots of jealous men, we see few who resemble Arnolphe]?

A set of assumptions about the creation of comic characters un-derlies Donneau de Visé's objections to *L'Ecole des femmes*. Molière would, he surmises, share these ideas but betrays them throughout his play. Donneau de Visé expects, above all, that characters will be fully coherent. If Arnolphe is intended to be jealous, he must at every moment behave like the jealous lover. Like Dom Garcie de Navarre, he should be intelligible by his jealousy, an inherent char-acteristic active no matter what others say or do. By their behavior, others can incite a jealous reaction or allay some of the jealous lov-er's worst fears, but the jealousy itself remains independent of oth-ers. The jealous character can do nothing more than control his passion. Knowing this, a reader or an audience ought to understand all of Arnolphe's actions by reference to his jealousy.

The Molière of *L'Ecole des femmes*, while maintaining a perspective that converges with Donneau de Visé's, moves in a different direction. In *Dom Garcie de Navarre*, he put on stage a character similar to the one Donneau de Visé has in mind. Dom Garcie *is* jealous. In the absence of a rival, he invents one. But *Dom Garcie de Navarre* was a resounding failure, because, according to Donneau de Visé, Molière "fut trouvé incapable de jouer aucunes pièces sérieuses" (*OC* 1:1018) [was found incapable of putting on any serious plays]. This may be true, but Molière also began, in his best plays, to draw more nuanced, more complicated characters. No longer can his best characters be portrayed in the essentialist terms that define Dom Garcie. Monsieur Jourdain in the *Bourgeois gentilhomme*, for instance, is the social climber par excellence, but his desire for social status is not an inherent quality that exists without reference to other people. On the contrary, Jourdain can make no decision without first ascertaining whether "les gens de qualité" [people of quality] would approve. While Dom Garcie appears impermeable to the will of others, the *bourgeois gentilhomme* relies totally on them. Arnolphe is cast from the same mold as his unhappy predecessor. Donneau de Visé's reservations reflect, however, that Arnolphe also has much in common with later characters like Monsieur Jourdain. What he fails to see is that in *L'Ecole des femmes*, Molière moves away from an essentialist, Cartesian notion of the individual and that Arnolphe reflects this change.

Arnolphe's very first words demonstrate his character. In response to Chrysalde's inquiry about his engagement, Arnolphe declares: "Oui, je veux terminer la chose dans demain" (1.1.2) [That's right. I want to sort things out without delay]. Here, then, is a man who would be affirmative, decisive, even aggressive. Once he has decided to act, he will brook no opposition. With a pride typical of Molière's comic heroes, he steps onto the scene saying, "Oui, je...." But why does a man, intent on domination of others, say "je veux" rather than "je vais terminer la chose dans demain"? The truth is that Arnolphe wants to marry Agnès, he wants to control her, he wants not to be a cuckold. He is driven by his desire for power rather than by a feeling of power. He wants, above all, to be different from others and superior to them.[6] His frustrated attempts to exercise the power he seeks are at the heart of the play's humor.

To avoid becoming a cuckold, Arnolphe has a plan: "Chacun a sa méthode. / En femme, comme en tout, je veux suivre ma mode" (1.1.123–24) [I'll do the thing my way. / I've chosen my own wife,

I'm going to have my say]. Whether or not he is conscious of all he has said here, Arnolphe reveals his obsessive desire to follow his "méthode" in everything he does. "En femme," the method could hardly be clearer. He is rich enough, he believes, to "choisir une moitié qui tienne tout de moi" [choose a wife who owes everything to me] and from whom he can, therefore, exact a "soumise et pleine dépendance" (1.1.126–27) [complete and obedient dependence]. (Translations by author) Just before showing Agnès the *maximes du mariage*, Arnolphe reminds her that marriage to him will rescue her from a lowly social status. This should make her immensely grateful:

> Je vous épouse, Agnès, et cent fois la journée
> Vous devez bénir l'heur de votre destinée,
> Contempler la bassesse où vous avez été,
> Et dans le même temps admirer ma bonté,
> Qui de ce vil état de pauvre villageoise
> Vous fait monter au rang d'honorable bourgeoise.
>
> (3.2.679–84)

> [I'm going to marry you, Agnes, and from now on
> You should thank God that your good fortune has begun,
> And bear in mind the lowness of your former state,
> And realize how good I am to contemplate
> Removing you from base and brutish village life,
> And making you a decent, bourgeois, lady wife.]

It is only natural that Agnès submit to her husband, for, as Arnolphe instructs her, "Votre sexe n'est là que pour la dépendance: / Du côté de la barbe est la toute-puissance" (3.2.699–700) [Your sex exists to be meek and subordinate, / Us men, who wear the beards, are here to dominate]. Her mission is to be dependent, his to lord it over her.

Arnolphe's talk of male omnipotence is neither idle nor exaggerated. He means exactly what he says. If his intent is not quite to become God, he does want to put himself on the same plane as God. The "sotte" (1.1.82) [fool] whom he hopes to marry may be empty-headed, but she must not be totally passive: "Et c'est assez pour elle, à vous en bien parler, / De savoir prier Dieu, m'aimer, coudre et filer" (1.1.101–2) [I want her ignorant, since all she needs to know / Is how to love me, pray God, and spin and sew]. Agnès's first duty will be to pray to God, but it is Arnolphe—not God—whom she is to love; and her obligation toward Arnolphe is of a quasi-religious nature. He compares her to a novice in a convent: Agnès must learn the *maximes du mariage* as a novice learns the Divine Office (3.2.739–43). Lest she have the slightest doubt about what her future husband envisions, Arnolphe issues a peremptory order: "Je suis maître, je parle: allez, obéissez" (2.5.642) [I'm master here. I've spoken. Come on now, obey!]. In his prenuptial exhortation, he compares the relationship of a good wife to her husband to that of a "valet à son maître" (3.2.707) [valet who serves his master]. The obedience owed by a friar to his religious superior can hardly approach the "profond respect où la femme doit être / Pour son mari, son chef, son seigneur et son maître" (3.2.711–12) [profound respect she must show, in a word, / To him, for he's her husband, ruler, chief, and lord]. So absolute is the proposed subjugation of Agnès that she will become "un morceau de cire" (3.8.810) [a lump of wax] in Arnolphe's hands, molded and shaped to his likes. Once married, Agnès will relinquish completely her personal autonomy in favor of the godlike power of her husband.

Arnolphe's method, like that of Descartes, is founded upon fundamental principles designed to accomplish a particular end. By raising Agnès in a state of ignorance and marrying her, Arnolphe expects to dominate her, to be the master of her personal life as well as his own. His marriage will be "foolproof."[7] In this, he will differ from other men, who are tricked by their wives and ridiculed for their foolishness. Ultimately, Arnolphe desires power to guarantee his independence from others. He imagines a life in which Agnès obeys him and in which he remains secure in the knowledge of her fidelity. Less fortunate men will be "des sujets de satire" (1.1.43) [subjects of satire] (Translation by author), while he, laughing at their unhappy lot, fancies himself an aloof "spectateur" (1.1.44). As James F. Gaines indicates, "Prédire, prévoir, précaution, prévention, toutes les modalités des verbes et des substantifs qui caractérisent la pensée d'Arnolphe trahissent le désir d'anticiper la vie même en vivant toute situation à l'avance dans un petit univers cérébral"[8] [Predict, foresee, precaution, preconception, all the forms of verbs and substantives that characterize Arnolphe's thought betray a desire to anticipate life itself by living out every situation in advance, in the closed little universe of his mind]. Arnolphe wants to create for himself the identity of a man apart, thoroughly different in at least one significant way from others. Agnès, too, must take care not to resemble others: "Mais ne vous gâtez pas sur l'exemple d'autrui. / Gardez-vous d'imiter ces coquettes vilaines / Dont par toute la ville on chante les fredaines" (3.2.718–20) [But you should never care what other people say. /

Don't try to imitate coquettes who make me frown: / Their shocking doings are the talk of all the town]. Radical individuality is Arnolphe's highest value. He defines who he is by what he is not, a cuckold.

Social pretension in Molière's theater often accompanies the will to power and the concomitant desire for self-distinction. Arnolphe does not go as far as Monsieur Jourdain, but he does take for himself a new and ennobling name, Monsieur de la Souche. His noble name is crucial to the play's plot, for her suitor, Horace, knows Agnès's guardian only as de la Souche. Horace does not, therefore, recognize that his confidant, Arnolphe, is also his rival. Max Vernet suggests that by choosing this ridiculous name, Arnolphe intends to "faire souche," to be at the origin of a noble house.[9] Arnolphe gives no convincing reasons for his abrupt change of name: "Mais enfin de la Souche est le nom que je porte: / J'y vois de la raison, j'y trouve des appas; / Et m'appeler de l'autre est ne m'obliger pas" (1.1.184–86) [But anyway my name is Monsieur de la Souche. / I changed it for a reason, I prefer it now: / You'd best forget the other, or we'll have a row]. What others think matters not a whit. When, for example, Chrysalde insists that it is an "abus de quitter le vrai nom de ses pères" (1.1.175) [madness to give up the name your fathers bore], Arnolphe tyrannically demands that his friend accept his new name. With Chrysalde, as with Agnès, he will have his way. The patent foolishness of the name de la Souche serves to demonstrate that once he has made up his mind, he is inflexible. He cannot order his friend to obey as he did his prospective bride (3.1.642), but his attitude toward Chrysalde is the same as toward Agnès.

In his extreme self-involvement, Arnolphe seems devoid of concern with the feelings and opinions of others, let alone their will. Always the distant observer, he is merciless in his satire of men cuckolded by their wives. Yet Arnolphe is not as self-sufficient as his apparent disdain of others might lead one to believe. In curious ways, he recognizes intimate ties to the community he scorns. Immediately after his first encounter with Horace, he frets about his own honor:

> J'y prends pour mon honneur un notable intérêt:
> Je la [Agnès] regarde en femme, aux termes qu'elle en est;
> Elle n'a pu faillir sans me couvrir de honte,
> Et tout ce qu'elle a fait enfin est sur mon compte.
>
> (2.1.381–84)

[My honour is at stake, I'm taking it to heart.
I see her as my wife, and that's what makes me smart.
Ah, if she's let me down, then I'll be filled with shame:
For everything she does, she's doing in my name.]

In other words, Agnès's actions will reflect upon Arnolphe, since others will observe them and judge him accordingly.

As Agnès is about to read the *maximes du mariage*, Arnolphe tells her that his honor will soon be in her hands: "Songez qu'en vous faisant moitié de ma personne, / C'est mon honneur, Agnès, que je vous abandonne" (3.2.723–24) [Just bear in mind that you're becoming half of me, / So you're the keeper of my honour, Agnes, see?]. He is convinced by her recitation of the *maximes* that he should marry her, for her innocence is less menacing to him than the wiles of some crafty woman. He knows that whether he is married to an unschooled innocent or a treacherous, deceitful woman, his reputation will depend on other peoples' perceptions of his wife: "Mais une femme habile est bien une autre bête; / Notre sort ne dépend que de sa seule tête" (3.3.820–21) [A clever wife is quite another kettle of fish—/ Our destiny depends upon her lightest wish]. As if to emphasize the role of women in establishing a man's reputation, he repeats virtually the same sentiment a mere ten lines later: "Une femme d'esprit est un diable en intrigue; / Et dès que son caprice a prononcé tout bas / L'arrêt de votre honneur, il faut passer le pas" (3.3.829–31) [A clever woman's learnt her mischief, long ago. / And when she makes her mind up, you can be quite sure / Your honour will be gone, all you can do's endure]. When he discovers that Agnès attached a letter to the stone he had ordered her to throw down on Horace, he is crestfallen. Her unfaithfulness is, of course, a blow to his love, but her pursuit of the *blondin* tarnishes his honor as well: "l'amour y pâtit aussi bien que l'honneur" (3.5.987) [my honour is at stake, / He's made off with her heart].

Furetière defines "honneur" as a "tesmoignage d'estime ou de soumission qu'on rend à quelqu'un par ses paroles ou par ses actions"[10] [a token of esteem or submission that one offers to another by words or actions]. Honor, in short, is granted by others. Meritorious comportment alone cannot attain it. To assure his, Arnolphe must be seen by other people as married to a faithful, devoted wife. In addition to defending his love for Agnès against the advances of Horace, he must ward off the ridicule he will attract if others become aware of his fiancée's infidelity. He dreams of being the only undeceived husband. On this achievement will his honor rest, much as that of Corneille's heroes resides in their unquestioned devotion to country or family. Arnolphe's desire for honor, that is, his desire to avoid cuckoldry, makes him dependent on others. Without their confirmation, his image of himself crumbles. But he has apparently discovered a sure path to success: "Epouser une sotte est pour n'être point sot" (1.1.82)[11] [To wed a fool is not to become one, as a rule]. He has not, of course, counted on the intervention of nature as Agnès grows up.[12] "L'amour," he soon learns, "est un grand maître" (3.4.900) [Love is the greatest teacher in the world].

Ironically, Arnolphe, the detached, derisive spectator, understands the need for recognition by others in the lives of his servants:

> On veut à mon honneur jouer d'un mauvais tour;
> Et quel affront pour vous, mes enfants, pourrait-ce être,
> Si l'on avait ôté l'honneur à votre maître!
> Vous n'oseriez après paraître en nul endroit,
> Et chacun vous voyant, vous montrerait au doigt.
>
> (4.4.1095–99)[13]

> [For right now you must know that there's a dreadful crime
> Been planned against my honour. Think about the shame,
> The sleaze of your poor master losing his good name!
> You wouldn't dare to show your faces in the street,
> And you'd be pointed at by everyone you meet.]

He attempts to make Alain and Georgette follow the dictates of another person, in this case, their master, rather than their own instincts. The servants should want what the master wants in order to avoid the public reprobation that will befall them should Arnolphe lose his honor. Arnolphe intervenes in this scene to influence his servants not with threats or violence, but by inciting them to attend to that most human of preoccupations, namely, what other people think. That his urging moves Alain and Georgette is doubtful. A larger issue is his articulation of a model of behavior more universal than he suspects, but one seemingly inimical to a character like himself, bent on dominating, not following, others. His domineering grasp on his servants as on Agnès will go for naught if he does not gain their obedience and, therefore, his mastery. The subservience of Alain and Georgette, like Agnès's fidelity, grants him a superiority that others must recognize.

Donneau de Visé's question about Arnolphe's invitation to Chrysalde to dine with Agnès warrants consideration. The invitation is in no way gratuitous. By issuing it, Arnolphe unknowingly uncovers the truth about himself. He has just told his friend about how he had acquired Agnès from a peasant woman, had her raised in an isolated convent, and then brought her to one of his city houses. Agnès, he is sure, will be the perfect wife, because she knows no better. Arnolphe now wants Chrysalde to see the product of his efforts:

> Le résultat de tout est qu'en ami fidèle
> Ce soir je vous invite à souper avec elle;
> Je veux que vous puissiez un peu l'examiner,
> Et voir si de mon choix on me doit condamner.
>
> (1.1.151–54)

> [And now I'd like to ask you, as a faithful friend,
> To dine with us tonight. Come, will you condescend?
> Then you'll see the result of my experiment,
> And judge if my precaution's worthy of contempt.]

He is not merely showing Chrysalde his handiwork. He also asks him to approve it, "voir si de mon choix on me doit condamner." Whether he has made the right choice in Agnès depends less upon her or himself than upon Chrysalde. He invites his friend to dinner with Agnès in order to gain Chrysalde's approval of his "méthode" and what it has produced. Far from being superfluous, Chrysalde has a vital function: to give his approval of Arnolphe and to confirm Arnolphe's difference from other men, including Chrysalde himself.[14]

The invitation to Chrysalde exposes in adumbrated form a pattern of behavior often associated in Molière's theater with jealous lovers. Donneau de Visé reproaches Molière for creating nothing but jealous heroes: "la jalousie est tout ce qui les fait agir depuis le commencement jusques à la fin de ses pièces sérieuses, aussi bien que de ses comiques" (*OC* 1:1111) [from the beginning to the end of both his serious plays and his comedies, jealousy is all that makes his heroes act]. What Georges Couton calls the "cycle de cocuage" (*OC* 1:297) [cycle of cuckoldry] begins with *Sganarelle ou le cocu imaginaire* and reaches a point of high comedy in *L'Ecole des femmes*. All the cuckolds, real or not, are jealous lovers. Their jealousy manifests itself in different ways but, in the end, always makes the cuckolds depend upon a rival for whatever personal fulfillment they seek. Donneau de Visé is puzzled about why Arnolphe does not dismiss Horace and proceed as he had planned. To judge by earlier plays, however, rivalry is necessary to advance the action of the play.

In *Le Cocu imaginaire* and *Dom Garcie de Navarre*, Sganarelle and the eponymous prince invent rivals where none exist. The plot of the former play moves from one improbable misunderstanding to the next until a *suivante* untangles a hopelessly confused knot of misapprehensions. Sganarelle imagines that his wife is having an affair with Lélie, while the wife finds evidence that her husband is courting Célie, whose father, Gorgibus, has promised her to Lélie. The young couple, in turn, is torn by similar fears. Célie is convinced that her lover has abandoned her for Sganarelle's wife. Lélie assumes that Célie has married Sganarelle. All this on the basis of what characters think they have observed, whence the play's concluding lines: "De cet exemple-ci ressouvenez-vous bien; / Et, quand vous verriez tout, ne croyez jamais rien" (sc. 24.656–57) [When all the evidence as you receive it / Adds up to one conclusion: don't believe it].[15] Jealousy becomes a contagion in *Le Cocu imaginaire*, spreading wildly from character to character. Before long, it has polluted everything; no one can escape it. Once jealousy has taken hold, all the characters mistrust each other, and only the intervention of an individual untouched by jealousy can bring them back to their senses. In *L'Ecole des femmes*, the leveling effect of jealousy makes Arnolphe view all men in the same light.[16] They are all potential rivals; they all desire Agnès. As Arnolphe's jealousy grows, different characters in the play behave in increasingly similar ways. Sganarelle and the other characters in *Le Cocu imaginaire* fall into error and allow themselves to be carried away by it. Arnolphe is closer in spirit to Dom Garcie than to Sganarelle. At times, he is a sad figure for whom the audience may even feel pity.[17] He differs from Dom Garcie in that a character flaw is not at the root of his preoccupation with rivals. It is his method that leads to rivalry. His will to dominate makes rivals of those whom he would control.

Arnolphe's jealous rivalry with Horace has about it something of the same compulsiveness as Dom Garcie's inability to love without rivals. Arnolphe loves a young girl whom he has raised to be the ideal wife, and a rival appears on the scene. Though resenting the rival, Arnolphe is unwilling to extricate himself from a demeaning relationship with him. At the same time that he uses against Horace whatever information he gathers from him, he encourages him by providing him with money. Although he takes no joy in his conversations with the loquacious Horace, he says little to discourage actively the young man's love for Agnès. So engaged is Arnolphe in his rivalry with Horace that, at times, it displaces his love for Agnès as the primary subject of his attention. Whether Arnolphe could love Agnès without a rival is doubtful. What is certain is that the rival is always present. One day, Horace unexpectedly comes upon Agnès on her balcony, and she invites him to her room. Hardly have the lovers entered her quarters when Arnolphe appears, distraught, "poussant de temps en temps des soupirs pitoyables" (4.6.1156) [And every now and then, he'd heave a heavy sigh]. Agnès hides Horace in her armoire, from which observation point he sees Arnolphe hit her dog, pound on the furniture, and throw her clothes about the room. Shortly after this violent scene, Horace meets Arnolphe and recounts the event to him. A dismayed Arnolphe reacts in one of his conspicuous monologues to what he has just heard.[18]

The closest Arnolphe comes in this speech to any mention of either Agnès or his love for her renders the girl mere chattel, a prize he owns and means to keep in his possession: "De l'objet qu'on poursuit je suis encore nanti; / Si son coeur m'est volé par ce blondin funeste, / J'empêcherai du moins qu'on s'empare du reste" (4.7.1207–9) [For you forget the object of desire is mine. / Although her heart's been won by that blond saboteur, / At least I can prevent him from taking all of her]. Although saddened at the prospect that Agnès might not love him, Arnolphe finds a silver lining in the cloud over his future: "Ce m'est quelque plaisir . . . que cet étourdi, qui veut m'être fatal, / Fasse son confidant de son propre rival" (4.7.1212; 1214–15) [it cheers me up to know / . . . though / We're both at daggers drawn, this scatterbrained gallant / Has made his deadly enemy his confidant]. His love for Agnès is subordinated to his rivalry with Horace. The most threatening aspect of his rival's seduction of Agnès is that despite twenty years of planning and vigilance, Arnolphe is now in danger of being cuckolded.[19] This means that he will be identical to other men whom he has for so long derided:

> Des disgrâces d'autrui profitant dans mon âme,
> J'ai cherché les moyens, voulant prendre une femme,
> De pouvoir garantir mon front de tous affronts,
> Et le tirer de pair d'avec les autres fronts.
>
> (4.6.1192–95)

> [I learnt from their misfortunes how to live my life.
> When it was time for me to find myself a wife,
> I thought that I could hold my cuckold's horns at bay:
> I'd be the one to keep those wretched boys away.]

It is impossible to separate Arnolphe's love for Agnès from his desire to be different, to be unique.[20] When Horace finally succeeds, as he must, in his seduction of Agnès, he will strip Arnolphe of both the young girl he loves and his individuality.

What pathos there is in *L'Ecole des femmes* has its source in Arnolphe's love for Agnès. Loving her causes him genuine pain. His love, not unlike Dom Garcie's, is heightened when an obstacle stands in its way. In his first conversation with Chrysalde, he claims that Agnès's gentleness led him to fall in love with her when she was only four years old (1.1.130). Although the love one feels for a child of four is not normally of the kind that would eventuate in marriage, Arnolphe's case is different, for this first allusion to his love for Agnès is folded into his explanation to Chrysalde of his "méthode." From the start, Arnolphe's quest for individualism and his love are inextricably connected.

His love becomes more intense as he recognizes his young rival's success with Agnès. Upon learning about her secret letter to Horace, he explicitly links his love and the opinion others will have of him:

> Je souffre doublement dans le vol de son coeur,
> Et l'amour y pâtit aussi bien que l'honneur,
> J'enrage de trouver cette place usurpée,
> Et j'enrage de voir ma prudence trompée.
>
> (3.5.986–89)

> [I'm suffering both ways—my honour is at stake,
> He's made off with her heart, and oh, how mine does ache!
> I'm furious: he's occupied my property
> And thwarted all my plans by sheer duplicity.]

By holding on to Agnès, he will vindicate his method and defy his rival:

> Non, parbleu! non, parbleu! Petit sot, mon ami,
> Vous aurez beau tourner: ou j'y perdrai mes peines,
> Ou je rendrai, ma foi, vos espérances vaines,
> Et de moi tout à fait vous ne vous rirez point.
>
> (4.1.1035–38)

> [No, damn it! You won't get away with it, you'll see,
> You stupid oaf! You'll fail, and I'll do everything
> To stop you. You deserve your share of suffering,
> You won't have the last laugh. Not now, at my expense.]

Rivalry, not love, moves Arnolphe here. It is as if the only reason to marry Agnès were to vanquish Horace, who now influences every move that Arnolphe makes.[21]

Just as Dom Garcie loves Done Elvire despite the unfaithfulness he sees in her—or is it because of it?—all the reasons for which Arnolphe should not love Agnès serve rather to magnify his love:

> Elle n'a ni parents, ni support, ni richesse;
> Elle trahit mes soins, mes bontés, ma tendresse;
> Et cependant je l'aime, après ce lâche tour,
> Jusqu'à ne me pouvoir passer de cet amour.
>
> (3.5.996–99)

> [She's got no family, no money, no support,
> But she's betrayed me, let me down without a thought.
> And yet I love her, even if she's led me on.
> I love her so, I'll be destroyed if she is gone.]

The impossibility of his match with her entices him: "J'étais aigri, fâché, désespéré contre elle: / Et cependant jamais je ne la vis si belle" (4.1.1020–21) [I felt embittered, helpless too, and sorrowful, / And yet I'd never seen her look so beautiful]. He is drawn to her in spite of the impediments in the way of his love, which he is quick to rehearse. In fact, these obstacles enflame his desire. That is why he recites them. Arnolphe wants what he cannot have, Agnès's subjugation and her love. Although he loves her, his love is tainted, by rivalry with Horace or by rivalry with the whole society of cuckolds.

Haunted by the fear of resembling others, he tells Chrysalde, "Quoiqu'il m'arrive, au moins aurai-je l'avantage / De ne pas ressembler à de certaines gens / Qui souffrent doucement l'approche des galants" (4.8.1225–27) [Whatever happens, I won't suffer the disgrace / Of realizing I'm just like some men I know, / Who most politely welcome in their ladies' beaux]. As Pierre Force writes, "chez Arnolphe, le désir d'échapper au sort commun constitue le sens profond de la crainte du cocuage. Pour Arnolphe, tous les maris sont cocus. Ce qui, au fond, le terrifie, n'est pas tant le cocuage lui-même que la perspective d'être confondu dans la masse des maris cocus"[22]. [In Arnolphe's case, his desire to escape the common fate constitutes the deeper meaning of his fear of cuckoldry. As far as Arnolphe is concerned, all husbands are cuckolds. At bottom, what terrifies him is not so much cuckoldry itself as the perspective of being blended into the mass of deceived husbands]. The extent to which Arnolphe resembles his opponents presages his ultimate failure. In their first conversation, Chrysalde foresees that the tables might well turn on Arnolphe: "Oui; mais qui rit d'autrui / Doit craindre qu'en revanche on rie aussi de lui" (1.1.45–46) [it's dangerous to chaff / Your victims will be keen to take their turn to laugh]. Is it possible to avoid what Chrysalde calls a "revers de satire" (1.1.56) [thought that it might turn against me], which would place Arnolphe in the same position as those he ridicules?

Chrysalde's warning resonates throughout *L'Ecole des femmes*, particularly in the scenes in which rivalry leaves competitors indistinguishable. As Arnolphe returns home in the play's first act, his servants, Alain and Georgette, compete with each other, first not to open the door for him, and then, when Arnolphe threatens to cut their rations, to welcome him. Their words, as well as their sentiments, are identical:

ALAIN. Ouvre là-bas.
GEORGETTE. Vas-y, toi.
ALAIN. Vas-y, toi.
GEORGETTE. Ma foi, je n'irai pas.
ALAIN. Je n'irai pas aussi.

(1.2.201–3)

GEORGETTE. Ôte-toi donc de là.
ALAIN. Non, ôte-toi, toi-même.
GEORGETTE. Je veux ouvrir la porte.
ALAIN. Et je veux l'ouvrir, moi.

(1.2.212–13)

[ALAIN. Open the door.
GEORGETTE. No. Open it yourself!
ALAIN. No, you go.
GEORGETTE. No, what for?
ALAIN. Well, I won't go, so there!

GEORGETTE. Get out of it!
ALAIN. No, you get out of it! This ain't for kicks!
GEORGETTE. I want to let him in.
ALAIN. That's what I want to do.]

Agnès and Horace meet when he sees her on the balcony and bows to her. She returns his bow and a farcical competition begins to see who will bow last. In Agnès's description of this curious scene, there is a genuine rivalry between the two. The bowing and scraping went on and on:

Tant que, si sur ce point la nuit ne fût venue,
Toujours comme cela je me serais tenue,
Ne voulant point céder, et recevoir l'ennui
Qu'il me pût estimer moins civile que lui.

(2.5.499–502)

[And if the evening hadn't come, I'm telling you,
I would have gone on standing there, till now. It's true—
I'd never once have given in, it couldn't be
That he should think me less polite and nice than he.]

References to "la révérence" [bowing] occur throughout the play. Agnès's bowing to Horace anticipates the later scenes in which Arnolphe tells her to bow before her husband-to-be (3.2.739) or, with grating sarcasm, proposes that she bow one last time to Horace (5.4.1720–21). Her motives in bowing to the two men are different, her gesture, the same.

Agnès may not be a great deal better off with Horace than she would have been with Arnolphe, for the two men do not differ as much as their intense rivalry might suggest. For Barbara Johnson, "Agnès will 'belong' to Horace no less surely, although more willingly, than she would have 'belonged' to Arnolphe."[23] According to Richard Goodkin, Horace is even more perverse than his rival, because the apparent openness of his discourse is, in reality, a sham.[24] Horace speaks the same language as Arnolphe. In a moment of candor, unaware he is addressing his rival, he enunciates his true intentions: "Pour moi, tous mes efforts, tous mes voeux les plus doux / Vont à m'en rendre maître en dépit du jaloux" (1.4.341–42) [Yes, she's my heart's desire: there's nothing I won't do / To get control of her, and give that brute his due]. He and Arnolphe share the desire to become Agnès's master. Both are motivated by their will to defeat a rival as well as by their love for Agnès. A good bourgeois, Arnolphe is convinced that money will bring his plan to fruition. His wealth enables him to have the wife he wants (1.1.125–26). Horace agrees that money, not love, conquers all. He tells Arnolphe:

Vous savez mieux que moi, quels que soient nos efforts,
Que l'argent est la clef de tous les grands ressorts,
Et que ce doux métal qui frappe tant de têtes,
En amour, comme en guerre, avance les conquêtes.

(1.4.345–48)

[An enterprise may fail, however hard we try,
And money is the key, you know as well as I.
It takes hard currency to turn a person's head:
In love as well as war it helps you get ahead.]

In affairs of the heart, as in those of the purse, Arnolphe and Horace are of one mind. Far from distinguishing them from each other, their rivalry brings out their similarities.

In other ways, too, the dashing young gallant, "de taille à faire des cocus" (1.4.302) [cut out to make cuckolds] (Translation by author), and the mean-minded old bourgeois panicked at the thought of being cuckolded, are more alike than either realizes. Despite their well-defined and seemingly opposite personalities, both look to others for confirmation of their character. Arnolphe knows what he wants to do but is incapable of following his carefully conceived method to accomplish his end. He is driven to display ostentatiously his own supposed virtue so that others will acknowledge his identity and superiority. For his part, Horace feels compelled to tell all. Even when he does not need Arnolphe's help, he keeps his rival informed of every step in his seduction of Agnès. He himself gives the reason for his garrulousness:

> Comme à mon seul ami, je veux bien vous l'apprendre:
> L'allégresse du coeur s'augmente à la répandre;
> Et goûtât-on cent fois un bonheur tout parfait,
> On n'en est pas content, si quelqu'un ne le sait.
>
> (4.6.1176–79)

[I'm telling you all this because you're my best friend:
I like to have things out—it helps me to unbend.
Whatever happens, I have always found it's true,
You can't be happy till you've talked about it too.]

Horace's love for Agnès demands that others know about it and recognize his conquest. He goes so far as to make Arnolphe participate in his affair by turning the poor girl over to his rival and asking that "dans votre maison, *en faveur de mes feux,* / Vous lui donniez retraite au moins un jour ou deux" (5.2.1426–27; emphasis added) [on behalf of my affection, you take her into your house for at least a day or two] (Translation by author).

Donneau de Visé sensed something amiss in the behavior of Arnolphe and Horace, who, by their actions, encourage, rather than neutralize potential rivals. When Arnolphe gives Horace money, he fails to realize that he is abetting his rival. But one can suppose that were he to know this, he would not turn down the opportunity to control Horace by providing him with funds. The underlying desire of both characters is for superiority over others, and this desire, by its very nature, makes them rivals for power. By discussing every detail of his affair, Horace seems almost to tempt his interlocutor into rivalry. Similarly, Arnolphe virtually plants in Agnès's mind the idea of infidelity when he introduces her to the *maximes du mariage* [maxims of marriage].

Jealousy, in *L'Ecole des femmes*, is famously—and vulgarly—defined as a tripartite relationship in which two rivals vie for the affections of a woman:

> La femme est en effet le potage de l'homme;
> Et quand un homme voit d'autres hommes parfois
> Qui veulent dans sa soupe aller tremper leurs doigts,
> Il en montre aussitôt une colère extrême.
>
> (2.3.436–39)

> [You see, a woman is a soup-bowl for her man;
> And when a fellow sees how other men begin
> To gather around his soup and dip their fingers in,
> He blows his top at once, it's driving him insane.]

Alain explains this to Georgette, who has no difficulty understanding the "potage" [soup] metaphor. Georgette agrees that violence ensues from rivalry, when Alain uses a military image to describe her reaction should some famished soul insist on sharing her soup with her: "Dis-moi, n'est-il pas vrai, quand tu tiens ton potage, / Que si quelque affamé venait pour en manger, / Tu serais en colère, et voudrais *le charger?*" (2.3.432–34; emphasis added) [Imagine if you've got a bowl of soup, / And then some greedy-guts comes running up to try / To help himself. Well? You'd go mad, you won't deny]. However, she also wonders why anger and hostility are the only responses possible. Perhaps it would be better if everyone shared his soup with others. Georgette points out that there are, after all, men quite happy to have their wives the mistresses of "les biaux Monsieux" (2.3.442) [handsome men]. This, Alain answers, shows only that "chacun n'a pas cette amitié goulue / Qui n'en veut que pour soi" (2.3.443–44) [every man doesn't have this greedy attachment that wants everything for itself] (Translation by author). Georges Couton indicates (*OC* 1:1273) that Alain would appreciate La Rochefoucauld's definition of love:

Il est difficile de définir l'amour: ce qu'on en peut dire est que, dans l'âme, c'est une passion de régner; dans les esprits, c'est une sympathie; et dans les corps, ce n'est qu'une envie cachée et délicate de posséder ce que l'on aime après beaucoup de mystères. (Max. 68)[25]

[Love is difficult to define. What can be said about it is that in the soul, it is a passion to rule; in the mind, it is an instinctive attraction; and in the body, it is nothing but a fine, hidden desire to possess what one loves after many mysterious words, thoughts, and deeds.]

This certainly describes the feelings of both Arnolphe and Horace, who want to possess Agnès body and soul. Their jealousy of one another and their rivalry are inevitable. Arnolphe actually views jealousy as a virtue. He criticizes cuckolds for not troubling to have "soin jaloux" [jealous care] (Translation by author) for the purity and fidelity of their wives (1.1.29).

Although in later plays, Molière will delve more deeply into the dynamics of jealousy and rivalry, in *L'Ecole des femmes*, he already understands the tendency of rivalry to level differences between competitors. With his social pretentiousness, Arnolphe mimics the very people from whom he hopes to distance himself. This is the portent of Chrysalde's warnings to his friend. He tells Arnolphe in no uncertain terms that by changing his name, he is doing the opposite of what he intends: "De la plupart des gens c'est la démangeaison" (1.1.177) [You're not the only fellow bitten by this bug].

Having instructed his servants regarding the importance to them of his honor, Arnolphe tests them by pretending to be Horace and tempting them with bribes, as his rival had done to gain access to Agnès (2.4.555–57). He imitates Horace well, taking a tack used to good effect by the young lover's matchmaker to arrange his initial meeting with Agnès. Like the go-between, Arnolphe in his role as Horace claims that a love unrequited will be fatal to him: "Ma mort est sûre, / Si tu ne prends pitié des peines que j'endure" (4.4.1112–13) [I'm sure to die / Unless you show some pity. Couldn't you just try?]. It is as if an unarticulated awareness of how the *blondin* operates makes it possible for Arnolphe to step, for a brief moment, into Horace's shoes. He can do this because his love for Agnès, no less than Horace's, is La Rochefoucauld's "passion de régner" [passion to rule]. The two rivals are brothers under the skin.

Chrysalde's overly complaisant advice on the subject of cuckoldry[26] disqualifies him as a character who speaks for Molière, a *raisonneur*, but his contention that cuckoldry may not be as bad as Arnolphe thinks merits attention. Chrysalde exaggerates when he claims that "Le cocuage n'est que ce que l'on le fait" (4.8.1303)[27] [cuckoldry is only what you make of it]. However, he treats with equal harshness those who parade their wives' misdeeds in public and those who forever talk about avoiding the "monstre plein d'ef-froi" (4.8.1242) [something monstrous, hideous, and base]. The former "tirent vanité de ces sortes d'affaires" [treat their wives' af-fairs as if they were a joke] and "De leurs femmes toujours vont citant les galants" (4.8.1253–54) [And always have the lovers' say-ings on their lips]. The latter kind of husband is not that different, for he "Attire au bruit qu'il fait les yeux de tout le monde" (4.8.1265) [attracts by his goings-on the whole world's eyes] (Trans-lation by author). Chrysalde decries in both their call for recogni-tion from others. A man's honor, he seems to be saying, is his own, and despite what Arnolphe believes, it cannot be so easily be-smirched by someone else, even his wife. To rely upon oneself for the evaluation of one's worth is the correct defense against cuck-oldry. Arnolphe mistakenly looks outside himself for definition, and that is why Chrysalde tells him to remember: "Quoi que sur ce sujet votre honneur vous inspire, / Que c'est être à demi ce que l'on vient de dire, / Que de vouloir jurer qu'on ne le [a cuckold] sera pas" (4.8.1320–22) [You're taking a high moral tone in this affair—/ Of you-know-what, I mean—but still, you're halfway there, / If you insist on swearing it can never be].

Jealous rivalry can erupt in violence. In *L'Ecole des femmes*, vio-lence and death are always close at hand. Aside from the bit of slap-stack in which Arnolphe receives a blow from his servant (1.2.217), there is the paving stone thrown at Horace, Alain and Georgette's beating of the *blondin*, and Arnolphe's barely restrained desire to strike Agnès (5.4.1564–67). The old woman who introduces the two young lovers claims that Agnès's eyes have the power to "causer le trépas" (2.5.521) [kill men] and later dies. Arnolphe re-peatedly declares that this or that will kill him (3.5.982, 4.1.1024, 4.7.1214). He tells Agnès that he will gladly commit suicide to gain her love (5.4.1603–4). Horace is obliged to pretend he has been slain so that Arnolphe's servants will not finish him off, and he de-scribes how "J'ai d'un vrai trépassé su tenir la figure" (5.2.1397) [I lay there like a lifeless corpse—no vital spark]. He inflicts no injury on Arnolphe, but given the way he talks about his rival, he would probably respond in kind to the old man's violence were he to real-ize that Arnolphe is his rival, not his friend and advisor.

Agnès is naturally different from her suitors. With the exception of her bowing in response to Horace when they first meet, all of her reactions emanate from herself alone. She does not think about how others feel, and she cannot, therefore, imagine that they might want and take away from her what she desires. She relies uniquely on her own feelings to direct her actions. She does not love Arnolphe, and it would not occur to her to pretend to do so. Her demeanor is neither defiant nor aggressively willful. Unlike Arnolphe and Horace, she has no wish to dominate the man she loves. She loves Horace for the pleasure of it, and this, in and of itself, suffices: "Le moyen de chasser ce qui fait du plaisir?" she asks Arnolphe (5.4.1527) [But how can you control the instincts of your heart?]. Agnès's desire is self-contained. She represents Chrysalde's model for human behavior. Although she recognizes the authority that others may have, it has little substantial effect on her. When Arnolphe, on the verge of violence, threatens to hit her, she replies simply: "Hélas! vous le pouvez, si cela peut vous plaire" (5.4.1568) [Oh, dear, I can't stop you. Go on. Do what you like]. Arnolphe answers with the single indication in the play that his love for Agnès is not entirely motivated by the need for power over her: "Ce mot, et ce regard désarme ma colère, / Et produit un retour de tendresse de coeur" (5.4.1569–70) [That look, those words. I'm quite disarmed, and I can't strike / The girl. Instead, my heart is filled with tenderness]. Several lines later, however, he calls her a "petite traîtresse" (5.4.1580) [you little villainess]. His love cannot for long transcend his jealousy.

At play's end, Agnès and Horace are to be united, but Agnès remains silent. Her last words affirm that she does not want to go off with Arnolphe, who still does not comprehend that he is about to lose her. When he finally realizes what has occurred, he is, for the first time, struck dumb. He can say no more than "Oh!" (5.9.1764).[28] Arnolphe has always used words as weapons to overwhelm others. His loss of the power of speech amounts to total defeat. His downfall and the plans for the marriage of Horace to Agnès restore the proper order of things, and the characters are enjoined to "rendre grâce au Ciel qui fait tout pour le mieux" (5.9.1779) [thank the Lord, that things came out right, in the end]. But again, as in Le Misanthrope, the restoration of the natural order is temporary. As the curtain falls, Chrysalde suggests reimbursing Arnolphe for the cost incurred in "educating" Agnès. Horace can be expected to behave very much like Arnolphe. Jealous rivalry has not, despite the natural goodness of Agnès, been put to rest.

3

Enemy Brothers: The Interdependence
of Orgon and Tartuffe

NOWHERE MORE THAN IN *TARTUFFE* DOES MOLIÈRE DEMONSTRATE SO
forcefully what happens when one fails to recognize differences or,
worse yet, intentionally disregards them. Juxtaposing good and
evil, truth and falsehood, appearance and reality, religious piety
and hypocrisy, the play is a meditation on difference.[1] Only at their
peril do individuals and society neglect differences. Cléante makes
the point repeatedly, buttressing it with examples drawn from the
lives of both the wicked and their victims. He reproaches his
brother-in-law, Orgon, for precisely this reason: "Hé quoi? Vous
ne ferez nulle distinction / Entre l'hypocrisie et la dévotion?"
(1.5.331–32) [Oh, Heavens! Can't you see there's a distinction / Between hypocrisy and true devotion?].[2] Though not a learned doctor, as he lays out his personal philosophy, Cléante sounds like
Descartes defining *bon sens*: "Mais, en un mot, je sais, pour toute
science, / Du faux avec le vrai faire la différence" (1.5.353–54)[3] [No,
all my learning can be summed up in a word: / I can tell truth from
falsehood, see through what's absurd].
   Contending that Molière attacks real piety in the play, the Compagnie du Saint-Sacrement succeeded for several years in having
public performances of *Tartuffe* banned. Molière's combative defense in his published preface echoes Cléante. He has done everything possible to "bien distinguer le personnage de l'hypocrite
d'avec celui du vrai dévot" (*OC* 1:884) [distinguish fully the character who is a hypocrite from the one who is a truly pious man]. Addressing the king directly in his first *placet* [petition], he reiterates:

> et pour mieux conserver l'estime et le respect qu'on doit aux vrais dé-
> vots, j'en ai distingué le plus que j'ai pu le caractère que j'avais à tou-
> cher. Je n'ai point laissé d'équivoque, j'ai ôté ce qui pouvait confondre
> le bien avec le mal. (*OC* 1:890)

[in order best to maintain the esteem and respect due to the truly pious, I have distinguished the character about which I was speaking as much as possible from them. I have left nothing ambiguous, I have removed anything that might lead one to mistake evil for good.] (Translation by author)

To condemn all comedy because some comedies lampoon true piety and corrupt sacred values is like not distinguishing between two women with the same name, one of whom is upstanding and the other dissolute. "De semblables arrêts," Molière warns, ". . . feraient un grand désordre dans le monde" (*OC* 1:887) [Decrees like that would create great disorder in the world] (Translation by author).

Cléante's principle of difference informs the play's structure. When Madame Pernelle, followed by her servant, Flipote, rushes on stage in the first scene and maligns everyone in her son's household, the audience immediately understands that the action of the play will center around two opposing camps of characters: Madame Pernelle, Orgon, and Tartuffe against the rest of the family. The former are wrong-headed and wrong. Tartuffe is an impostor, a hypocrite, but Orgon, blinded by his desire for salvation, will not see this. Having sworn allegiance to Tartuffe, Orgon and his mother risk being no better than he. All three are insensitive and tyrannical in their dealings with others. Anyone who does not conform to their will is anathema to them. Orgon's wife, Elmire, his children, Mariane and Damis, as well as Mariane's suitor, Valère, and Cléante, all more moderate and normal, oppose the machinations of Tartuffe.[4] Truth is on their side, and the audience is led to identify with them.[5] The distinction between truth and falsehood is the play's major theme.[6] Molière sets them in opposition in the very first scene.

Complications arise from the fact that in *Tartuffe*, the truth is neither so absolute nor always so convincing as might be expected, given the clear demarcation in the first scenes between truth and its opposite. Even when good or wronged characters tell the truth, one may question their motives. For example, everything that Damis says about Tartuffe is true, but whether Damis acts and speaks in the service of truth or out of rivalry with Tartuffe and, ultimately, with Orgon, gives pause. Tartuffe, whose whole life is a lie, is quite capable of telling the truth, and the usually misguided Orgon accurately perceives his family as a unified front against Tartuffe. Molière does not preach one truth, sacred and absolute, to which all must adhere. To do that would be to approach in attitude his enemies in the Compagnie du Saint Sacrement. What interests him is how the difference between opposites defines his characters and their behavior. For both the characters and the audience, difference forms the primary structural element of *Tartuffe*.

The source of Tartuffe's power over Orgon and Madame Pernelle lies in his uncanny ability to blind them to differences starkly apparent to everyone else, and Tartuffe understands his skill at this game. It is not that he tricks them into believing what is manifestly untrue. That would be bad enough. Tartuffe goes one step further: he shows his victims the whole truth and arranges for them not to see it, even to reject it as untrue. The most extreme example of Tartuffe's brand of deception and his ability to bring it off occurs in the famous scene where Orgon, hidden under a table, watches Tartuffe try to seduce Elmire. In an attempt to cool down her suitor and give herself a chance to prod her husband into reacting, Elmire asks Tartuffe to check outside the door to see whether Orgon might not be nearby. Tartuffe finds such precautions unnecessary: "De tous nos entretiens il est pour faire gloire, / Et je l'ai mis au point de voir tout sans rien croire" (4.5.1525–26) [He's pleased as punch we're having meetings such as these—/ And I've made sure he won't believe the things he sees]. This sets forth Tartuffe's technique explicitly and accurately. He brags about leading Orgon around by the nose (4.5.1524) and tells exactly how he has done it.

When Tartuffe finally leaves the room for a moment, Elmire berates her husband for his inaction. Has he not yet seen enough? Adopting Tartuffe's language of vision, she taunts Orgon: "Attendez jusqu'au bout pour voir les choses sûres" (4.6.1533) [Hear him to the end, make sure / You're not assuming things]. As if to confirm Tartuffe's description of his modus operandi, Orgon later uses the same language to explain to his mother that he has at last been disabused: "Je l'ai vu, dis-je, vu, de mes propres yeux vu, / Ce qu'on appelle vu . . ." (5.3.1676–77) [I say I saw him, saw him, with my own eyes saw / Him; do you know what seeing means?]. Unpersuaded, Madame Pernelle retorts, "Il ne faut pas toujours juger sur ce qu'on voit" (5.3.1680) [The things you see you ought not always to believe] and then, ironically, repeats the words of her daughter-in-law: "Et vous deviez attendre à vous voir sûr des choses" (5.3.1686) [Just wait and see, don't be so hasty to provoke]. Madame Pernelle would certainly not have wanted Elmire to succumb to Tartuffe, let alone desire that her son witness such a scene. However, for the time being, she is still under the rogue's sway.

The discord Tartuffe sows in Orgon's household leaves nothing untouched. He is a voracious parasite, who gobbles up everything in sight: "A table, au plus haut bout il [Orgon] veut qu'il [Tartuffe] soit assis; / Avec joie il l'y voit manger autant que six" (1.2.191–92)[7] [At meals, he sits him in the place of honour, then / Rejoices when the fellow eats enough for ten]. Whence his enormous size. Before enumerating the dishes of Tartuffe's gluttonous repast in the presence of a weak, ailing Elmire (1.4.237–39), the servant Dorine describes her nemesis as a picture of corpulent good health: "Gros et gras, le teint frais, et la bouche vermeille" (1.4.234) [With rosy cheeks and scarlet lips, all sleek and stout]. Tartuffe's bloated figure is a physical image of his greed, an all-encompassing greed that nearly brings down Orgon and his family. Like many parasites, Tartuffe not only sucks nourishment from his hosts. He also secretes a powerful venom, which is how he does his worst damage. The most noxious ingredient of the poison Tartuffe injects into the body of Orgon's family is the inability to focus on difference. Michel Serres calls Tartuffe the canonic example of the parasite that the host cannot reject.[8] Indeed, the host has hardly an inkling that a foreign object has entered his body:

> To avoid the unavoidable reactions of rejection, exclusion, a (biological) parasite makes or secretes tissue identical to that of its host at the location of contact points with the host's body. The parasited, abused, cheated body no longer reacts; it accepts; it acts as if the visitor were its own organ.[9]

Disorder inevitably follows the parasite's introduction into the body.[10]

Without realizing how much he discloses of the true dynamic underlying his relationship with Tartuffe, Orgon recalls his first encounter with the *faux dévot* (1.5.281–98) [hypocrite]. Tartuffe had sought out his victim in church and put on for him an ostentatious display of piety. His success owes much to Orgon's susceptibility to being duped. As James Gaines aptly remarks, "It is the host Orgon who makes the arch-parasite possible."[11] Orgon tries to satisfy vicariously his need to exercise supremacy over his family by promoting Tartuffe. Like Madame Pernelle, he perceives Tartuffe as a man who dominates others, and identifies with the hypocrite's power. A paterfamilias, Orgon already has the power he seeks. The head of a family in seventeenth-century France held substantial authority over its members. If Orgon decides, for instance, to break off the engagement of his daughter to Valère, he may do so.

Mariane acknowledges and accepts Orgon's paternal control. When Dorine asks her why she had not objected more strongly to her father's proposal that she marry Tartuffe, Mariane explains: "Contre un père absolu que veux-tu que je fasse? . . . Un père, je l'avoue, a sur nous tant d'empire, / Que je n'ai jamais eu la force de rien dire" (2.3.589, 597–98) [He's so inflexible, so what else can I do? . . . A father can control his daughter, I confess. / I can't hold out—it takes more strength than I possess]. The play's conclusion confirms the legitimacy of the institution of the family,[12] which forms the base of the social order and relies upon paternal authority for its well-being. Why does Orgon not appreciate this and rest secure in the very real power he possesses?

Like Louis XIV, the ultimate model for behavior in seventeenth-century France, Orgon is an absolutist.[13] The normal differences in the social order, such as the superiority enjoyed by the head of a household, cannot satisfy him. It is one thing to be master of a well-ordered family, quite another to assert that one's mastery is absolute. That Mariane does not strongly resist her father's plan to have her marry Tartuffe is not, for Orgon, a sufficient show of submission. Not only must she yield to his will. She must also agree that what her father wants is right for her. Orgon explodes at Mariane's refusal to confirm that his design for her future will make her happy: "Mais je veux que cela soit une vérité; / Et c'est assez pour vous que je l'aie arrêté" (2.1.451–52) [The thing is, though, you see, I want it to be true, / And doing what I say should be enough for you]. As the arbiter of truth itself, he insists that others concede his power. Lionel Gossman maintains that Orgon desires, in the end, "to have himself recognized by all around him as divinely absolute and self-sufficient."[14] Orgon seeks a grossly exaggerated power and will believe he has attained it only when others assure him he has. In his eyes, Tartuffe has such power. Orgon, therefore, clings to the hypocrite, who becomes his model and, ultimately, his rival. Orgon never really comprehends what sustains his attachment to Tartuffe, and until the impostor tries literally to seduce his wife and steal his money, he does not see how dangerous Tartuffe is.

The head of the household is the only member of the family who fails to grasp Tartuffe's will to dominate, to control others, to be the master. For Dorine, Tartuffe is a "gueux" (1.1.63) [beggar] who would "contrarier tout, et . . . faire le maître" (1.1.66) [oppose everything . . . and act like the master]. Damis refers to Tartuffe's having grabbed "un pouvoir tyrannique" (1.1.46) [a tyrannical power], and even Madame Pernelle, comparing him to his servant,

Laurent, calls Tartuffe "le maître" (1.1.74)[15] [the master]. She, of course, believes that "tout ce qu'il contrôle est fort bien contrôlé" (1.1.52) [everything he supervises is well supervised] (Translations by author). Orgon's blindness to the central characteristic of Tartuffe's personality directly relates to the bourgeois's not realizing that he too wants absolute power over his family. Without Orgon's assent and active assistance, Tartuffe would be powerless. Orgon invites Tartuffe into his household, turns Elmire over to him for safekeeping, and disinherits his son in favor of the hypocrite. Tartuffe is a creature of Orgon as surely as Orgon is Tartuffe's primary victim. Neither could exist without the other. Orgon allows Tartuffe to seize power and then uses him to reinforce his own authority. Thanks to Tartuffe, Orgon has become a new man: "Oui, je deviens tout autre avec son entretien" (1.5.275) [I've learnt from him, the truth is clearer in my eyes]. What has changed is that Orgon has begun to feel something of the personal superiority he has long sought. The lesson that Tartuffe teaches deeply affects Orgon: "Qui suit bien ses leçons goûte une paix profonde, / Et comme du fumier regarde tout le monde" (1.5.273–74) [If you sat at his feet, he'd bring you peace, for sure; / The world would seem to you a great heap of manure]. To enhance and sustain his power, Orgon unconsciously imitates his unholy guest. This imitation draws the two men closer and closer together in their similarity.

Tartuffe does not appear on stage until the third act, and by the time he and Orgon confront each other in dialogue, the scoundrel has already made his first attempt to seduce Elmire. Hidden in a closet, Damis witnesses the seduction scene. Elmire pleads in vain with Damis not to report Tartuffe's wayward behavior to his father. She would strike a bargain with the impostor: in return for her silence, he will encourage Orgon to allow Mariane to marry Valère. But in the presence of Tartuffe, Damis cannot resist the opportunity to displace the would-be seducer. Orgon's initial reaction to the accusation against Tartuffe is a predictable question: "Ce que je viens d'entendre, ô Ciel! est-il croyable?" (3.6.1073) [Oh, Heavens, is it true? Eh? What's all this I hear?]. Tartuffe's answer is unforeseen: "Oui, mon frère, je suis un méchant, un coupable, / Un malheureux pécheur, tout plein d'iniquité, / Le plus grand scélérat qui jamais ait été" (3.6.1074–76) [Yes, brother, I'm a guilty, wicked man, I fear, / A miserable, evil sinner, of no worth, / The greatest scoundrel that has ever walked the earth]. Tartuffe's moral self-flagellation is, as the author of the "Lettre sur la comédie de l'*Imposteur*" [Letter on the Comedy of the *Impostor*] says, extremely general. It mentions no specific faults.[16] But the dark picture Tartuffe paints of himself does not lie. He is wicked, guilty, and a sinner. He lays all this before Orgon, who will not accept the truth and, instead, threatens violence against Damis. With his "malédiction" (3.6.1140) [curse], he throws his son out of the house. Tartuffe's ploy has worked. Truth and falsehood are indistinguishable for Orgon. Nor is this the only confusion in these scenes.

Damis's refusal to beg Tartuffe's forgiveness undermines Orgon's parental authority, and Tartuffe quickly appropriates the role of the father, addressing Damis as his son: "Oui, mon cher fils, parlez; traitez-moi de perfide, / D'infâme, de perdu, de voleur, d'homicide" (3.6.1101–2) [Yes, my dear son, go on, call me a perjurer, / A sinner, infamous, a thief, a murderer]. Orgon raises no objections, thus tacitly ceding his position to the impostor. Following Tartuffe's presumption, the two repeatedly refer to one another as "mon frère" [brother] in their first meeting on stage (3.6.1107, 1109, 1112; 3.7.1154, 1161). For Tartuffe, this brotherhood extends to sharing authority over the family. By calling Orgon his brother, he becomes less an intruder and more a member of the household, on an equal footing with Orgon. Integrating Tartuffe into the family also serves the purpose of Orgon, who seizes control by aggressively defying his family and, in the process, portrays himself just as others have portrayed Tartuffe: "Ah! je vous brave tous, et vous ferai connaître / Qu'il faut qu'on m'obéisse et que je suis le maître" (3.6.1129–30) [Ah! I defy you all. You'll see—I'll make you learn / I'm going to be obeyed. I'm master now—my turn!]. In yet another challenge hurled at the family, Orgon insists that Tartuffe frequent Elmire: "Faire enrager le monde est ma plus grande joie, / Et je veux qu'à toute heure avec elle on vous voie" (3.7.1173–74) [My greatest joy on earth is making people squirm: / You'll see her all the time, I promise, I'll stand firm]. As if this were not enough, "pour les mieux braver tous" (3.7.1175) [I'll defy them all], Orgon disinherits Damis and declares Tartuffe his sole heir. His family becomes an undifferentiated mass of resisters whose individuality is lost on him: "Vous le [Tartuffe] haïssez tous; et je vois aujourd'hui / Femme, enfants et valets déchaînés contre lui" (3.6.1119–20) [You all detest him, I can see that the whole pack, / Wife, children, servants, all, have joined in the attack]. When Orgon measures his family against Tartuffe, he endows the hypocrite with an individual identity worthy of affection: "Un bon et franc ami, que pour gendre je prends, / M'est bien plus cher que fils, que femme, et que parents" (3.7.1179–80) [My future son-in-law, my dear and honest friend, / Means more to me than wife and children, in the end]. He does not distinguish among the others, who are all alike in their opposition to Tartuffe and, by extension, to Orgon himself. Differences among characters and among their functions blur. In this episode, Orgon imitates Tartuffe in his will to mastery, and Tartuffe achieves the status of brother (to Orgon), father (to Damis), son (as Orgon's heir), potential lover (to Mariane), and surrogate husband (to Elmire).[17]

Cléante's appeals to reason fall on deaf ears when he speaks to Orgon and Tartuffe. Convinced of his house guest's show of piety, Orgon pays no heed to his brother-in-law's lengthy admonition and, with a dismissive "Je suis votre valet" (1.5.409) [I'm your humble servant], prepares to leave. Cléante immediately raises the question of Orgon's pledge to have Mariane marry Valère but has no better luck with this. Orgon merely replies as Tartuffe might, that he will "faire / Ce que le Ciel voudra" (1.5.422–23) [do / What Heaven ordains], and utters a terse "Adieu" to end their conversation (1.5.425). When later, Orgon pleads with Tartuffe to be his heir and to watch over Elmire, the hypocrite's typical response recalls Orgon's earlier words: "La volonté du Ciel soit faite en toute chose" (3.7.1182) [May Heaven's will be done, in this and everything!]. Cléante's entreaty that Tartuffe not allow Damis to be disinherited meets with an equally abrupt dismissal. Rational argument failing him, Tartuffe simply absents himself to attend to "certain devoir pieux" (4.1.1267) [pious duties]. What motivates Orgon and Tartuffe to speak and behave similarly is less self-interest than a rivalry that, as in other plays by Molière, leads the characters most at odds with each other to behave similarly. And the two men are locked into a progressively deepening rivalry for the family's wealth, for power, and for Elmire.

La Bruyère's portrait of Onuphre, the perfect *faux dévot* [hypocrite], implicitly criticizes Tartuffe for the conspicuousness of his hypocrisy and his inattention to his own best advantage. Onuphre, like Tartuffe, is a parasite, but he never competes with his host:

> S'il se trouve bien d'un homme opulent, à qui il a su imposer, dont il est le parasite, et dont il peut tirer de grands secours, il ne cajole point sa femme, il ne lui fait du moins ni avance ni déclaration . . . Il est encore plus éloigné d'employer pour la flatter et pour la séduire le jargon de la dévotion. (*De la mode*, 24)[18]

> [If he is comfortable at the house of a rich man whom he can deceive, whose parasite he is, and from whom he may derive great advantages, he never cajoles his patron's wife, nor makes the least advances to her, nor declares his love . . . still less will he make use of devotional cant to flatter and seduce her.]

While Tartuffe's victim ultimately becomes his rival, Onuphre's remains a dupe. Onuphre would never say, as does Tartuffe, that he wears a hairshirt and flagellates himself; he would find a more subtle way to inform others of his self-mortification. Nor would he move to disinherit a man's children, because a direct attack on children's claims to their father's estate might subject Onuphre to public scrutiny: "il y a là des droits trop forts et trop inviolables: on ne les traverse point sans faire de l'éclat (et il l'appréhende)" (*De la mode*, 24)[19] [their rights are too strong and inviolable to be upset without loud clamours, which he dreads]. La Bruyère paints a hypocrite more calculating, more self-conscious, and, one imagines, more svelte than Molière's. He makes no reference to Onuphre's appetite. One visualizes him thin. In Erich Auerbach's view, Onuphre would not work well on the stage.[20] His acute awareness of who he is and what he is about distinguishes him markedly from Tartuffe. Onuphre stands securely apart from his victims. In his extreme devotion to his role, which entails imitating piety in its every detail, indeed to perfection, Onuphre has something of the ascetic.[21] He avoids personal entanglements, especially those that could loosen his firm control over himself and eventuate in his unmasking.

By not disciplining his appetites or his outlandish behavior, Tartuffe descends from the pedestal of absolute authority on which Orgon has placed him and becomes an ordinary, if overly self-satisfied rival. No one is more horrified by this turn of events than Orgon, who needs Tartuffe to maintain his own identity as master of his household and, therefore, refuses at first to see the truth. After Damis accuses him of the attempted seduction of Elmire, Tartuffe pretends that he must leave the house. Orgon's reaction— "Non, vous demeurerez: il y va de ma vie" (3.7.1165) [No, you'll stay here with me—my whole life is at stake]—proves that he cannot live without Tartuffe, not, at least, as the all-powerful paterfamilias he wants to be. Only when he has seen for himself that Tartuffe intends to seduce Elmire does Orgon order the impostor out: "Allons, point de bruit, je vous prie. / Dénichons de céans, et sans cérémonie" (4.7.1553–54) [Oh, stop fooling about. / I've had enough of this. It's high time you got out]. For a brief moment, Tartuffe appears to consider using a ploy to mollify Orgon, as he has in the past. Orgon interrupts him and again orders him to leave. Tartuffe's retort signals that the two rivals think alike:

TARTUFFE. Mon dessein . . .
ORGON. Ces discours ne sont plus de saison:
   Il faut, sur-le-champ, sortir de la maison.

TARTUFFE. C'est à vous d'en sortir, vous qui parlez en maître:
  La maison m'appartient, je le ferai connaître.

                                           (4.7.1555–58)

[TARTUFFE. No, listen to my plan . . .
ORGON.   There's nothing to discuss.
  Get out of here, and do it quick. Don't make a fuss.
TARTUFFE. No, you get out. Go on. You're not the master here.
  This house belongs to me, as everyone will hear.]

This dialogue ends with Tartuffe's informing Orgon and the
stunned Elmire that he has his ways to make those who are trying
to chase him away regret their foolishness (4.7.1563–64). Whatever exalted place Tartuffe once held in Orgon's mind, parasite
and host, because of their rivalry, can now do nothing more than
toss back and forth the same threat of expulsion, the words of each
mimicking those of his enemy "brother."

    At last, Orgon sees through Tartuffe. He looks back on his
friendship with the hypocrite and reminds the family of all he has
done for the ungrateful wretch. Tartuffe has turned Orgon's charity against him. Orgon's resentment boils over:

        Il m'ose menacer de mes propres bienfaits,
        Et veut, à ma ruine, user des avantages
        Dont le viennent d'armer mes bontés trop peu sages.

                                           (5.3.1652–54)

        [And now he holds my goodness to him in contempt,
        And wants to use the weapons I put in his hand,
        By trusting him too much, to bring about my end.]

Orgon and Tartuffe have shared a symbiotic relationship in which
they nourished each other and thrived through each other.[22] But
all that is changed. Tartuffe's theft of Orgon's money and belong-
ings will "me réduire au point d'où je l'ai retiré" (5.3.1656) [leave
me as he was when first I helped him out]. In other words, Tartuffe's machinations have produced an earlier version of himself.
Orgon wanted to be like the Tartuffe of his mind's eye, pious and,
by dint of his piety, powerful—but not impoverished. Now he may
indeed become like Tartuffe, but not that Tartuffe and not the Tartuffe he has created with his gifts and adulation.[23] Underlying the
irony in his present circumstances is a larger truth: Orgon and
Tartuffe, in their rivalry, are more alike than different. Orgon fears

a role reversal with Tartuffe rich and himself poor. That, of course, would suit his rival perfectly. Dorine's ironic salvo to Orgon's plaintive account of all he has done for Tartuffe recalls her master's earlier and persistent concern for "Le pauvre homme!" (5.3.1657) [Poor fellow!]. But which of the two is truly "le pauvre homme"?

Tartuffe asserts certain rights, including ownership of Orgon's house, and assumes that the Exempt, who represents the king, will confirm those claims, as M. Loyal, the bailiff come to evict Orgon, has just done. Tartuffe means to benefit from the king's intervention in much the same way that Orgon has profited from the parasitical Tartuffe's invasion of his household. By identifying his own authority with that of the absolute monarch, Tartuffe will become master over what had once been Orgon's domain. It cannot be by chance that Tartuffe's expression of fidelity to the monarch recalls Orgon's mean-spirited confession of his faith in Tartuffe. "Mais l'intérêt du Prince," Tartuffe tells the Exempt, "est mon premier devoir" [But I must first act in the King's best interest] and to it, he would willingly sacrifice "Ami, femme, parents, et moi-même avec eux" (5.7.1880, 1884) [For him I'd give up parents, friends, and wife]. From Tartuffe, Orgon claimed to have learned to detach himself from all worldly affections, even toward his family: "Et je verrais mourir frère, enfants, mère et femme,/ Que je m'en soucierais autant que de cela "(1.5.278–79) [And I could watch my mother, child, wife all die, / And, shall I tell you? I just couldn't care less]. These references to biblical passages from Matthew and Luke in which Christ tells his disciples what they must give up to follow Him, suggest how both Orgon and Tartuffe raise a figure to godlike proportions, only to use him to advance their own causes. The devotion of Orgon to Tartuffe and of Tartuffe to the king is, of course, bogus, and never an end in itself. It does, however, demonstrate that Tartuffe and Orgon's rivalry intensifies their similarity. They play the same tricks, speak the same words.

Roger Planchon's controversial 1973–74 production of *Tartuffe* raises the possibility that Orgon has a homosexual attachment to Tartuffe. Dorine complains to Cléante that her master calls Tartuffe his brother and loves him "cent fois plus qu'il ne fait mère, fils, fille, et femme" (1.2.186) [A thousand times more . . . than husband, child, or wife]. Orgon treats Tartuffe like a mistress, according to Dorine: "Il le choie, il l'embrasse, et pour une maîtresse / On ne saurait, je pense, avoir plus de tendresse" (1.2.189–90) [He's in thrall / To him, he cherishes, embraces him. It's like / A lover doting on his mistress, if you like]. Tartuffe and Orgon are alone on stage only once in the play when Tartuffe, accused by Damis, insists he must leave and Orgon pleads with him to stay. Planchon has Orgon sit next to Tartuffe on the stage floor and enfold him with a gesture of reassurance that suggests a homosexual relationship.[24] Planchon's reading is speculative, unsupported by textual evidence other than Dorine's remarks. It nevertheless dramatizes the strength of the link tying Orgon to Tartuffe. The parasite and his host form an interdependent couple who cannot survive without each other.

In one of the play's most troubling scenes, Orgon watches in hiding for an inordinately long time as Tartuffe tries to seduce Elmire. Preparing to receive Tartuffe, Elmire puts her husband on notice; it will be up to him to decide how far Tartuffe goes. Orgon can stop him when he has seen enough: "Ce sont vos intérêts; vous en serez le maître" (4.4.1385) [I leave it up to you—you're master in this place]. Here as elsewhere, Orgon the paterfamilias has the upper hand, but he clings to a Tartuffe above reproach to use against his family. If Tartuffe proves innocent, as Orgon anticipates, Elmire and the others will have to relinquish their claims against him and endorse Orgon's faith in the hypocrite. Orgon imagines that his paternal authority will then be absolute. Because so much is at stake, he finds it impossible to abandon hope. He has turned Tartuffe into an idol, expecting to empower himself. When he at last emerges from his hiding place, he tells Tartuffe: "J'ai douté fort longtemps que ce fût tout de bon, / Et je croyais toujours qu'on changerait de ton" (4.7.1547–48) [For ages I could not believe that this was real, / I kept on hoping that you would amend your spiel]. Finally, what makes him see the truth is Tartuffe's mocking disdain for him.[25] Planchon's Orgon is "profondément transformé" [profoundly transformed] by what he sees Tartuffe do.[26] The pillar of strength on which Orgon leaned has crumbled, and with it, his own authority and image of himself. All seems lost: "Ma foi, je suis confus, et n'ai pas lieu de rire" (4.8.1566) [This is no laughing matter. I should have foreseen . . .].

Although the primary victim of Tartuffe's imposture, Orgon is not the only one. In carrying out his scheme, Tartuffe imperils the good order of the entire family. From the moment in the first scene that Madame Pernelle boxes the ears of her servant, Flipote, violence that could disrupt the household looms. Orgon, like his mother, is inclined to hit his servant when she defends Mariane's right not to marry Tartuffe (2.2). He wants to take a stick to his son (3.6) and, later, pummel Tartuffe (5.4.1797–1800). Damis is tempted to cut off Tartuffe's ears (5.2.1634) and give M. Loyal a sound thrashing (5.4.1767–68). Mariane twice threatens suicide (2.3.614, 2.3.681–82).

Elmire takes the lead in ridding her family of Tartuffe, but in order to do so, she must place herself in the most compromising of positions. The author of the "Lettre sur la comédie de l'*Imposteur*" portrays Elmire as "une vraie femme de bien, qui connaît parfaitement bien ses véritables devoirs et qui y satisfait jusqu'au scrupule" (*OC* 1:1151)[27] [a truly upright woman who knows her real duties perfectly well and who carries them out scrupulously]. Unless one adopts the perspective of Elmire's mother-in-law, the text gives little reason to contradict this view. On the other hand, Elmire appears to enjoy lavish entertaining. She obviously does not love her husband and may well be a bit of a coquette. She seems to have an instinctive understanding of Tartuffe and takes steps to undo him that many women of her class would reject out of hand. Elmire has, as Ralph Albanese observes, a somewhat ambiguous character.[28] Lionel Gossman suggests that "we do not know what she really is."[29] Elmire cannot engage Tartuffe as she must without raising questions about her own character. Such is the corrupting influence of Tartuffe's presence in her household.

Andrew McKenna has convincingly shown how the atmosphere of rivalry in the family contaminates Damis.[30] The son's opposition to Tartuffe and, thereby, to his father is modeled on Orgon's defiance of his family and celebration of the *faux dévot*. Having witnessed Tartuffe's first attempt to seduce Elmire, Damis cannot resist the urge to defeat Tartuffe, his rival for Orgon's attention. He strikes out against Tartuffe with the same words that his father will later speak to oppose the family, and believes—or, like Tartuffe and Orgon, claims to believe—that his wrath is an expression of God's will: "Et la bonté du Ciel m'y [to the seduction scene] semble avoir conduit / Pour confondre l'orgueil d'un traître qui me nuit" (3.4.1023–24) [It seems that Heaven's goodness brought me here / To catch him out before he tries to interfere]. Orgon gives his daughter to Tartuffe for the same reason, "pour confondre l'orgueil de toute ma famille" (3.6.1126) [so I'll utterly confound my family's pride]. The duel between father and son, on close observation, looks more like a spectacle in which both play the same part. Damis only seems to have right on his side. In truth, rivalry is no less at the root of his choleric behavior than of his father's.

The second act of *Tartuffe* has, since Molière's time, appeared problematic, indeed unnecessary, to many critics. John Cairncross calls it "padding—an afterthought," and Henry Carrington Lancaster thinks that the lovers' quarrel, the act's main event, is "superfluous."[31] "Ce charmant deuxième acte" [this delightful second act], in the words of Jacques Scherer, is very different from the others in that its "contenu rationnel . . . n'a évidemment pas beaucoup intéressé Molière, et la motivation des personnages n'y est pas prise très au sérieux"[32] [rational content . . . clearly did not much interest Molière, and the characters' motivation is not taken very seriously]. The subject of the second act is the love affair between Mariane and Valère, who, in good comic tradition, must overcome an obstacle to their happiness. The obstacle is twofold: a meddlesome father who has chosen a bad mate for his daughter and rivalry between the two lovers. The rivalry deepens into a quarrel that threatens their relationship. Orgon, trying to inflict his will on Mariane, refuses to listen to Dorine's rational arguments against his plot. Mariane, in despair, almost gives in to her father. Her weak resistance to him infuriates Valère, with whom she quarrels. Dorine must step in to save the day. Orgon's bullying, the outbreak of rivalry, and the need for an outside force to restore order are all elements of the second act with parallels in other scenes. The *dépit amoureux* [lovers' quarrel] demonstrates schematically what happens when two characters compete for dominance and imitate each other to achieve it. In this sense, the scene mirrors the action of the entire play.

Toward the end of the dispute, Valère blames Mariane for his behavior: "c'est vous-même / Qui contraignez mon coeur à cet effort extrême" (2.4.745–46) [you'll have to take the blame / For this—it was your fault, yes, you and your new flame]. In forcing himself to forget about Mariane, he will do little more than imitate her: "le dessein que mon âme conçoit / N'est rien qu'à votre exemple" (2.4.747–48) [to find a cure for my distress, / I'm following your example]. He mimics her, she follows him, and they begin to sound identical. Mariane's passivity in the face of her father's plan outrages Valère, who matches her seeming lack of concern with a feigned nonchalance of his own. Mariane asks what he would have her do. Why, marry the man, of course, he replies. "Hé bien! c'est un conseil, Monsieur, que je reçois" (2.4.699) [Well, Sir, I may pursue the course you advocate]. Frustrated, Valère bids her farewell and prepares to leave. Rather than convince him to remain, she makes way for his departure: "Il souffre à me voir, ma présence le chasse, / Et je ferai bien mieux de lui quitter la place" (2.4.761–62) [It's because I'm here he's going, I believe. / The best thing I can do is turn my back, and leave]. If she will leave, so will he: "Je vois bien que ma vue est pour elle un supplice, / Et sans doute il vaut mieux que je l'en affranchisse" (2.4.765–66) [It's clear that she's disgusted at the sight of me. / The best thing I can do is go, and leave her be]. Dorine intervenes, and the lovers ask her what she is about to do (2.4.769). Her desire to unite them meets with similar reactions from Valère—"N'as-tu pas entendu comme elle m'a parlé?" (2.4.772) [No, but, look here, you have heard the awful things she said]—and from Mariane—"N'as-tu pas vu la chose, et comme il m'a traitée?" (2.4.774). [Well, you saw how it was, and what he said to me]. The two are beyond rational help. Dorine, therefore, takes one hand of each, joins them together, and tells the lovers how to salvage their future. Only the servant's smart gesture averts a crisis. Dorine mediates the dispute from her position at the lowest end of the social scale. Louis XIV will soon intervene from above. Neither the servant nor the king can be ensnared in the rivalry. Her place is too low in the social hierarchy—no one in the family would compete with her—his too high—no one *can* compete with him. Dorine resolves a small conflict within the family; the king restores order to the entire household. The lovers' quarrel represents in microcosm the dynamics of the rivalry at the center of *Tartuffe*.[33]

Despite the praise lavished on it by the "Lettre sur la comédie de l'*Imposteur*," the denouement of *Tartuffe* has often been criticized as artificial and facile. Whether, in writing it, Molière had really "égalé tous les anciens et surpassé tous les modernes" [equaled all the ancients and surpassed all the moderns] and then outdone even himself (*OC* 1:1168) is debatable. There can be no doubt that the king appears intelligent, discerning, and just. It has been suggested that the play's ending was intended to flatter Louis XIV. The king had, after all, supported Molière in the cabal against *Tartuffe* and allowed it to be performed publicly. Molière was certainly not above flattering the monarch.[34] He also understood that the dynamics of rivalry at the heart of his play's action, once set in motion, could be stopped only by an external force, a character not susceptible to being drawn into rivalry's vortex. The king always remains at a remove from the actions of his subjects. In the play, he does not even appear himself but is represented by the Exempt. Tartuffe's appeal to the king with flattery does not succeed. Louis XIV, although the ultimate model on whom his subjects pattern their behavior, will not be engaged in their rivalry.

The several rivalries within the household unfold to destroy all semblance of order. It should be possible to call upon the law to restore order, especially when dealing with a known criminal, as the Exempt reveals Tartuffe to be, but the character who comes closest to representing the law, M. Loyal, heightens the tension and increases the danger of violence. Orgon would like to strike him: "pouvoir, à plaisir, sur ce mufle assener / Le plus grand coup de poing qui se puisse donner" (5.4.1799–1800) [I'd like the joy, not to be missed, / Of flattening this devil's fat face with my fist]. For once, Damis agrees with his father: "J'ai peine à me tenir, et la main me démange" (5.4.1802) [My hand itches to fetch the creep a hefty smack]. Dorine's ire flares, as she tells M. Loyal that "Quelques coups de bâton vous siéraient pas mal" (5.4.1804) [A sharp smack with a stick would do no harm at all]. The king alone is above the law and above everyone subject to it. In addition to all his other crimes, Tartuffe has replaced the king as Orgon's model. To save himself from punishment for his collaboration with a *frondeur* [participant in the Fronde], Orgon had handed over to Tartuffe compromising documents. The king forgives Orgon his crime and thus replaces the condemned Tartuffe; it is now he who shares Orgon's secret. The royal decree demotes Tartuffe from "maître" [master] to "traître" [traitor]: "Oui, de vos papiers, dont il se dit le maître," the Exempt proclaims, "Il [Louis] veut qu'entre vos mains je dépouille le traître" (5.7.1933–34) [I'm to take all your papers from this traitor, who / Claims they belong to him, and give them back to you]. And Orgon, modeling himself on the king, turns to Tartuffe and hurls at him the Exempt's very word: "Hé bien! te voilà, traître . . ." (5.7.1947) [So, traitor, now you see . . .]. Tartuffe's imprisonment saves Orgon and his family, but one wonders what it will be like to live with an Orgon whose model, whose "maître," is no longer the "traître," but the king.

4

"Grand seigneur méchant homme": Dom Juan and the Credo of Conquest

DOM JUAN IS A FIGURE OF MYTHIC PROPORTIONS[1] WHOM MOLIÈRE AP-propriates and, in a very real sense, domesticates. The occasional heroic gestures of Molière's Dom Juan are undercut by the charac-ter's knavery. Nor does he acquire the stature of the great libertine despite his ostentatious defiance of death, present in the guise of the Statue of the Commandeur, and his challenge to God Himself. In fact, the don's dramatic experiences with the Statue seem hardly out of the ordinary, since once they have occurred, they are barely mentioned again.[2] Like the vulgar, bourgeois characters of other Molière plays, Dom Juan is self-centered and obsessive. His desire to be as prodigious a lover as Alexander was a warrior re-places Jourdain's social pretensions in the *Bourgeois gentilhomme* and Harpagon's money box in *L'Avare*, but in keeping with the so-cial climber and the miser, Dom Juan fails to understand that what he really desires is the submission of others to his will, for that alone can convince him that he is who he wants to be. Each of his victories, like theirs, is so fleeting a sign of power that another con-quest must follow it swiftly.

The play is a continuation of *Tartuffe*,[3] although, unlike Tartuffe, Dom Juan is a man of real convictions. Tartuffe's pursuit of money and pleasure leads him to practice an overt form of hypocrisy. To dupe a poor fool like Orgon, he slips on the mask of piety and haunts churches. To seduce Elmire, any patter will do, even the inappropriate language of religious devotion, which in this con-text, is particularly laughable. Though no more high-minded than Tartuffe, Dom Juan does have a distinct set of beliefs that he un-hesitatingly articulates. In *Dom Juan*, the protagonist reflects upon his motivation and speaks explicitly about the tenets underlying his behavior. His hypocrisy is more than just a means to an end. It becomes a creed.[4] If Dom Juan does not always understand every ramification of his declaration of faith, it is, nonetheless, given for the audience to probe, analyze, and measure his actions and words against. In his words and in his actions, there is a schematic element that has the effect of making the goals of his behavior and its results immediately apparent. Tartuffe's presence infects Orgon's household with a contagion that leaves Damis sounding very much like his hated rival for his father's wealth and attention. Dom Juan incorporates the same leveling of differences between rivals into his credo and, with Monsieur Dimanche, goes so far as to explain it to his victim. The don is more vicious than Tartuffe, because he is more aware. He knowingly engages in biological warfare, attacking his rivals with the germ that Tartuffe carried.

To validate his own identity, Dom Juan must compete with other characters in the play. The stakes are high, the struggle to win fierce. The outcome will, of course, affect others as well as himself. Elvire, Charlotte, and Mathurine, for example, all stand to win—or lose—their man. Sganarelle's freedom and money are on the line. Monsieur Dimanche thinks only of hard cash, but Francisque believes his eternal salvation threatened. Far from being intimidated by the odds against him in such personal struggles, Dom Juan eagerly confronts them, sabotaging order as he fights a diverse array of battles. A despicable character, he lies, he cheats, he coldheartedly plays off one of his victims against another. He would exchange wedding vows with any woman he comes across. In fact, Sganarelle, in a comic exaggeration, tells Elvire's squire, Gusman, that Dom Juan would hardly hesitate to marry "toi, son chien et son chat" (1.1) [you, his dog, and his cat].[5] The noble rake is an atheist, grossly irreverent and sacrilegious in the extreme. He abducted Elvire from a convent and tempts the poor hermit, Francisque, to blaspheme. He reneges on his debts, disrespects his father, and has committed murder. Notwithstanding his malevolence, however, he has a certain engaging charm. Quick-witted and at times honorable, he often seems winningly spontaneous. Until, that is, he embraces hypocrisy. Although far from being his most heinous crime, this is the misdeed that turns the tide against him. Molière saves his protagonist's espousal of hypocrisy for the last act of the play, as if all the rest of Dom Juan's reprehensible behavior culminates in his cynical announcement that he will henceforth be a hypocrite. Hypocrisy, he declares, is a "vice à la mode, et tous les vices à la mode passent pour vertus" (5.2) [fashionable vice, and all fashionable vices pass for virtues]. Furthermore, a hypocrite is doubly protected, by his own clever lies and by the connivance of "tous les gens du parti" (5.2) [all the other members of the party].

Molière does not miss the mark; the latter are precisely the "dé-
vots" who had successfully attacked *Tartuffe*.[6] Still smarting from
the controversy over the earlier play while writing *Dom Juan*, Molière uses his "grand seigneur méchant homme" (1.1) [great lord
who is a wicked man] to vilify his opponents. An audience can at
moments put aside Dom Juan's wickedness to find him funny or
engaging but cannot forgive him his hypocrisy. Molière calls attention to that flaw by making the don's last acts his most dastardly.
In his final encounters with his father and Elvire's brother, Dom
Carlos, Dom Juan has none of the earlier seductiveness of the man
unflinchingly devoted to his own pleasure. He is simply perverse
as he pretends to have undergone a dramatic change of heart.
That he dupes his father, Dom Louis, only makes the hypocrisy
worse. Molière's intention is unmistakable, and it was not lost on
his detractors.

The "Observations sur une comédie de Molière" [Observations
on a Comedy of Molière] is a diatribe against *Dom Juan*, although
its author, Rochemont, seems at times more incensed by *Tartuffe*
than by the work most directly in his line of fire. Granting that Molière "parle passablement français" (*OC* 2:1200) [speaks tolerable
French] but angered by his determination to perform *Tartuffe* in
public (*OC* 2:1206), Rochemont maliciously accuses him of plagia-
rism, an absence of poetic genius, and impiety. Molière taunts his
critics with Dom Juan's sudden conversion to hypocrisy, and the
playwright's defiance stings them. If only because he is, on top of
everything else, a murderer, Dom Juan is more evil than the *faux
dévot* [hypocrite], but, for Molière's critics, Dom Juan's hypocrisy
emphasizes his direct lineage from Tartuffe and overrides all else.

The will to supremacy motivates both Tartuffe and Dom Juan.
With Elmire, Tartuffe attempts sexual domination, unsuccessfully.
Dom Juan's life is an unbroken line of sexual exploits. Tartuffe's
false piety is his weapon against the pious and the not so pious. Not
until the end of the play does Dom Juan wear the mask of piety,
but even before the curtain rises, his abduction of Elvire from a
convent has put him into rivalry with God. Dom Juan's histrionic
displays of independence and freedom from all social and moral
constraints hide his inability to do anything without first thinking
of others.[7] His own desire for absolute superiority has him "perpetually on the lookout for rivals"[8] with whom he must compete to
prove to himself and others that he stands above the law, above
society's legitimate expectations, and, ultimately, above the will of
God. Tartuffe does not believe in God but neither does he have a
particular desire to take Him on. Dom Juan, on the other hand,

feels compelled to proclaim his atheism and his unwillingness to be intimidated by God or subservient to Him. Others must know that in this most extraordinary rivalry, Dom Juan will stand his ground. When confronted by the Spectre, who tells him to repent, Dom Juan fearlessly rejects Sganarelle's plea that he comply: "Non, non, il ne sera pas dit, quoi qu'il arrive, que je sois capable de me repentir" (5.5) [No, no, it shall not be said, come what may, that I am capable of repenting]. Appropriately, it is the king who punishes Tartuffe, the *Ciel* [Heaven] that brings down Dom Juan.[9]

His pursuit of superiority does not allow Dom Juan to distinguish among his rivals. This explains the curious combination of characters who cross his path and the disjointed plot that their often unexpected appearances create. From Dom Juan's perspective, everyone is a rival to be subdued, and like Pascal's hunter, he loses all interest in his quarry once it has been bagged. Critics have often remarked that his noble wife, Elvire, and the peasants, Charlotte and Mathurine, are equally attractive to the great seducer. He tricks Monsieur Dimanche and humiliates his own father; he is dismissive of those strange characters in direct contact with the *Ciel*—Francisque, the Statue, and the ghost. Dom Juan's encounters with others are not only the occasion for him to demonstrate his superiority over them. They also represent a real danger that he will not appear in the eyes of others as all he claims to be. Sganarelle might see the deficiencies in his master's projected image of himself; Francisque could—and does—choose God over Dom Juan, and Monsieur Dimanche could conceivably insult him by insisting that his debts be repaid. Dom Juan parades before his audience a contradictory nature in which swaggering self-assuredness and a vulnerability born of deep-seated feelings of weakness come together. Although his will to power makes him a dashing, single-minded character, much of what Dom Juan discloses about himself undermines the façade he so carefully constructs.

Pierre Force compares Molière's characters to patients on a psychoanalyst's couch, who, without realizing it, divulge their innermost truths to an attentive audience.[10] Nowhere does this occur more vividly than in the famous speech in which Dom Juan defends his promiscuity against Sganarelle, who finds it indescribably shabby. The speech builds in brassiness as the don, with great bravado, wishes for other worlds where he might extend his sexual prowess: "je me sens un coeur à aimer toute la terre; et comme Alexandre, je souhaiterais qu'il y eût d'autres mondes, pour y pouvoir étendre mes conquêtes amoureuses" (1.2) [I feel a heart in me fit to love the whole world; and like Alexander, I could wish there were other worlds, so that I might extend my amorous conquests there]. The warrior-like lover speaks a bellicose language whose tone communicates that love is a battle to be won by courageous soldiers. Dom Juan is happiest when he can "réduire . . . le coeur d'une jeune beauté . . . combattre . . . l'innocente pudeur d'une âme qui a peine à rendre les armes . . . forcer pied à pied toutes les petites résistances" [(be) overcoming a young beauty's heart . . . combating . . . the innocent modesty of a soul loath to surrender it arms . . . forcing, step by step, the little obstacles], and "vaincre les scrupules" [(be) conquering the scruples] of any woman foolhardy enough to resist his advances (1.2). And having won the battle, Dom Juan, propelled by "l'ambition des conquérants, qui volent perpétuellement de victoire en victoire" (1.2) [the ambition of the conquerors who perpetually fly from victory to victory], moves on in search of new conquests. The don portrays himself here as a he-roic figure, valorous in battle and never content to rest on past lau-rels.

Alongside the bombast in this speech runs a current of feckless-ness that betrays a character quite different from the public Dom Juan. His much vaunted freedom from all constraint is "of a singu-larly negative kind."[11] His language accents, for example, his inca-pacity for personal commitment: "J'ai beau être engagé, l'amour que j'ai pour une belle n'engage point mon âme à faire injustice aux autres" (1.2) [I may be bound; but the love I have for one beautiful woman does not bind my soul to do injustice to the oth-ers]. He is not just an unusually aggressive suitor. He cannot pre-vent himself from being attracted to all women: "je ne puis refuser mon coeur à tout ce que je vois d'aimable" (1.2) [I cannot refuse my heart to anyone I see to be lovable]. His is a paradoxical form of impotence in which desire burns hotly but always beyond his control: "Il n'est rien qui puisse arrêter l'impétuosité de mes dé-sirs" (1.2) [There is nothing that can arrest the impetuosity of my desires]. Beauty overcomes him, and he surrenders to it: "la beauté me ravit partout où je la trouve, et je cède facilement à cette douce violence dont elle nous entraîne" (1.2) [beauty entrances me wherever I find it, and I easily yield to the sweet violence with which it sweeps us along]. This would-be Alexander shows himself to be exceedingly weak willed.

In the absence of both commitment and the fidelity that accom-panies it, Dom Juan does not distinguish among the women he tries to seduce. As Sganarelle explains, "Dame, damoiselle, bour-geoise, paysanne, il ne trouve rien de trop chaud ni de trop froid pour lui" (1.1) [Grown lady, young lady, bourgeoise, peasant girl, he finds nothing too hot or too cold for him]. It would be foolish, the don asserts, to pledge himself to the "premier objet qui nous prend" (1.2) [first object that captivates us] and establish a precedence that would limit his desire: "toutes les belles ont droit de nous charmer" [every beautiful woman has the right to charm us], and they all have "justes prétentions . . . sur nos coeurs" (1.2) [just claims . . . on our hearts]. The right is theirs, not his. He draws no distinctions among the relative merits of his potential partners, nor can he: "je conserve des yeux pour voir le mérite de toutes, et rends à chacune les hommages et les tributs où la nature nous oblige" (1.2)[12] [I still have eyes to see the merit of them all, and I pay to each one the homage and tribute that nature requires of us]. What is normally a lover's free choice becomes for Dom Juan an obligation imposed by nature itself. Love invigorates Charlotte, Mathurine, and Elvire. It enervates Dom Juan.

The conquest energizes the victorious soldier, but love has the opposite effect. When the battle is won, when "l'innocente pudeur d'une âme" [the innocent modesty of a soul] has been overcome, "lorsque on en est maître une fois . . . nous nous endormons dans la tranquillité d'un tel amour" (1.2) [once we are the master . . . in the tranquillity of such a love we fall asleep]. The soldier's greatest enemy is the eternal sleep of death, and Dom Juan explicitly associates fidelity with a living death: "La belle chose de vouloir se piquer d'un faux honneur d'être fidèle, de s'ensevelir pour toujours dans une passion, et d'être mort dès sa jeunesse à toutes les autres beautés" (1.2) [That's a fine thing, to want to pride ourselves on some false honor of fidelity, to bury ourselves forever in one passion, and to be dead from our youth on to all the other beauties that may strike our eyes!]. In the exchange between Sganarelle and Dom Juan that precedes the Alexander speech:

> SGANARELLE. Je sais mon Dom Juan sur le bout du doigt, et connais votre coeur . . . il se plaît à promener de liens en liens, et n'aime guère à demeurer en place. . . .
> DOM JUAN. Quoi? Tu veux qu'on se lie à demeurer au premier objet qui nous prend? . . . (1.2)
>
> [SGANARELLE. I have my Don Juan at my fingertips, and I know your heart . . . It loves to ramble from bond to bond, and doesn't much like to stay put. . . .
> DOM JUAN. What? Do you want us to bind ourselves for good to the first object that captivates us . . .]

one is tempted to recall Pascal's discovery that "tout le malheur des hommes vient d'une seule chose, qui est de ne savoir pas demeurer

en repos, dans une chambre" (fragment 139)[13] [all of man's unhappiness comes from one thing alone, which is not knowing how to
stay in a room quietly]. "Demeurer en repos"—not insignificantly,
both Sganarelle and Dom Juan use this verb—with its parallel to
death is what Dom Juan most fears—and flees. His life, like that of
Pascal's fallen man, is thus filled with diversions that help him
avoid seeing death, even when, ironically, he tries to face it down,
as he does with the Spectre and the Statue.

Dom Juan's *divertissements* [diversions], to borrow Pascal's word,
rely heavily for their success upon the cooperation of others, all of
whom are, or quickly become, his rivals. Of the play's twenty-seven
scenes, Dom Juan appears in twenty-five, never alone. His servant,
Sganarelle, is always at his side.[14] Not unlike Orgon and Tartuffe,
the two men form a comic couple, although Sganarelle is not
duped by his master.[15] Indeed, when Sganarelle does not imitate
the don's behavior, he sees right through it. His penetrating comments regularly serve to explain Dom Juan's actions. Sganarelle's
response to the Alexander speech is a critique of Dom Juan's
method: "vous tournez les choses d'une manière, qu'il semble que
vous avez raison; et cependant il est vrai que vous ne l'avez pas"
(1.2)[16] [you turn things in such a manner that you seem to be right;
and yet the truth is that you're not]. If the protagonist of Molière's
later *George Dandin* feels victimized by appearing to be wrong when
he is right, Dom Juan consciously confuses right and wrong, diminishing the difference between them. To confound his rivals, he
erases differences on which they rely as the foundation of order in
their lives. Dom Juan needs Sganarelle as a witness to his conquests. The servant's role is to validate his master's superiority by
affirming it.[17] If Sganarelle does not do this or if Dom Juan does
not perceive that he is doing it, the servant, like everyone else, becomes a rival in the eyes of his master. When this happens, Dom
Juan uses against Sganarelle the same tactic he employs against
others. Only Sganarelle's independence keeps him from falling
prey to his master and allows the servant to see the truth.

Dom Juan opens with one of the play's most perplexing scenes.
Elvire's attendant, Gusman, appeals to Dom Juan to return to his
abandoned wife. Sganarelle knows that this will not happen, but
before trying to explain his master to Gusman, he launches into
the praise of tobacco. Critics have long been puzzled by this bizarre
glorification of the virtues of tobacco. Ralph Albanese sees in it the
servant's quest for moral superiority.[18] The Compagnie du Saint-
Sacrement opposed the use of tobacco, so the speech might be read
as an attack against that society.[19] Patrick Dandrey takes it as a pri-

mary example of the pseudo-encomium, a rhetorical device that is a major topos in the play.[20] For Jacques Guicharnaud, the speech anchors the comedy in farce, and Ronald Tobin interprets Sganarelle's first words as a parody of the sacrament of Holy Communion.[21] The brief speech is clearly open to a variety of readings.

Michel Serres advances the idea that the praise of tobacco establishes the fundamental law of a system of communication that Dom Juan breaks at every opportunity. Instead of exchanging tobacco for tobacco and money for money, the don repays his debts with words.[22] But Sganarelle also proposes that to become an "honnête homme" [gentleman], one need only participate in the exchange of tobacco, which has the power to guarantee the "vertu" [virtue] that attends social status. By exchanging tobacco, everyone, presumably even a servant like Sganarelle, can become an "honnête homme." Tobacco touches all, and all respond identically, giving freely of what they have received. Desire, which normally promotes rivalry and the delineation of differences, is diminished, for one "court au-devant du souhait des gens" [anticipates people's wishes] to offer others tobacco before it occurs to them to want it. In Sganarelle's utopian vision, everyone is happy not because desire is fulfilled, but because everyone is the same. The individuality that makes for different desires and causes conflict has disappeared: "le tabac inspire des sentiments d'honneur et de vertu à tous ceux qui en prennent" (1.1) [tobacco inspires sentiments of honor and virtue in all those who take it]. Dom Juan, in his weakness, functions like tobacco, except that while tobacco elevates its users, his indiscriminate pursuit of women reduces them to the same level.

Despite his pride in displaying how well he knows his master's way with others—"Je n'ai pas grande peine à le comprendre" (1.1) [I don't have much trouble understanding it]—Sganarelle is more than once subjected to Dom Juan's method of defeating his rivals. Just after Dom Juan delivers his ringing denunciation of constancy, Done Elvire arrives to ask her husband why he has left her. Taken aback by her unexpected presence and, no doubt, by the directness of her question, he insists, against Sganarelle's futile protestations, that his servant explain the master's infidelity. The best the baffled Sganarelle can offer is the comic response that "les conquérants, Alexandre et les autres mondes sont causes de notre départ" (1.3) [the reasons for our departure are conquerors, Alexander, and other worlds]. Contrary to Dom Juan's order to account for his departure, the fearful servant provides an explanation of "notre départ," thereby associating himself with his master's malicious behavior. Lest Sganarelle's innocence stand in too stark contrast with Dom Juan's culpability and lead Elvire to judge the servant as morally superior to his master, the don lowers Sganarelle to his own level by allying his servant with himself in evil. As he seduces Charlotte, he again brings Sganarelle into the action by demanding that he confirm the girl's physical beauty and his master's honorable intentions. Dom Juan is certainly playing to his servant in the hope of beguiling him, along with Charlotte, Mathurine, and everyone else.[23] At the same time, he limits Sganarelle's individuality and independence of spirit by drawing him into the libertine's sphere and minimizing the differences that separate them.

Dom Juan often compels Sganarelle to act on his behalf or to accompany him on a perilous mission. It is Sganarelle who is commissioned to invite the Statue to dinner (3.5), and he must stay in the room when the Commandeur comes to dine (4.8). With an ironic politeness, the Statue asks his host to dinner the following evening. "Oui," the don answers, "j'irai, accompagné du seul Sganarelle" (4.8) [Yes, I'll come with only Sganarelle for company]. That Dom Juan has earlier had his servant sit down at table with him alone indicates that more is involved in these episodes than his display for Sganarelle of fearlessness, courage, and superiority. Social mores dictate that master and servant not eat at the same table. By breaking this convention, Dom Juan de-emphasizes the difference between his servant and himself. When, to flee twelve horsemen pursuing him, he suggests that Sganarelle disguise himself as the master (2.5), it appears that their separate identities will, by this exchange of roles, be momentarily conflated. Sganarelle wisely declines the honor of dying for his master: "Ô Ciel . . . fais-moi la grâce de n'être point pris pour un autre" (2.5) [O Heaven . . . grant me not to be taken for someone else!]. On the other hand, he accepts the disguise of a doctor and, in the very next scene, shows both his susceptibility to Dom Juan's infringement on his individual identity and how he counters it.

Though he recognizes that disguising himself as a doctor does not make him one, he cannot resist prescribing remedies to the peasants who approach him (3.1). His doctor's clothes also embolden him to argue against his master's skepticism about medicine and religion. His identity, in other words, is unstable, subject to the influence of mere appearances. A simple-minded faith in what he calls the "miracles" of contemporary medicine and his belief in legendary characters like the Moine-Bourru help protect Sganarelle from Dom Juan's powers over him.[24] In the scene with the Pauvre, Sganarelle actively collaborates with Dom Juan by encouraging the hermit to swear, and he imitates his master again when Monsieur Dimanche calls in a debt owed by Sganarelle. The servant seems always on the brink of losing his independence to Dom Juan's will to dominate all rivals. Sganarelle is not a heroic figure who puts up strong psychological barriers against his master. His only defense is his intellectual naïveté and a mundane desire to be paid for his work. "Mes gages, mes gages, mes gages!" he cries out at play's end (5.6) [My wages! My wages! My wages!]. In his subservience to another master, money, Sganarelle manages to retain his identity against Dom Juan's relentless efforts to make his servant's thoughts and actions coincide with his own.

Others are not nearly so fortunate. Having rid himself of Charlotte's fiancé, Pierrot, Dom Juan is about to conclude his successful seduction of her when her rival, Mathurine, appears. Intense rivalry replaces love and dictates every word in what follows, as the don is challenged by two women, both of whom expect to marry him. So schematically drawn are Dom Juan's tactics, the defeat of the two female rivals, and Sganarelle's intervention at the end of the scene that the audience readily grasps how rivalry unfolds and undoes its victims. Dom Juan has promised marriage to both Charlotte and Mathurine, each of whom now demands that he confirm his commitment to her in front of the other. He replies to each, sotto voce, that she is right and her rival wrong. Dom Juan says the same thing to Charlotte that he says to Mathurine, treating them identically. To Mathurine, he declares, "Je gage qu'elle va vous dire que je lui ai promis de l'épouser" [I'll bet she'll tell you I've promised to marry her] and to Charlotte, "Gageons qu'elle vous soutiendra que je lui ai donné parole de la prendre pour femme" (2.4) [Let's bet that she'll maintain that I've given her my word to make her my wife]. This satisfies neither. Mathurine presses Dom Juan to declare his love for her in order to convince and thereby defeat her rival. Whether or not Dom Juan actually loves Mathurine is beside the point. Nor does Charlotte seem to care much about the don's feelings for her. Her only desire is the same as Mathurine's, acceptance of her victory by her rival. Dom Juan's strategy makes mirror images of the rivals. Mathurine and Charlotte sound more and more alike as they appeal to their "fiancé" to end the confusion:

CHARLOTTE. Oui, Mathurine, je veux que Monsieur vous montre votre bec jaune.

MATHURINE. Oui, Charlotte, je veux que Monsieur vous rende un peu camuse.
CHARLOTTE. Monsieur, vuidez la querelle, s'il vous plaît.
MATHURINE. Mettez-nous d'accord, Monsieur.
CHARLOTTE. *à Mathurine.* Vous allez voir.
MATHURINE. *à Charlotte.* Vous allez voir vous-même.
CHARLOTTE. *à Dom Juan.* Dites.
MATHURINE. *à Dom Juan.* Parlez. (2.4)

[CHARLOTTE. Yes, Mathurine. I want Monsieur to show you how naïve you are.
MATHURINE. Yes, Charlotte. I want Monsieur to take you down a peg.
CHARLOTTE. Sir, settle the quarrel, please.
MATHURINE. Clear us up, sir.
CHARLOTTE. (*to* Mathurine). You'll see.
MATHURINE. (*to* Charlotte). You'll see yourself.
CHARLOTTE. (*to* Don Juan). Tell her.
MATHURINE. (*to* Don Juan). Speak up.]

In effect, Dom Juan robs Charlotte and Mathurine of whatever individuality they may once have possessed.

Having undermined their capacity for certainty, he extricates himself from the dilemma by telling the women that they must rely upon what they themselves know and believe: "Est-ce que chacune de vous ne sait pas ce qui en est, sans qu'il soit nécessaire que je m'explique davantage?" (2.4) [Doesn't each of you know what the truth is, without my needing to explain myself further?]. Words have no potency when it comes to bringing meaningful order to situations like these: "Pourquoi m'obliger là-dessus à des redites? . . . Tous les discours n'avancent point les choses; il faut faire et non pas dire, et les efforts décident mieux que les paroles" (2.4) [Why make me repeat myself on this? . . . All this talk doesn't get us anywhere; we must do, not say, and actions speak louder than words]. Of course, everyone, except perhaps Charlotte and Mathurine, knows that Dom Juan's actions are as worthless as his words. The nature of rivalry in Molière's theater is to destabilize the rivals' sense of who they are. Dom Juan's behavior demonstrates how this happens, and Sganarelle underscores the point, making it impossible for the women to trust language. The servant tells Charlotte and Mathurine that "Mon maître est un fourbe; . . . c'est l'épouseur du genre humain" [My master is a cheat . . . he's the marrying kind—of the whole human race], but spying Dom Juan, who might overhear him, he quickly utters the opposite: "Mon maître n'est point l'épouseur du genre humain, il n'est point fourbe" (2.4) [My master is not the marrying kind—of the whole human race—he's not a cheat]. What are Charlotte and Mathurine to believe? Which of Sganarelle's contradictory statements? The only certainty is that words no longer speak a reality on which the characters can rely.

Dom Juan reneges on his financial obligations in much the same way that he turns aside the appeals of women he has lured. He understands that to greet Monsieur Dimanche's unwelcome visit with hostility will only leave the two men at odds over a debt that Dom Juan has no intention of repaying. To deal with creditors, "Il est bon de les payer de quelque chose . . . sans leur en donner un double" (4.2) [It's good to give them some satisfaction . . . without paying them a penny]. Instead of refusing to receive Monsieur Dimanche, the don invites him inside and treats the rich bourgeois as a social equal. Having settled him into an armchair, to which only a noble would be entitled, he inquires after his guest's family and dog. No secret is made of the strategic move employed to dispense with the troublesome creditor: "je ne veux point qu'on mette de différence entre nous deux" (4.3) [I don't want any distinction shown between the two of us]. It is a small, if not altogether logical, step from the contention that Dom Juan and Monsieur Dimanche are socially equal to the conclusion that there is no difference between creditor and debtor and, therefore, no debt to be repaid. Dom Juan's skillfully executed pretense of equal social status completely disrupts the system of financial exchange.

Even when Dom Juan chooses to observe the social code of the nobility, he represents a danger to the well-being of his class. He is shocked that Elvire would visit him dressed in clothes more suitable for the country. In encounters with her two brothers, he instinctively comes to the aid of Dom Carlos, who is about to be robbed by a band of thieves, and he does not deny his identity when Dom Alonse, who, with his brother, is hunting him down to avenge their sister's disgrace, recognizes him. Thinking of himself as a man of honor, Dom Juan poses as the protector and friend of Dom Carlos. At the same time, he is Carlos's bitter enemy. Friend and enemy, "grand seigneur" [great lord] and "méchant homme" [wicked man], Dom Juan cannot but sow discord within the ranks of the nobility. Dom Alonse and his brother disagree over whether retribution should be exacted from Dom Juan on the spot or later. Their dispute goes to the core of what it means to be noble, and Dom Juan stands by quietly as the brothers quarrel about whether honor or life itself is more important. Once again, he has, by his actions, pitted his rivals against each other and shown the underlying fragility of the social order to which both he and his rivals adhere. That order will be hard-pressed to survive the obliteration of distinctions essential to it. When all is said and done, Dom Carlos and Dom Louis share a preoccupation with how others view them, and in this they are not different from Dom Juan himself.[25]

Dom Louis holds firmly to his belief in an aristocratic order and castigates his son for not living up to its values: "Apprenez enfin qu'un gentilhomme qui vit mal est un monstre dans la nature, que la vertu est le premier titre de noblesse" (4.4) [In short, know that a gentleman who lives badly is a monstrosity in nature, that virtue is the first title of nobility]. Dom Juan's corruption so degrades the nobility that his father would prefer the "fils d'un crocheteur qui serait honnête homme" [the son of a porter who was a decent man] to a monarch's son "qui vivrait comme vous" (4.4) [who lived as you do]. By this statement, Dom Louis tacitly admits that nobility has no essence separating it from the people and is, therefore, vulnerable to the attacks of his son and those like him. Though annoyed when told his father has come to call on him, Dom Juan knows perfectly well how to neutralize the old man. If Dom Louis degrades his own son to a status below that of a porter's child, Dom Juan returns the favor by treating his noble father as he had treated Monsieur Dimanche, dignifying Dom Louis's lengthy diatribe with no more than a "Monsieur, si vous étiez assis, vous en seriez mieux pour parler" (4.4) [Sir, if you sat down, you would be more comfortable for talking]. A meddlesome father with whom he shares social rank and a pushy bourgeois creditor pose the same problem for Dom Juan, and he dispenses with them in the same way.

When the don meets a representative of his ultimate rival, God, his behavior remains consistent (3.2). He refuses to acknowledge the superiority of his rival and does what he can to shrink the immense difference between himself and God. Francisque is a poor hermit who offers advice to travelers and begs for alms to maintain his meager existence. Understanding that charity will not bring the hermit over from God's camp, Dom Juan insists that Francisque swear in order to receive a gold coin. Were the poor man to utter an oath, Dom Juan would be victorious, but Francisque would rather die of hunger. Dom Juan disdainfully tosses him the coin, with the famous line, "je te le donne pour l'amour de l'humanité" (3.2) [I'll give it to you for love of humanity]. The words confirm Dom Juan's atheism[26] and his willingness to incur the wrath of God. More importantly, they deny the implied precedence of a good act performed for the love of God over a gesture in the name of humankind alone. Dom Juan rejects the hierarchy in which God or, for that matter, anyone other than himself, is superior.[27] The don's verbal adroitness carries the day, but his success is short-lived.

In his desire to distinguish himself from others by his superiority over them, Dom Juan fits the mold of Molière's great comic protagonists. Unlike most of them, he is not subjected to ridicule,[28] because, in part at least, for a seventeenth-century audience, his explicit rivalry with God raises his evil behavior to high seriousness. Tartuffe's religious hypocrisy is equally scandalous, especially when he manipulates the language of piety in pursuit of sexual gratification, but his rivals, on the other hand, are always very much of this world. By feigning piety, Tartuffe bears out La Rochefoucauld's maxim that "l'hypocrisie est un hommage que le vice rend à la vertu" (Max. 218)[29] [Hypocrisy is the homage that vice pays to virtue]. Dom Juan surpasses Tartuffe by adopting his predecessor's hypocrisy to have his way with the world and then tempting God to punish him. Abducting Elvire from a convent, proudly trumpeting his atheism to Sganarelle, and showing contempt for Francisque's piety are all offenses against God. When, finally, Dom Juan refuses to repent and grandly offers his hand to the Statue, who leads him down into Hell, God at last takes revenge.

The don's boldness in the face of certain death might, at first glance, appear heroic, and he is, in fact, steadfast in his unwillingness to change. But when he assumes the mask of the hypocrite, he falls into the same trap he has set for his rivals: he loses his personal distinction, becoming just like everyone else. Hypocrisy, as he himself says, is in style. Now, imitating others rather than being imitated by them, he becomes just another clone of the likes of Tartuffe. Despite his earlier cynicism, Dom Juan sounds like a whining child as he explains his hypocrisy: "Et pourquoi non? Il y en a tant d'autres comme moi, qui se mêlent de ce métier, et qui se servent de même masque pour abuser le monde" (5.2) [And why not? There are so many others like me who ply that trade, and use the same mask to take advantage of people!]. What he reveals to Sganarelle is that the master is no different from anyone else; all wear the very same mask.[30] Dom Juan looks to his servant to approve his new behavior: "Je veux bien, Sganarelle, t'en faire confidence, et je suis bien aise d'avoir un témoin du fond de mon âme et des véritables motifs qui m'obligent à faire les choses" (5.2)[31] [I'm willing to confide this in you, Sganarelle, and I'm very glad to have a witness of my inmost soul and of the real motives that oblige me to do things]. Sganarelle is adamant in his condemnation. His "reasoning" is nonsensical and merits Dom Juan's dismissive "Ô le beau raisonnement" (5.2) [Oh, what fine reasoning!], but his conclusion makes perfect sense: "vous serez damné à tous les diables" (5.2) [you will be damned to all the devils in Hell].

This is not the first time that Sganarelle disapproves of his master's behavior, but, from this point on, there will be none of the reversals of judgment that so often followed the servant's earlier outbursts of indignation. He rebukes the don for telling Dom Carlos that Heaven prevents his returning to Elvire (5.4) and entreats his master to repent once the Spectre appears (5.5). Dom Juan's most effective strategy for nullifying his rivals has suddenly lost its potency. In becoming like those he has decided to imitate, he subjects himself to the same punishment that will, in the end, be theirs. There is, once again, a right and a wrong, a true and a false. Dom Juan is on the wrong side of these reinstituted norms and will suffer the consequences. Albeit imperfectly, for a moment, the order that Dom Juan has shattered is restored. United against him, "tout le monde est content" (5.6) [everyone is happy]—except Sganarelle. He alone is still miserable, for the wages his master owes him remain unpaid.

As Dom Juan confronts his rivals, one after the other, he, like Tartuffe, tries to break down their individual identities. He does not always succeed. Pierrot never relents in his opposition to Dom Juan. Francisque does not abandon his faith. Elvire finally gives up the hope of having Dom Juan and, for altruistic reasons, counsels repentance. Sganarelle is now firm in his indignation. The rapid movement from episode to episode overshadows Dom Juan's repeated failures. As the curtain falls, Sganarelle's complaint, "Mes gages, mes gages, mes gages!" (5.6), bears witness to the impossibility of Dom Juan's realizing his project of absolute superiority over others. Sganarelle's real master is money, not Dom Juan. The don's attempt to control his servant in order to identify himself through the eyes of another fails for a flimsy reason—hard cash. By taking on all comers, Dom Juan lays bare the mechanisms by which rivalry functions. He too falls prey to it.

5

The World Turned Upside Down: Rivalry and *Ressentiment* in *Amphitryon*

To HAVE THE ONLY WIFE WHOSE FAITHFULNESS IS GUARANTEED, TO live a life purged of all that is bourgeois, to be sick, to be more devout, richer, or more clever than others—these are but some of the poses struck by Molière's characters who strive for superiority by making a show of difference. In *Amphitryon*, distinction and superiority are givens, since not only is Jupiter a god, but the greatest god among the Olympians. There can be no question of equating or, for that matter, comparing him with a mere mortal like Amphitryon. Rivalry between them would seem, therefore, unthinkable. Jupiter represents power; both gods and men acknowledge his might. What Alceste and Monsieur Jourdain want Jupiter has. The god's higher position in the universe is securely established, as is his superiority to all humankind. Jupiter certainly need not prove himself stronger, more ingenious, more masterly than Amphitryon. Yet that is precisely what he does, for this god is not without desire. He falls head over heels in love with Amphitryon's new wife, Alcmène, whom he will at whatever cost possess.

The world has been turned upside down in *Amphitryon*, more dramatically even than in *Dom Juan*. It is one thing for a noble to be attracted physically to a pretty peasant girl but quite another for a god to be so smitten with a mortal that he must play the jealous lover to the husband she continues to adore. Jupiter himself confesses this: "Et c'est moi, dans cette aventure, / Qui, tout dieu que je suis, dois être le jaloux" (3.10.1903–4) [And it is I, in this affair, / Who, god though I am, must utter jealous sighs].[1] By putting a jealous god on stage, Molière pushes to the limit the situation he created in *Dom Juan*, that of a character whose desire overwhelms his superiority. Though Dom Juan loses something of his nobility by his shameless pursuit of Charlotte, his brief rivalry with Pierrot is structured in the most normal of ways. To woo Charlotte, he emphasizes the difference between himself and his rival: "Quoi? une personne comme vous serait la femme d'un simple paysan! Non, non: c'est profaner tant de beautés . . . Vous méritez sans doute une meilleure fortune, et le Ciel, qui le connaît bien, m'a conduit ici tout exprès pour empêcher ce mariage, et rendre justice à vos charmes" (2.2) [What? A person like you should become the wife of a mere peasant? No, no: that would be a profanation of so much beauty . . . There's no question you deserve a better lot; and Heaven, which knows this well, has brought me here on purpose to prevent this marriage and do justice to your charms]. Charlotte underlines the distinction when she reproaches Pierrot for not wanting her to have the very best: "Si tu m'aimes ne dois-tu pas être bien aise que je devienne Madame?" (2.3) [If you love me, shouldn't you be mighty pleased to see me become a real lady?]. Jupiter's approach is diametrically opposed to Dom Juan's. Rather than flatter Alcmène by courting her as a god, he disguises himself as her husband. The rivalry between Amphitryon and Jupiter is as intense as any in Molière's theater, but here, the similarity of the rivals takes precedence over their difference as the central problem of the play. Thus, Jupiter first appears on stage disguised as his rival, and only at play's end does he divulge his true identity.

Critics have proposed a number of reasons for which Molière might have chosen to write a play based on Plautus's *Amphitryon*. The most colorful—and fanciful—is that of Roederer, the first to suggest that Molière saw in the story of Jupiter's love for the wife of Amphitryon a parallel with the attachment of Louis XIV to Madame de Montespan, whose husband reacted badly to her infidelity.[2] Despois and Mesnard believe that Molière may have reached a stage in his career at which Plautus appealed to his creative sensibilities. He had, after all, recently written *L'Avare* under the influence of the Latin master. The editors of the Grands Ecrivains de la France edition add to this supposition a more substantial explanation of the playwright's affinity to Plautus's subject: its theatrical durability.[3] For Georges Couton, *Amphitryon*, written during the War of Devolution, is an example of the kind of lighthearted works often inspired by the events associated with wars and produced at the same time as more somber writings.[4] Gérard Defaux prefers to see in the play a continuation of Molière's pondering over the problem of appearances so central to understanding *Tartuffe*.[5] Whatever the reason for Molière's choice of his subject, one thing is certain. The story Plautus tells touches directly upon preoccupations at the heart of Molière's comic vision.

Jupiter, first among the gods and, therefore, responsible for the order of the universe, threatens that very order as his desire leads him into rivalry with Amphitryon.[6] Moreover, this rivalry reduces the world of mortals to chaos not as a result of the difference separating the rivals, but rather because they are so much alike. As he confronts the story of Amphitryon, Molière again comes to grips with the dynamics of rivalry and the danger inherent in it.[7] His instinct is to be more radical than his Roman predecessor. In Plautus's play, the audience can distinguish Jupiter from Amphitryon by the gold tassel the god wears on his hat. Mercury has a plume on his, lest he resemble too completely his human counterpart.[8] In Molière's play, Amphitryon and Jupiter look exactly alike, as do Sosie and Mercure.

At the origin of Jupiter's ambivalent relations with humans is, of course, his desire.[9] Asking for a delay in the onset of daylight so that Jupiter can prolong his tryst with Alcmène, Mercury reminds La Nuit that the master of the gods "Aime à s'humaniser pour des beautés mortelles, / Et sait cent tours ingénieux, / Pour mettre à bout les plus cruelles" (Prologue 56–58) [likes to put on human guise / When there are mortal beauties to pursue, / And how he's full of tricks and lies / That purest maids have yielded to]. La Nuit, aware of the god's celebrated propensity to masquerade as someone other than himself to seduce beautiful women, cannot, despite her admiration for Jupiter, understand why he does this. Mercure's explanation, in both its language and substance, is richly suggestive. Mercure speaks in an overly familiar way of his master's disguises as gestures of a "Dieu qui n'est pas bête" (Prologue 79) [god who is not stupid] (Translation by author). He would consider Jupiter quite wretched (Prologue 81) if the god never abandoned his formidable mien and "au faîte des cieux il fût toujours guindé" (Prologue 83) [let the jeweled bounds of Heaven confine him]. As Robert Jouanny indicates in his edition of Molière, the word "guinder" [to hoist] smacks of disrespect and ought not be used in reference to Jupiter.[10] Nor would one normally think of the greatest of the gods as "emprisonné toujours dans sa grandeur" (Prologue 85) [Always . . . imprisoned in . . . splendor]. Mercure's deprecating talk debases the esteem in which this king of the gods (Prologue 34) should be held. To him, Jupiter's godliness is a hindrance when it comes to love, and he congratulates his master for coming down from the heights of glory for the sake of dalliance. Amorous desire in *Amphitryon* functions much as the desire for power in Corneille's *Cinna*, where Auguste feels trapped in his absolute authority:

L'ambition déplaît, quand elle est assouvie,
D'une contraire ardeur son ardeur est suivie,

> Et comme notre esprit jusqu'au dernier soupir
> Toujours vers quelque objet pousse quelque désir,
> Il se ramène en soi n'ayant plus où se prendre,
> Et monté sur le faîte, il aspire à descendre.
>
> (2.1.365–70)[11]

> [Ambition palls once it is accomplished;
> And an opposing passion takes its place.
> So now our spirit, having striven ever
> To the last breath to gain some certain end,
> Turns on itself, with nothing more to conquer,
> And having reached the peak would fain descend.][12]

The absence of limits itself becomes, paradoxically, a limitation to be overcome for both the king and the god driven by desire.

Despite his omnipotence, Jupiter derives little personal gratification from the identity bestowed upon him by his exalted rank. His disguises, as Mercure tells La Nuit, allow the god to "goûter . . . toutes sortes d'états" (Prologue 78) [sample every state of being]. In different guises, he may achieve the pleasures and objectives sought as well by his human rivals. That he, a god, should feel compelled to share the experience of the mortal Amphitryon can only be explained by obsessive desire, the same desire that inhabits all of Molière's theater. Indeed, Molière's Jupiter differs from his other characters only in having at his disposal more efficacious means of attaining his ends. Monsieur Jourdain cannot transform himself into a nobleman to conquer Dorimène, but Jupiter is capable of becoming Amphitryon, if that is the way to win the heart of Alcmène. Ironically, this very power disadvantages Jupiter, who cannot completely assuage his desire by indulging it, because his mask, while granting him entrée to Alcmène's bed, also makes it impossible for her to love him for or as himself. Whence Jupiter's jealousy of a rival inferior to the god. Mercure's description of Jupiter once the god has transformed himself into a mortal is very much to the point: "Et pour entrer dans tout ce qu'il lui plaît / Il sort tout à fait de lui-même, / Et ce n'est plus alors Jupiter qui paraît" (Prologue 90–92) [When he would enter into any new / Delight, he lays his selfhood by, / And Jupiter the god is lost to view]. In his imitation of Amphitryon, Jupiter loses a firm grip on his being. His desire is, in one sense, fulfilled. On the other hand, he enjoys Alcmène's love only in the person of the mortal he is imitating. Alcmène remains faithful in spirit to her husband. Jupiter succeeds, as a god must, but at the same time he fails. The contradiction is symptomatic of the disease epidemic among Molière's characters who are seized by a desire they try to placate through imitation of others.

What is particularly interesting about *Amphitryon* is that the identity between rivals does not emerge gradually as characters move to distinguish themselves from each other. It is, rather, the central feature of the dramatic action from the start. On the contrary, the profound similarity between Alceste and his rivals—they all seek personal validation in the eyes of others—is initially hidden by the protagonist's insistence on his higher principles. Likewise, the *femmes savantes* [learned women] at first appear very different from their opponents. Only little by little does it become evident that Philaminte and company hunger after power just as surely as the oppressive dullards they so abhor. In *Amphitryon*, this similarity, more dangerous than the struggle of seeming opposites that often hides it, rivets the attention of the audience. By imitating Amphitryon, Jupiter brings the community of mortals to the brink of chaos. His charade and the momentary elimination of differences caused by his behavior threaten the family, social order, and the integrity of the individual self. In the third act, Jupiter himself sums up the dilemma when he promises to clarify the mystifying confusion: "Alcmène attend de moi ce public témoignage: / Sa vertu, que l'éclat de ce désordre outrage, / Veut qu'on la justifie, et j'en vais prendre soin" (3.5.1691–93) [Alcmena asks of me that explanation. / Her virtue, sullied by this confrontation, / Asks to be proven pure, and that's my aim]. "Désordre" [disorder] describes perfectly the state of the community infected by Jupiter's virus. His transformation into a human manifests not only his frailty, his susceptibility to the same whims of desire as mortals, but also the fragile nature of the order on which humans found their existence. Plautus and Rotrou, in his *Sosies*, conclude their plays by recalling the tale of how Hercules, the son born of Jupiter's cohabitation with Alcmène, strangles the serpents attacking him in his cradle. Molière allows Jupiter to forecast the birth of Hercules but goes no further with the myth. The omission, coupled with Sosie's words— "Et chez nous il doit naître un fils d'un très grand coeur: / Tout cela va le mieux du monde" (3.10.1938–39) [And we shall have . . . / A son with whose renown the world shall ring; / And all that's very fine, I guess]—brings into prominence the human,[13] for when god and man become indistinguishable from each other, the problem that ensues falls to man.

Jupiter descends into the company of mortals and brings with him a linguistic precept that disrupts human discourse and throws the community into disarray. As Mercure explains to La Nuit, whose modesty is offended by his request that she conspire, even indirectly, in Jupiter's escapade:

> Un tel emploi n'est bassesse
> Que chez les petites gens.
> Lorsque dans un haut rang on a l'heur de paraître,
> Tout ce qu'on fait est toujours bel et bon;
> Et suivant ce qu'on peut être,
> Les choses changent de nom.
>
> (Prologue 126–31)

> [To do such service isn't base
> Except in those of low degree.
> When one is blessed with high estate and standing,
> All that one does is good as gold,
> And things have different names, depending
> On what position one may hold.]

According to this formula, the identity of the speaker rather than his language or the nature of the object in question determines meaning. On the surface, of course, Mercure says nothing very complicated. He simply makes another cynical declaration of the ageless verity that power imposes itself on every aspect of human existence, including language. It is, however, also literally true in this play that the stability of names—what a person is called, how one is identified—cannot be counted upon. Mercure, for example, assumes the role of Sosie by stealing from the servant both his looks and his name—"En lui volant son nom, avec sa ressemblance" (1.2.281)[14] [stealing . . . / Not only his appearance but his name]. With his name gone, Sosie does not know who he is; he is adrift in a world in which the name Sosie no longer situates him. The undermining of human language forms a major component of the turmoil that results from Jupiter's perfect imitation of his rival.

Shortly after Mercure forbids Sosie to be Sosie, the servant has his first encounter with his master, Amphitryon, who wants to get to the bottom of all the "confusion" (2.1.703). Sosie has learned the lesson of servitude at the violent hand of Mercure. Seeing the anger of Amphitryon, Sosie assures him that "vous aurez toujours raison" (2.1.695) [The truth shall be exactly what you please]. Before his anxious master questions him about events in the household, Sosie wants to understand how the interrogation will proceed:

Parlerai-je, Monsieur, selon ma conscience,
Ou comme auprès des grands on le voit usité?
    Faut-il dire la vérité,
    Ou bien user de complaisance?

(2.1.709–12)

[Shall I speak, Sir, from my conscience and my heart,
Or as the hangers-on of great folk do?
    Shall what I say be simply true,
    Or shall I speak with flattering art?]

Sosie, it seems, is nimble enough to adjust either to a language in which words represent the truth or to one in which what is said is dictated by his interlocutor's influence and power. But he must ascertain the rules of the game. Amphitryon claims to want nothing but the truth from his servant, but when Sosie begins to sound confused, his master accuses him of drunkenness and orders him to be silent. As if he had overheard Mercure's word to La Nuit, Sosie responds to Amphitryon's contention that he has been speaking nonsense:

Tous les discours sont des sottises,
Partant d'un homme sans éclat;
Ce serait paroles exquises
Si c'était un grand qui parlât.

(2.1.839–42)

[All speech is foolish if it's framed
By someone of obscure estate:
But the same words, uttered by the great,
Would be applauded and acclaimed.]

Seen in context, Sosie's conclusion is more than a recognition of the power of a "grand." He has just been told by Mercure that he is not Sosie, and now Amphitryon says that the truth he speaks amounts to meaningless gibberish. The solid underpinnings of Sosie's existence give way to utter confusion.

The gods' assault against the world of Amphitryon and Sosie does violence to meaning and, therefore, to human communication. When Sosie talks about "himself," he is incomprehensible to anyone not aware of his encounter with his "other self," Mercure; and Sosie can never assume that the words of Amphitryon or Mercure really mean what they seem to mean. As elsewhere in Molière's theater, the corrosive effects of power gone awry take their toll on characters' ability to resolve problems by using language.

Mercure, even as he unmasks himself at the play's conclusion, would have Sosie believe that the violence of the gods is not so bad after all: "Et les coups de bâton d'un Dieu / Font honneur à qui les endure" (3.9.1878–79) [For it's an honor to have one's back / Lambasted by a deity]. "Coups de bâton," obviously intended to inflict pain, suddenly become harmless and, more than that, honorific. Like words, they lose their real meaning in Mercure's description of them. Sosie, who has suffered too often from Mercure's indulgence in gratuitous violence, replies with appropriate irony: "Ma foi! Monsieur le dieu, je suis votre valet: / Je me serais passé de votre courtoisie" (3.9.1880–81) [My goodness, Mister God, I thank Your Grace; / But I could have done without your gracious favor]. Similarly, Jupiter's words, revealing his true identity, fly in the face of the legitimate outrage that has been at the root of Amphitryon's behavior:

> Un partage avec Jupiter
> N'a rien du tout qui déshonore;
> Et sans doute il ne peut être que glorieux
> De se voir le rival du souverain des dieux.
>
> (3.10.1898–1901)

> [To share a love with Jupiter
> Has surely no dishonor in it;
> And surely it must seem a glorious thing
> To be the rival of Olympus' king.]

Jupiter tries to have his cake and eat it too. In the process, he contributes to the erosion of the important distinction between gods and men. The words and deeds of gods differ qualitatively from those of mortals, who should, therefore, be honored by the deities' intervention. On the other hand, these same gods, who claim to be so different in nature, act like men, take on the looks of men, and admit to such human feelings as jealousy. To accept Jupiter's vision is to embrace chaos, to reject it, is futile. Once again, nothing has changed fundamentally at the end of a Molière play. Mercure's flippant retort to La Nuit in the Prologue—"Et suivant ce qu'on peut être, / Les choses changent de nom" (130–31) [And things have different names, depending / On what position one may hold]—returns to haunt the characters in the play's final lines. The silence of Amphitryon and his wife and Sosie's last words, bringing the play to its end—"Sur de telles affaires, toujours / Le meilleur est de ne rien dire" (3.10.1942–43) [Regarding matters of this sort, / It's wisest always to be still]—signal the suspended status of the momentary return to order expected by the audience after Jupiter divulges the truth that has so confounded his human victims. Order is indeed restored, but it seems unlikely to endure beyond the point at which silence gives way to language.

Not by chance did Molière assign to himself the role of Amphitryon's servant, Sosie. The master experiences the chaos that comes from rivalry and the elimination of difference. Amphitryon lives an incomprehensible dilemma. His lot is to contend with the crisis rather than to apprehend it. He does not and cannot know what is happening around him, because he is not confronted by his double until the end of the play. The truth dawns on Amphitryon slowly. Sosie, on the other hand, meets his double almost immediately and is more than once called upon to explain his own behavior. If his explanations often bewilder his interlocutor and amuse the audience, what he says reveals much about the structure and inherent danger of imitative rivalry. The rivalry between Sosie and Mercure is also more elemental than that between Amphitryon and Jupiter. The king of the gods wants to seduce Amphitryon's wife. Mercure has no interest at all in Sosie's wife, Cléanthis. He desires the very being of Sosie, who, therefore, has more at stake than his master. The battle between Jupiter and Amphitryon clearly engages the individuality of both combatants. Were Jupiter to succeed, Amphitryon would lose his self-esteem as well as his wife. Still, Amphitryon's experience of the rivalry centers on the object of the two rivals' desire, Alcmène. In the case of Sosie, that object is his name, his very self. A victorious Mercure, "ce moi plutôt que moi" (2.1.741) [Sosia; another me], would subsume the identity of Sosie, replacing the servant in his totality, rather than in the bed of Cléanthis.

The instability of Sosie's identity is manifest as soon as he steps on stage. In the play's first scene, the servant has returned home to deliver to Amphitryon's wife news of her husband's victory in battle. Sosie complains of being sent off to do this errand on the darkest of nights—La Nuit has obliged Mercure—and bemoans the fate of those who, like himself, are subjected to the will of the great for whose benefit everyone else must sacrifice (1.1.168–71). His musings imply that Sosie thinks he would do well to quit the service of Amphitryon. What keeps him on the job is neither fidelity to his master nor pride in his work. He is seduced by his master's presence, by "la moindre faveur d'un coup d'oeil caressant" (1.1.186) [their least nod, or smile, or show of grace]. The opinion of others counts more than his own:

> . . . notre âme insensée
> S'acharne au vain honneur de demeurer près d'eux,
> Et s'y veut contenter de la fausse pensée
> Qu'ont tous les autres gens que nous sommes heureux.
>
> (1.1.178–81)

> [. . . foolishly we cling and cleave
> To the empty honor of being at their side,
> And strive to feel what other men believe,
> That we are privileged and full of pride.]

Being seen as happy has greater value to him than being happy. He lives under the gaze of others and allows it to determine his situation, despite his awareness that what others think is dead wrong, a "fausse pensée." Sosie, however, is more than just another seventeenth-century fop worried about appearances. His preoccupation with them derives, above all, from his will to be seen by others, since their view of him determines his view of himself. His identity has, in effect, been decentered; it has lost its place as the core of his being. He lives, in Pascalian terms, a diffused, imaginary existence over which he no longer retains control. Although discontented with his lot, he carries on, because others believe he is lucky to be able to keep company with the likes of his master. Pascal explains this kind of behavior: "Nous ne nous contentons pas de la vie que nous avons en nous et en notre propre être: nous voulons vivre dans l'idée des autres d'une vie imaginaire, et nous nous efforçons pour cela de paraître" (fragment 147)[15] [We are not satisfied with the life that we have within ourselves and in our own being: we want to live an imaginary life in the mind of others, and to do that we strive to appear]. Appearance becomes a sign, in *Amphitryon* as in the *Penseés*, of the dissipation of individual identity as it gives way to the need for recognition from others. It is impossible to answer the question "Who is Sosie?" by looking at the character himself. To the extent that he molds himself to fit the view of others, he has no fixed identity. The appearance of Mercure disguised as Sosie is a logical dramatic development in the portrayal of Sosie's protean nature. It forces the servant, as nothing else could, to face the issue of his identity.

Even before Mercure dispossesses Sosie of his identity, Molière has Amphitryon's servant freely step outside himself to take on the roles of others. In a long monologue, Sosie rehearses his announcement to Alcmène of her victorious husband's return, assumes the role of Alcmène receiving news of her husband and responding to it, pretends to be himself recounting Amphitryon's

adventures, and, finally, muses favorably on his ability to play himself. He surprises himself by the aplomb with which he answers Alcmène's questions:

> *"Que dit-il? que fait-il? Contente un peu mon âme."*
>   "Il dit moins qu'il ne fait, Madame,
>   Et fait trembler les ennemis."
> (Peste! où prend mon esprit toutes ces gentillesses?).
>
> (1.1.223–26)

> ["How does he speak, or act? I long to know."
>   Madam, he'd sooner act than speak, and so
>   His enemies have cause to dread him.
> (Listen to that! Am I not the prince of wits?)]

The scene, which foreshadows Sosie's unhappy fate, demonstrates
the instability of his character. Nothing here is firmly grounded in
reality. Sosie is split between the imaginary Sosie and the actor who
stands back and comments on his own acting. Alcmène, who is not
present, is represented by a lantern with the voice of Sosie. And
the details of Amphitryon's actions are pure invention, since Sosie
has never been on the field of battle with his master. The actual
meeting between Sosie and Alcmène, were it to take place as
planned, would be no more real than the rehearsal. Sosie puts on
this little drama to prepare for that future encounter in which he
will once again only play at being himself: "Pour jouer mon rôle
sans peine, / Je le veux un peu repasser" (1.1.200–201) [I must rehearse a bit, and groom / Myself to give this role my best].
  At Mercure's first appearance in the guise of Sosie, the servant
calls up his limited courage in order to mount a defense of his own
individuality. Though he relies only upon appearances to defend
himself—"Si je ne suis hardi, tâchons de le paraître" (1.2.305)
[Though I'm not brave, I can dissimulate]—he responds to Mercure's "Qui va là?" [Who goes there?] with a simple, but not insig-
nificant, "Moi" (1.2.309) [I]. Sosie may well be a coward, but, in
this brief moment, he is Sosie, he is himself. He conjures up an
image of the brave Amphitryon to give substance to his false claim:
"Il [Mercure] est seul, comme moi; je suis fort, j'ai bon maître"
(1.2.307) [The man's alone; I'm strong; my master's great]. Moments later, he tries to solidify an otherwise playful description of
himself by telling Mercure, "j'appartiens à mon maître" (1.2.319)
[I . . . am my master's man]. Sosie's assertion of his identity ties it
closely to that of his master. There is in the servant an emptiness
that can be filled only by reference to others. Since what distin-

guishes Sosie from Mercure is appearances or inconsequential facts about his past—his meal while Amphitryon was on the battlefield or the contents of the box containing Amphitryon's gift to Alcmène— Mercure can, with a good disguise and a bit of knowledge, easily replace him. Sosie clings to his individuality but neither experiences nor articulates it in ways that secure it against the incursions of his double.

The affirmation, in his initial encounter with Mercure, that he is Sosie, albeit "Sosie battu" (1.2.382) [Sosia *frappé*], yields place to the servant's recognition that he cannot prevail in the struggle for his identity against the odds of his double's violent pugnacity: "Hélas! je suis ce que tu veux; / Dispose de mon sort tout au gré de tes voeux: / Ton bras t'en a fait le maître" (1.2.389–91) [I'll be whatever you insist. / Make of me what you will. Your arm and fist / Have gained you that prerogative]. However alarming the prospect, Sosie may have to "renoncer à moi-même" (1.2.400) [renounce myself] and surrender his name. But, he wonders: "Être ce que je suis est-il en ta [Mercure's] puissance? / Et puis-je cesser d'être moi?" (1.2.426–27) [How can you be the person that I am? / Can I cease to be myself?]. And if this is possible, where does that leave him? For he must have some identity: "Mais si tu l'es [Sosie], dis-moi qui tu veux que je sois? / Car encore faut-il bien que je sois quelque chose" (1 2.511–12) [But if you're he, tell me who *I* am, then——/ Because I must be someone, mustn't I?]. Sosie, standing there on stage being Sosie, talks as if he might evaporate into thin air only to be drawn up short by the realization that he is still something. He seems, as servants at times do in Molière's theater, to be talking nonsense. In fact, his prattle, if taken seriously for a moment, exposes what Lionel Gossman calls the two major themes of the play: "the nature of the self and the nature of relations with others."[16] It remains to Sosie to solve the puzzle of his own identity.

More perspicacious than literary critics and psychologists, Sosie recognizes instinctively what has happened to him. The difference between himself and others, which had once constituted his identity as an individual, has, in his contact with Mercure, disappeared. Resemblance has replaced difference, and Molière returns to an image from the work of Plautus that, by exaggerating similarity, warns implicitly of the dangerous collapse of difference:

> Des pieds jusqu'à la tête, il est comme moi fait,
> Beau, l'air noble, bien pris, les manières charmantes;
> Enfin deux gouttes de lait
> Ne sont pas plus ressemblantes.
>
> (2.1.783–86)[17]

[From head to foot he's like me—handsome, clever;
Well-made, with charms no lady could withstand;
    In short, two drops of milk were never
    As much alike as we are.]

The confusion produced by this doubling is a source of amusement to the audience, but beneath the comedy, the participants in the story witness the breakdown of the order that has lent a measure of meaning to their lives. Sosie earlier imitated others without losing a sense of himself. Now uncertainty confounds him. Violence supplants reason as the guiding principle of human behavior. Sosie finally succumbs, beaten into submission by Mercure:

Je ne l'ai pas cru, moi, sans une peine extrême;
Je me suis d'être deux senti l'esprit blessé,
Et longtemps d'imposteur j'ai traité ce moi-même.
Mais à me reconnaître enfin il m'a forcé:
J'ai vu que c'était moi, sans aucun stratagème.

(2.1.779–82)

[I too was doubtful and inclined to take
My doubleness as a sign of mental strain;
I thought my other self a fraud, a fake;
But at last he made me see that I was twain;
I saw that he was I, and no mistake.]

To survive in any sense, Sosie must accept "ce moi plutôt que moi" (2.1.741) [that I who's not I] (Translation by author) who rules by force.

    Sosie's acquiescence to the uncanny resemblance between himself and Mercure has the effect of establishing a new perspective from which to view the servant's dilemma. Thematically, *Amphitryon* does not differ greatly from other Molière comedies, but the context of resemblance in which the themes appear is novel and radical. Jealousy is a particularly interesting case in point, because as he wrote *Amphitryon*, Molière evidently had in mind *Dom Garcie de Navarre ou le prince jaloux*, from which he again borrowed extensively.[18] Babbling on to Amphitryon about Mercure, Sosie goes right to the root of the relationship between the doubles when he calls the god "Sosie, un moi, de vos ordres jaloux" (2.1.736) [Sosie, another me, jealous of your orders]. Shortly thereafter, Sosie refers to himself and Mercure as "ces deux moi, piqués de jalousie" (2.1.755) [those two selves, their jealousy aroused]. Amphitryon's inability to understand why Sosie did not see Alcmène as he had been ordered to do so frustrates the servant that he assails his master with a hilarious litany of descriptions of Mercure, each beginning with the words "ce moi." Among these is "ce moi de moi-même jaloux" (2.1.815) [this self jealous of myself] (Translations by author). Mercure, according to Sosie, is jealous of him. Unaware of the true identity of his adversary, Sosie quite naturally assumes that "ce moi" wants to usurp his place in Amphitryon's household. Jealousy and rivalry here, as elsewhere, are one. Sosie jealously clings to his threatened identity, and Mercure jealously covets it. They are rivals, Sosie comically supposes, for the position of servant to Amphitryon, whose orders each would have barked at him. What disappears in the competition between two combatants is their difference. One is a human servant, the other a god. Mercure, however, uses his godly powers to make himself identical to Sosie. This is the import of Sosie's words. The physical resemblance between Mercure and himself substantiates a metaphysical dimension of their relationship that Sosie calls jealousy. It is a jealousy that makes them identical and leads to chaos.

Amphitryon, the successful warrior and happy bridegroom, is no less a victim of the gods' shenanigans than his servant. The master's attention focuses on his wife rather than on his identity, but the sentiment aroused in him is the same:

> Ma jalousie, à tout propos,
> Me promène sur ma disgrâce;
> Et plus mon esprit y repasse,
> Moins j'en puis débrouiller le funeste chaos.
>
> (3.1.1462–65)

> [Incessantly, my jealous brain
> Dwells on my dark vicissitudes,
> And yet, the more it mulls and broods,
> The less it can untangle or explain.]

Amphitryon knows for certain that he has been replaced in his wife's bed by another man, for she herself tells him that "nous nous fûmes couchés" (2.2.1019) [we two retired to bed] during the period when he was still off at war. He has also begun to understand that his rival bears a physical resemblance to him. Yet he cannot fathom the complete breakdown of difference that has caused the dilemma he rightly characterizes as chaotic:

> La nature parfois produit des ressemblances
> Dont quelques imposteurs ont pris droit d'abuser;

Mais il est hors de sens que sous ces apparences
Un homme pour époux se puisse supposer,
Et dans tous ces rapports sont mille différences
Dont se peut une femme aisément aviser.

(3.1.1470–75)

['Twixt men, there can be similarities
Whereby impostors manage to deceive;
But that some crafty rascal could with ease
Impersonate a husband, I can't conceive;
There'd be innumerable disparities
Which any wife would readily perceive.]

Difference orders Amphitryon's thought and makes his world comprehensible to him. If nature permits resemblance to intrude on this order, it is only in the form of appearances, which are, by definition, superficial and, therefore, subject to penetration. Beyond appearances lie hard realities, the truth. That mere appearances based on resemblance might, in the eyes of his wife, erase the difference between her husband and another man is "hors de sens." The only explanations Amphitryon can imagine for the strange phenomenon confronting him are that some sort of magic has taken place, which he believes unlikely, or that Alcmène has lost her mind. Rational understanding of the events requires that difference remain intact. Its absence leads to distraction—"Je ne sais plus que croire, ni que dire" (3.4.1604) [I don't know what to say or to suppose], Amphitryon finally declares—and signals the reign of chaos.[19]

Mercure, in a particularly nasty bit of fun at Amphitryon's expense, locks the valiant soldier out of his own house and taunts him with a warning not to disturb the "douces privautés" (3.2.1556) [secret joys] going on inside between Alcmène and her "real" husband. Mistaking Mercure for Sosie—they do look exactly alike, after all—Amphitryon threatens "his servant" with the violent consequences of such insubordination: "Quels orages de coups vont fondre sur ton dos" (3.2.1530) [What a shower of blows your back is going to take!]. Although in one sense, nothing more than a comic elaboration of Mercure's malicious urge to harass Amphitryon, this scene is also a microcosm of what happens in the play before the mystery of resemblance between gods and men unravels. Mercure is neither fully a god nor totally human, for at the same time he teases Amphitryon unmercifully, and with impunity, he must hear himself threatened by a mere mortal. Amphitryon, on the other hand, thinks of himself as Sosie's master and is mystified by his supposed servant's disobedience. Just as Amphitryon had earlier blamed Sosie's double-talk on drink (2.1.821–22), Mercure accuses Amphitryon of drunkenness: "Dis-nous un peu: quel est le cabaret honnête / Où tu t'es coiffé le cerveau?" (3.2.1539–40) [Tell me, in what fine pothouse, or what inn, / Has drinking turned your wits askew?]. Roles are reversed all around: a god lowers himself to bickering with a mortal, a servant mistreats his master, a man would give a god a sound thrashing. Violence looms, with god and man ready to attack each other and Amphitryon crying out for vengeance: "Et toute mon inquiétude / Ne doit aller qu'à me venger" (3.3.1569–70) [Let bitter hate be all I feel, / And vengeance be my only theme]. Amphitryon's fear of chaos is not, it would seem, misplaced. Impending physical violence and its psychological counterpart turn the world upside down.

Jupiter himself is not untouched by the mischief he has wrought. First among the gods though he be, loving Alcmène quickly leads him to experience human feelings. He is not satisfied, for example, that Alcmène thinks of him as the husband to whom she owes her love. Jupiter draws a neat line between the role of husband and that of lover, and despite his disguise as Alcmène's husband, wants her to desire him as she would a lover. As her lover, "Il veut de pure source obtenir vos ardeurs, / Et ne veut rien tenir des noeuds de l'hyménée" (1.3.597–98) [He would obtain your love at its pure source, / And not be way of nuptial bonds and rights]. Her love and his person must be sufficient for Jupiter to obtain the physical and metaphysical favors he wants from her (1.3.571–76). Physical desire alone cannot explain Jupiter's quest:

> Cet amant, de vos voeux jaloux au dernier point,
> Souhaite qu'à lui seul votre coeur s'abandonne.
>   Et sa passion ne veut point
>   De ce que le mari lui donne.

(1.3.593–96)

> [The lover, fiercely jealous of your heart,
> Would be the only one for whom you care,
>   And will not settle for some part
>   Of what the husband deigns to share.]

So manifestly superior is the god to Amphitryon that Alcmène is Jupiter's for the asking. He insists, however, that she *choose* him over her real husband, thereby demonstrating that his rivalry with Amphitryon is not just a squabble over sexual favors, which he has, in any event, already won. Jealousy overpowers the god just as it

does mortals. He will later, like Dom Garcie de Navarre, threaten
to commit suicide if Alcmène rejects his love. Not only does Jupiter's jealousy reveal his personal insecurity and thus undermine
his claim to power, to mastery over the world. It also dooms him
to ultimate failure. Jupiter can succeed with Alcmène only by being
disguised as her husband. But the mask itself makes it unnecessary
for Alcmène to take seriously Jupiter's distinction between lover
and husband.

His insistence on the difference between "amant" and "mari"
clearly indicates how Jupiter sees the universe. Like the mortals he
imitates, he thinks along the lines of difference. Since he is a god,
he permits himself to take liberties with Amphitryon's wife without
ever a thought about his behavior. For Jupiter differs fundamentally from the mortals whose world he has invaded. Jupiter uses his
superiority, upon which the essential difference between himself
and the likes of Amphitryon is founded, to overcome an impediment concomitant with that very difference. Difference is at once a
blessing, because it makes Jupiter omnipotent, and a curse, because it isolates him from the object of his desire. To have what he
wants, Alcmène, he violates the status separating him from mortals
by assuming all the attributes of a man, even as he continues to
think of himself as a god. This disruption of the organizing principle of difference, however, is as dangerous for a god as for a mortal. By becoming the rival of Amphitryon, Jupiter momentarily
surrenders to his desire and abdicates his godly prerogatives. He
is ineluctably drawn into the snare of jealous rivalry that levels all
difference. Adopting the dichotomy between "ressemblance" and
"différence" enunciated earlier by Amphitryon, Jupiter tells the
Theban captain, Naucratès, who confirms the physical likeness of
the two rivals:

> Oui, vous avez raison; et cette ressemblance
> A douter de tous deux vous peut autoriser.
> Je ne m'offense point de vous voir en balance:
> Je suis plus raisonnable, et sais vous excuser.
> L'oeil ne peut entre nous faire de différence,
> Et je vois qu'aisément on s'y peut abuser.
>
> (3.5.1669–74)

> [Well said. Our strange resemblance justifies
> Your having doubts of both of us—him, and me.
> I'm far too reasonable to criticize
> Your hesitation and uncertainty.
> Since the eye can't tell us two apart, it's wise
> Not to act rashly. Sirs, we quite agree.]

Like Amphitryon, Jupiter stands fast by the existence of a real difference between the jealous lovers. Unlike him, he understands what is happening, but even the god is obliged to admit that, to the naked eye, the difference between himself and his rival has disappeared, with the result that general consternation ensues. His rivalry with a human being has made Jupiter behave as a mortal and share the same feelings.

Alcmène is the only major character in *Amphitryon* who stays above the fray engendered by jealous rivalry. Recently married to Amphitryon, she loves him and believes she has remained faithful. Alcmène is victimized by both Jupiter, with whom she unwittingly violates her vow of marital fidelity, and Amphitryon, who, initially at least, blames her for occurrences that he cannot comprehend. As the object of desire of the two rivals, Alcmène becomes an innocent victim of both men. Her role is to remain outside the action dictated by the rivalry between Jupiter and Amphitryon and shed light by her innocence on the flaw in their thinking. During her first meeting with Jupiter disguised as her husband, she rejects his attempt to distinguish between a husband and a lover: "Je ne sépare point ce qu'unissent les Dieux, / Et l'époux et l'amant me sont fort précieux" (1.3.620–21) [What the gods have joined, I shall not separate; / For husband and lover both, my love is great]. Later, she will have an opposite reaction to both lover and husband, but will, nevertheless, continue to reject the dichotomy urged upon her by Jupiter:

> Je ne distingue rien en celui qui m'offense,
> Tout y devient l'objet de mon courroux,
>   Et dans sa juste violence
> Sont confondus et l'amant et l'époux.
> Tous deux de même sorte occupent ma pensée,
> Et des mêmes couleurs, par mon âme blessée,
>   Tous deux ils sont peints à mes yeux:
> Tous deux sont criminels, tous deux m'ont offensée,
>   Et tous deux me sont odieux.
>
> (2.6.1332–40)

> [I'll spare no part of him who does me wrong;
> It's the whole man at whom my rage takes aim,
>   And to my anger, just and strong,
> The husband and the lover look the same.
> Both of them, in my thoughts, combine and fuse;
> And both are painted in the same dark hues
>   By the heart which they have violated;

> Both have insulted me; both I accuse,
>> And both, by me, are fiercely hated.]

Needless to say, Alcmène is unaware that the person to whom she speaks in these scenes is not her husband. She simply reacts to people and events as they appear to her.

Alcmène is neither blind to differences among men nor foolish in her encounters with them. She would know perfectly well how to deal with a man other than her husband who made unacceptable advances. She possesses none of the traits that typically induce Molière's characters to exaggerate the difference between themselves and others and, in the process, come to resemble those from whom they feel most distant. Alcmène loves Amphitryon but has not the slightest concern about how others see either of them. She has no desire to be superior to anyone, and she has no rivals. She is, most importantly, devoid of jealousy. The motives for her actions are straightforward; she is never calculating. For this reason, she goes so far as to tell Jupiter that a jealous lover, if his feelings are spontaneous, can be forgiven:

> Des véritables traits d'un mouvement jaloux
>> Je me trouverais moins blessée.
>
> . . . .
> De semblables transports contre un ressentiment
> Pour défénse toujours ont ce qui les fait naître,
>> Et l'on donne grâce aisément
>> À ce dont on n'est pas le maître.
>>>>> (2.6.1274–75, 1286–89)

> [The transports of an honest jealousy
>> Would trouble me far less.
>
> . . . .
> Yes, he who offends us by a jealous fit
> Can always plead its origin in love,
>> Which no man is the master of,
>> And therefore be absolved of it.]

"Véritables traits," though associated with jealousy, are what Alcmène looks for and accepts instinctively. Her freedom from desire and her self-assuredness hold out a possibility for resolving the kinds of conflicts that plague the other characters. Why, then, does Alcmène leave the stage at the end of act 2, never to reappear? The play's comic denouement is brought about by Jupiter's revelation of his true identity and his declaration that having had him as a rival carries with it a certain honor. The outcome, he admits, leaves him—"tout dieu que je suis" (3.10.1904) [god though I am]—not Amphitryon, as the jealous party. Moreover, Amphitryon's house is about to be glorified by the birth of Hercules:

> L'éclat d'une fortune en mille biens féconde
> Fera connaître à tous que je suis ton support,
>   Et je mettrai tout le monde
>   Au point d'envier ton sort.
>
> (3.10.1918–21)

> [Your future days, replete with all good things,
> Will show the world that you are in my care,
>   And lesser mortals everywhere
>   Will envy what my favor brings.]

If, as the god proclaims, "Les paroles de Jupiter / Sont des arrêts des destinées" (3.10.1925–26) [For when the voice of Jove sings out, / His words are the decrees of Fate], what do his words to Amphitryon mean? Chaos has been averted and order restored by the voluntary unmasking of Jupiter and Mercure. On the other hand, the play's final moments hold no promise of the elimination of the rivalry and jealousy so central to the work's action. On the contrary, Jupiter has arranged for everyone else to envy Amphitryon. The cuckoldry that might have turned Amphitryon into a social pariah has redounded to his glory. The ending is a happy one, but it is a conclusion in which nothing is concluded. Rather, everything starts all over again. The restoration of difference between gods and humans reestablishes order, but the envy of Amphitryon that Jupiter predicts foretells a reenactment of what has happened in the play. Alcmène's absence is a sign that desire, rivalry, and jealousy have not been rooted out and banished once and for all. For Molière, it is difficult to imagine an enduring order. The quest for order will always have to be renewed.

6

Dark Comedy: Disorder and Sacrifice
in *George Dandin*

AMONG THE MANY EARLY CRITICS OF MOLIÈRE'S THEATER ARE TWO
names rarely associated with each other, the Jesuit homilist Bourdaloue and Jean-Jacques Rousseau. Both mount vigorous attacks
against theatrical spectacles and against Molière in particular.
Rousseau's commentary generalizes the threat to the social order
contained in Molière's theater:

> Voyez comment, pour multiplier les plaisanteries, cet homme [Molière]
> trouble tout l'ordre de la Société; avec quel scandale il renverse tous
> les rapports les plus sacrés sur lesquels elle est fondée; comment il
> tourne en dérision les respectables droits des pères sur leurs enfans,
> des maris sur leurs femmes, des maîtres sur leurs serviteurs![1]

> [Look how this man, in order to multiply the number of jokes, disturbs
> the whole order of society; how he scandalously turns upside down all
> the most sacred relations on which society is founded; how he holds up
> to ridicule the rights of fathers over their children, of husbands over
> their wives, of masters over their servants, all of which ought to be re-
> spected!]

Not unexpectedly, Bourdaloue has greater religious concerns, but
he might easily have written the same words. In *George Dandin ou
le mari confondu*, it is specifically the description of order that
prompts their negative criticism. Comparing the vices that Molière
attacks with those that the dramatist seems to consider less harm-
ful, Rousseau turns to this play to ask:

> Quel est le plus criminel d'un Paysan assés fou pour épouser une De-
> moiselle, ou d'une femme qui cherche à déshonorer son époux? Que
> penser d'une Pièce où le Parterre applaudit à l'infidélité, au mensonge,
> à l'impudence de celle-ci, et rit de la bêtise du Manan puni?[2]

[Which is the more criminal, a peasant crazy enough to marry a lady or a woman who tries to dishonor her husband? What is one to think of a play whose pit applauds marital infidelity, lies, and the impudence of such a wife, and laughs at the stupidity of the yokel punished for his foolishness?]

For Bourdaloue, the play has a corrosive power:

Le comble du désordre, c'est que les devoirs, je dis les devoirs les plus généraux et les plus inviolables chez les païens mêmes, soient maintenant des sujets de risée. Un mari sensible au déshonneur de sa maison est le personnage que l'on joue sur le théâtre, une femme adroite à le tromper est l'héroïne que l'on y produit; des spectacles . . . qui corrompent plus de coeurs que jamais les prédicateurs de l'Evangile n'en convertiront, sont ceux auxquels on applaudit.[3]

[The crowning disorder is that duties, those that I would call the most generally accepted and the most inviolable even by pagans, are now subjects of mockery. A husband sensitive to the dishonor brought upon his household is the character played on stage, a wife deft at tricking him is the heroine of the piece; entertainments . . . that corrupt more hearts than preachers of the gospel could ever convert are those applauded.]

The priest and the philosopher understood eminently well that in *George Dandin*, order is shaken to its very core.

It is in the nature of comedy that a reigning order, whether social, familial, religious, or other, be endangered. Molière's theater, early and late, proves the point. *George Dandin* underlines it. Indeed, in *George Dandin*, the disruption has occurred before the play opens. The protagonist's first words address the source of the already present disorder: Dandin's desire to be what he is not, a member of the family of a *gentilhomme*. The audience, particularly one versed in other Molière comedies, is left to wonder just how order will be restored.

Three of Molière's important works appeared in 1668: *Amphitryon*, *George Dandin*, and *L'Avare*. In the first, a god upsets the order of the universe when he lowers himself to the level of mere mortals in order to seduce the wife of Amphitryon, who, as a result of this escapade, becomes the god's rival. George Dandin, on the other hand, seeks to rise to noble rank. And from the start, he suffers the unhappy consequences of his success in this endeavor. He knows that "La noblesse de soi est bonne, c'est une chose considérable assurément" (1.1) [Nobility is, of itself good; it is certainly a thing worthy of consideration],[4] yet his noble wife is unfaithful, he cannot punish her, and his in-laws hold him in contempt. By breaching the boundary separating the classes, Dandin sets off a series of events that batter the family, social, and linguistic structure on which he depends in order to understand and control his life, which quickly falls into disarray. As Ralph Albanese notes, "Dandin éprouve un sentiment profond d'étrangeté à l'égard de lui-même, et la prise de conscience de son dilemme ne fait que renforcer l'impression d'aliénation qui s'opère à l'intérieur de son moi"[5] [Dandin experiences a deep feeling of strangeness with regard to himself, and his becoming conscious of his dilemma only reinforces the impression of alienation at work deep inside his self]. To withstand his personal trial, Dandin organizes his life around a compulsion to force his in-laws to see and accept their daughter's guilt and his disgrace. However irrational this proclivity, it consumes him. Believing himself cuckolded, he wants above all to prove, in a quasi-legal way, that that is the case. The obstinacy with which he maintains and attempts to demonstrate his wife's betrayal while at the same time unwittingly underscoring his own dishonor makes him ridiculous.

Dandin is convinced that at the root of all his problems is his desire to ally himself with a noble family, a desire that has led to his wretched marriage with a faithless woman of a social class higher than his own: "mon mariage est une leçon bien parlante à tous les paysans qui veulent s'élever au-dessus de leur condition, et s'allier, comme j'ai fait, à la maison d'un gentilhomme!" (1.1) [my marriage is an eloquent lesson for any peasant who wants to rise above his rank and, as I did, form a connection with the house of a gentleman]. More self-aware than similar characters in Molière, Dandin identifies himself with all those of his class who would follow his path. Nowhere more than in his explicit warning to them does he express so clearly his vision of the world. He sees and thinks in terms of categorical, polar differences. There are nobles and commoners, masters and subjects, the happy and the unhappy. Dandin's desire is to effect a change in the fundamental conditions of his life. A commoner, he had hoped, in marrying Angélique, to rise to the ranks of the masters; now, oppressed by a cruel, unfaithful wife, he wants to dominate her, to alter her behavior. He acknowledges his role in his own misery and vigorously berates himself for yielding to his desire: "Vous l'avez voulu, vous l'avez voulu, George Dandin, vous l'avez voulu, cela vous sied fort bien . . . vous avez justement ce que vous méritez" (1.7) [You wanted it, you wanted it, George Dandin, you wanted it, and it's really quite becoming to you . . . you have just what you deserved].

Unfortunately for George Dandin, the model on which he bases his desire for nobility is the Sotenvilles, and he succeeds in getting what he wants, an aristocratic wife and nobiliary trappings. But he gets more of what he doesn't want. The closer he comes to the objects of his desire, the more they become obstacles for him. Dandin wanted to be like the Sotenvilles. For this privilege—and his marriage—he has bailed them out of "assez bons trous" [real holes], but the sole benefit he has received is "un allongement de nom" (1.4) [a lengthening of his name]. Monsieur de la Dandinière now feels obliged to extract from his haughty mother-in-law the recognition of what should, in fact, be a given, his full membership in the Sotenville family. Madame de Sotenville wants the same thing as her son-in-law, namely, to be recognized as noble, and she believes that to accomplish this she must not accept him as an equal. Their rivalry will reveal, as so often in Molière's works, that behind the supposed and at times real differences among the characters, there is a sameness that outweighs differences.

The Sotenvilles are even more ridiculous, more exaggerated, than Dandin himself. As obsessed with nobility as their son-in-law, they share with him a predisposition to think and to act according to their personal perceptions of inalterable differences between themselves and others. Since he has married their daughter, Dandin is part of the Sotenville family, but in the eyes of Madame de Sotenville, he remains hopelessly beyond acceptance into the family circle: "tout notre gendre que vous soyez, il y a grande différence de vous à nous" (1.4) [son-in-law though you be, there remains a great difference between you and us]. Angélique insists on the same distinction of class: "Que dans tous leurs discours et dans toutes leurs actions les gens de cour ont un air agréable! Et qu'est-ce que c'est auprès d'eux que nos gens de province?" (2.3) [In all that they say and all that they do, people at the court are so pleasing! And next to them, what can mere provincials be like?]. She feels inferior to the nobility and, like her husband, wants to "s'élever au-dessus de [sa] condition" (1.1) [rise above her condition]. Dandin remains proud of his origins and family, because they represent for him a mark of distinction. He refuses to brook Angélique's little affairs, since "les Dandins ne sont point accoutumés à cette mode-là" (2.2) [the Dandins are not accustomed to this kind of thing]. In this, the wannabe noble would have his common family not only different from, but superior to, his fickle wife. Dandin, the Sotenvilles, and their daughter all want to distinguish themselves from others and show themselves better. They have the same desire, and their efforts to satisfy it are the same.

Angélique and her lady's maid, Claudine, are obviously from different social categories, and the social distinction between servant and mistress is never in doubt. In their relations with men, however, Molière portrays two women very much alike. Claudine wants freedom, which she promises not to abuse: "Lorsqu'un mari se met à notre discrétion, nous ne prenons de liberté que ce qu'il nous en faut" (2.1) [When a husband puts himself at our disposition, we take only the liberties we need to]. Lubin, her suitor, understands this desire for freedom on the part of his mistress. He responds to it unhesitatingly: "Hé bien! Je te donnerai la liberté de faire tout ce qu'il te plaira" (2.1) [Well then, I'll give you the freedom to do whatever you like]. Angélique too lays claim to freedom of action. Like Claudine, she rejects the "tyrannie de Messieurs les maris" (2.2) [tyranny of husbands], which, for her, would be a kind of death: "je les [Messieurs les maris] trouve bons de vouloir qu'on soit morte à tous les divertissements . . . et ne veux point mourir si jeune" (2.2) [I find it just great that husbands want us dead to all diversions . . . but I don't want to die so young]. The marriage of Dandin and Angélique had been arranged by the Sotenvilles without the agreement of their daughter, who does not feel "obligée à me soumettre en esclave à vos [Dandin's] volontés" (2.2) [obliged to submit as a slave to your will]. She defends her right to "prendre les douces libertés que l'âge me permet" (2.2) [take the sweet liberties that age allows me].

Women in Molière's theater often need to defend themselves against men, and it would appear that Claudine and her mistress want only to protect their personal freedom against masculine authoritarianism. However, Angélique also wants Dandin to accept her infidelity, and Claudine, who explains to her suitor that "c'est la plus sotte chose du monde que de se défier d'une femme, et de la tourmenter" (2.1) [it's the most foolish thing in the world to distrust a wife and to torment her], detests "les maris soupçonneux" [suspicious husbands], and wants one "qui ne s'épouvante de rien, un si plein de confiance, et si sûr de ma chasteté, qu'il me vît sans inquiétude au milieu de trente hommes" (2.1) [who will be upset by nothing and so full of confidence and so sure of my innocence that he could see me surrounded by thirty men without worrying]. In other words, she would like her husband to accept without jealousy conduct that would normally arouse it. Angélique also expects her husband to accept other men's attentions to her. Their interest in her pleases Angélique, and she says as much. When

Dandin asks her "Mais quel personnage voulez-vous que joue un mari pendant cette galanterie?" [But how do you expect a husband to act while this intrigue is going on?] she replies in a way that betrays the resemblance between her servant and herself: "Le personnage d'un honnête homme qui est bien aise de voir sa femme considérée" (2.2) [like an upstanding man who is at ease seeing his wife paid attention to by others]. Freedom, then, is not all these women desire. They want to impose their freedom on their men and force them to acknowledge it. Rather than hiding their peccadillos, the women prefer to display them before husband and lover. The difference of social class between Claudine and Angélique counts for little by comparison to what makes their behavior so similar.

George Dandin rightfully asks what role he might best play in such circumstances. His wife's response to his question leaves much unsaid. Angélique feels that she is her husband's slave and is angry at her parents for having delivered her over to such a tyrant. When she defies Dandin, she does not threaten him with what will happen once she has her freedom but rather speaks of her desire for freedom. She cannot affirm a freedom that will, at some time in the future, be acquired and fully realized: "*je prétends* n'être point obligée à me soumettre en esclave . . . *je veux* jouir, s'il vous plaît, de quelque nombre de beaux jours que m'offre la jeunesse" (2.2; emphasis added) [I intend not to be obliged to submit as a slave . . . I want, if you don't mind, to enjoy the good days that youth offers me]. Far from being independent of everything related to her husband, her desire for freedom ties her closely to Dandin, whose recognition of that freedom is essential to its having meaning for her. While "she . . . sees him and tries to govern him as an object,"[6] as he does her, Angélique and her husband, contemptuous though they are of each other, need each other to fulfill their desire. They are engaged in a bitter rivalry to see which one will control the other.

In the final analysis, Dandin and his wife are equally unlikeable. By his marriage, Dandin hoped to dominate his wife and achieve superiority over a woman of noble rank. His definition of marriage more than hints at his intention: "Je vous dis encore une fois que le mariage est une chaîne à laquelle on doit porter toute sorte de respect, et que c'est fort mal à vous d'en user comme vous faites" (2.2) [I'll tell you again that marriage is a bond to which one owes every respect, and it is very bad of you to act as you do]. "That Angélique does not love him," as Lionel Gossman notes, "causes him no pain, only that she does not recognize him as her master."[7]

To force his wife to respect him, Dandin dredges up his family origins, the very ones from which he had hoped to escape by marrying Angélique: "Si je ne suis pas né noble, au moins suis-je d'une race où il n'y a point de reproche" (2.2) [If I was not born noble, at least my ancestry is without reproach]. Since she has nothing but contempt for her husband, his ranting leaves her unmoved. Her interest is in Clitandre, who is hidden at the back of the stage. When Dandin sees Clitandre, he lights into his wife, who disdainfully replies: "Hé bien, est-ce ma faute? Que voulez-vous que j'y fasse?" [Well, is it my fault? What do you want me to do about it?]. Dandin knows very well what he wants her to do: "Je veux que vous y fassiez ce que fait une femme qui ne veut plaire qu'à son mari" (2.2) [I want you to do what a wife who wants to please only her husband does]. This little dialogue is almost identical to the one in which Dandin asks his wife what role he should play in the face of her unfaithfulness. A similar question elicits a similar answer from both husband and wife. The implication is clear: your behavior should please me so as to prove that my need to dominate prevails over yours.

Order in George Dandin's world depends upon difference, but the desire for distinction of each of the characters attenuates the differences between them and testifies to their resemblance. In sum, Dandin had admired the Sotenvilles and wanted to marry their daughter to satisfy his desire to belong to a social class higher than his own. He felt a need to be recognized by his future in-laws, but if the Sotenvilles accepted him into their family, it was only because they needed him, or, rather, his money. The ridiculous names of these two families newly elevated to noble rank—de Sotenville et de la Dandinière—indicate the similarity that binds them together despite the difference that separates them and on which Madame de Sotenville insists so much.[8] This collapse of differences runs parallel to the crumbling of order in the play. Already in the first act, Dandin understands that "je serai cocu, moi, si l'on n'y met ordre" (1.4) [I'll end up a cuckold if things are not put back in order], and Madame de Sotenville believes that her son-in-law's behavior threatens good order. Fooled by her daughter at the end of the second act, Madame de Sotenville sees the possibility of a reconciliation between Angélique and George. "Je suis ravie de voir vos désordres finis," she tells him (2.8) [I am delighted to see the end of your troubles].

One of the essential signs of the disintegration of order in *George Dandin* is the instability of language. The principal character can no longer comprehend what people say to him, nor is he any longer capable of communicating with others what is for him the most obvious of truths.[9] The simplest words lose their normal meaning for Dandin, whose comic frustration is, in large part, linguistic. The lesson he receives from the Sotenvilles on the respect he owes aristocrats is couched in linguistic terms: to "appeler les gens par leur nom" [call people by their name] or to "dire 'ma femme'" [say "my wife"] when speaking about Angélique shows a lack of respect. Aristocratic politesse completely escapes Dandin, for whom his mother-in-law's words constitute nothing less than a shattering of meaning: "J'enrage," he declares, "Comment? ma femme n'est pas ma femme?" (1.4) [That enrages me. How can it be? Isn't my wife my wife?]. If one does not know the code at the root of her linguistic pretensions, as Dandin certainly does not, Madame de Sotenville's explanation of the rule forbidding Dandin to call Angélique his wife is hardly reassuring: "Oui, notre gendre, elle est votre femme; mais il ne vous est pas permis de l'appeler ainsi, et c'est tout ce que vous pourriez faire, si vous aviez épousé une de vos pareilles" (1.4) [Yes of course, son-in-law, she is your wife, but you're not allowed to call her that. That's what you could do if you'd married one of your own kind]. The logic of differences is such that if one recognizes the distinction between the aristocracy and the lower ranks as well as the linguistic protocols that regulate communication within each group, everything Madame de Sotenville says makes sense. However, Madame de Sotenville is herself but a pale imitation of a true aristocrat, and the only idea of nobility that Dandin has comes from the Sotenvilles. A real social difference between the interlocutors in such a conversation might make it possible for the dialogue to have some lucidity. Without that, confusion reigns.

In the sixth scene of the first act, Angélique, Clitandre, and Claudine confront Dandin in the presence of the Sotenvilles. George has already denounced Clitandre to Monsieur de Sotenville, and he expects that Angélique's father will punish his daughter. Dandin is sure of the truth of his accusation against Clitandre and Angélique, but it is he himself who ends up being treated as the guilty party. This injustice provokes his wrath: "J'enrage de bon coeur d'avoir tort, lorsque j'ai raison" (1.6) [It really enrages me to be wrong when I'm right]. In his rage, he perceives that "avoir tort" and "avoir raison" have lost their distinct meanings. If one takes him literally, his inference is that he is, at one and the same time, both right and wrong. What distinguishes right from wrong can no longer be apprehended. Language has lost its transparency. Angélique is a liar whose parents are easily taken in by her lies, but she is also capable of tricking others by telling the truth and simply changing the tone of her voice. At the beginning of this scene in which Dandin is infuriated by the aura of guilt that surrounds him despite his innocence, his wife explicitly invites Clitandre to become her lover: "Je voudrais bien le voir vraiment que vous fussiez amoureux de moi. Jouez-vous-y, je vous en prie, vous trouverez à qui parler. C'est une chose que je vous conseille de faire" (1.6) [I'd be quite willing to see you pay me court. Go ahead and try it; you'll see what will happen. It's something I advise you to do]. If he is prepared to come to her when her husband is away, "vous serez reçu comme il faut" (1.6) [you'll be received appropriately]. Claudine suggests that he "faire l'amour à ma maîtresse" [pay court to my mistress]. The Sotenvilles hear in all this a tone of irony that is to them proof of Angélique's innocence. For Dandin, nothing could be further from the truth, but he is utterly powerless, in the face of the opacity of language, to make his in-laws understand the truth.

Mistaken identities are a commonplace in comedy, so it is no surprise that in their first meeting at the beginning of the play, Lubin mistakes the true identity of Dandin and therefore tells him secrets the husband should not know. In the farcical scenes at end of the play, Clitandre mistakes Claudine for Angélique, Lubin makes the opposite mistake and, at one point, goes to the extreme of thinking he is speaking to Claudine when, in fact, he is talking to Dandin. These errors highlight the confusion and disorder that prevail over reason. They are attributable in part to the darkness of the night, but Molière surely appreciated the need to lighten up a situation that could become lugubrious. Moreover, they are a sign of the upheaval provoked by Dandin's desire to transgress the social barrier separating him from the Sotenvilles. By mistaking the mistress for the servant and the servant for her mistress, Lubin and Clitandre suspend for a brief moment the difference of class between Angélique and Claudine, but all these farcical elements are founded on the disappearance of differences fundamental to order. Such farce incites laughter; it also signals a crisis. In George Dandin's world, as in Amphitryon's, everything is topsy-turvy.

Outbreaks of violence, another characteristic of Molière's farce, serve the same purpose as mistaken identities. Early on, Dandin imagines a violent solution to his problem, and in the end, he falls victim to violence. He looks back with regret on his desire to "tâter de la noblesse" [have a taste of nobility], for had he married a woman of his own social class, he would be able to "en faire la justice à bons coups de bâton" (1.3) [set her right with a good, hardy stick]. When Angélique goes on the attack, reminding him that he had consulted only her parents before marrying her, Dandin has "des tentations d'accommoder tout son visage à la compote" (2.2) [the temptation to beat her to a pulp]. Power and force should, according to Dandin, restore an order in which the distinction between the master of the house and his wife—who, needless to say, must occupy an inferior station—would be clear. Angélique transforms Dandin's "tentations" into gratuitous violence inflicted on her husband. She pretends, in the presence of her parents, to reproach Clitandre for paying her court and to beat him, but it is Dandin who finishes on the receiving end of her stick. This bit of farce once again temporarily jumbles the differences between the characters. Violence, which is intimately linked to disorder, always holds out the danger of sliding into chaos.

A recurring image in the play, justice and the legal system, its guarantor, represents the hope of reestablishing order. The task of justice is to settle disputes among characters, and, in principle, resolve conflicts without their erupting into violence. A judicial system that functions properly prevents conflicts from escalating to the point at which violence explodes and leads to unending, reciprocal acts of vengeance, which, in turn, threaten the very life of society.[10] In other words, there must be a superior authority that will mediate between opposing interests and thus maintain order. Dandin invests the Sotenvilles with this authority. Since he cannot "faire la justice" [set her right] by beating his wife, he will "faire mes plaintes au père et à la mère" (1.3) [lodge my complaint with her father and mother] so that they can decide in his favor. He repeats this same phrase to his in-laws: "Je vous ai dit ce qui se passe pour vous faire mes plaintes, et je vous demande raison de cette affaire-là" (1.4) [I have told you what is happening to lodge my complaint, and I am asking you for satisfaction in this affair]. The Sotenvilles are only too happy to play the role of judge: "nous serons les premiers, sa mère et moi, à vous en faire la justice" (1.4) [her mother and I will be the first to do you justice]. In the second act, when the Sotenvilles come on stage just as Dandin discovers Clitandre and Angélique together in his house, he explicitly assigns to his in-laws a quasi-legal role: "Le sort me donne ici de quoi confondre ma partie; et pour achever l'aventure, il fait venir à point nommé les juges dont j'avais besoin" (2.6) [Fate is presenting me with a way to confound my opponent; and to put an end to all this, it's making the judges I need arrive just in the nick of time]. Evidence in hand, the plaintiff goes to court.

Angélique and Clitandre speak a similar language to the Sotenvilles, and they both expect that it will be Dandin who is judged guilty. For Angélique, it is "bien horrible d'être accusée par un mari lorsqu'on ne lui fait rien qui ne soit à faire" (1.6) [really horrible to be accused by a husband when you haven't done anything to him that oughtn't have been done]. Clitandre complains of having been "faussement accusé" [falsely accused] and asks his mistress's father to act as judge: "vous êtes homme qui savez les maximes du point d'honneur, et je vous demande raison de l'affront qui m'a été fait" (1.6) [you are a man who knows the rules of honorable conduct, and I am seeking redress at your hands for the insult against me]. Be it a point of honor or legality, it is up to Monsieur de Sotenville to determine the innocence or guilt of the individuals who plead their cases before him.

Unfortunately, the Sotenvilles are ridiculous creatures, and it is inconceivable that any judgment at which they arrive could be taken in the least seriously. The potential influence of their judgments would be undermined also by the incapacity of language to signify in a fixed and definitive fashion. Furthermore, the very characters who want the Sotenvilles to serve as judges lack confidence in them. Angélique's criticism of her parents calls into question both the Sotenvilles and the idea of justice. She explains to Clitandre that husbands are not freely chosen by their wives: "On les prend, parce qu'on ne s'en peut défendre, et que l'on dépend de parents qui n'ont des yeux que pour le bien mais on sait leur rendre justice, et l'on se moque fort de les considérer au-delà de ce qu'ils méritent" (3.5) [We take husbands because we can't shield ourselves against them and we depend on our parents, who have eyes only for possessions; but we know how to do them justice, and it would never occur to us to give them more credit than they're due]. Justice for Angélique surely is not justice for Dandin, and a judgment rendered by the Sotenvilles could hardly be respected by both husband and wife. The judicial system called upon to restore order to the family's affairs and to which plaintiff and defendant both appeal is ineffective, incapable of resolving the dilemma that troubles the good order of the entire family.

Critics have more than once demonstrated that each of the play's three acts is organized around the same set of circumstances: Dandin discovers his wife in flagrante delicto; he accuses her before her parents and asks that they condemn her; he is found guilty by a lie or a trick perpetrated by Angélique or Clitandre. The play's action is directed toward finding some way of putting an end to this baneful repetition of accusations and condemnations with their inevitable result, but the more the essential differences among the characters fade, the more they all behave reprehensibly or ridiculously and the more the repetition is assured. At the end of the play, none of the players are likeable. George Dandin is a spiteful soul who tries to subjugate his wife. Angélique and Clitandre, a couple of adulterers, respect no one, and the Sotenvilles are so foolishly pretentious as to attract only disdain. All the characters are possessed by an idée fixe that prescribes their actions and prevents them from behaving differently. To reach a denouement, the cycle of repetitive actions must be interrupted. The judgment that can make this happen is one that will reinstate the differences among the characters. However, given that everyone is wrong, order can be reestablished only by an arbitrary judgment. When all are blameworthy, how can one party legitimately be found guilty and held responsible for what has happened?

In the absence of an authority that can pass a judgment acceptable to all, recourse to a quasi-legal resolution of the dilemma gives way to a rite at once legal and sacrificial in character. The first act of *George Dandin* concludes with a declaration of Dandin's culpability and a portent of the sacrificial rite that will occur at play's end. Having pronounced that Dandin's conduct has justifiably set everyone against him, Monsieur de Sotenville demands that his son-in-law grant satisfaction to Clitandre by repeating an apology dictated by Sotenville himself:

> MONSIEUR DE SOTENVILLE. Répétez après moi: "Monsieur."
> GEORGE DANDIN. "Monsieur."
> MONSIEUR DE SOTENVILLE. *Il voit que son gendre fait difficulté de lui obéir*: "Je vous demande pardon." Ah!
> GEORGE DANDIN. "Je vous demande pardon."
> MONSIEUR DE SOTENVILLE. "Des mauvaises pensées que j'ai eues de vous."
> GEORGE DANDIN. "Des mauvaises pensées que j'ai eues de vous."(1.6)

> [MONSIEUR DE SOTENVILLE. Repeat after me: "Sir."
> GEORGE DANDIN. Sir.
> MONSIEUR DE SOTENVILLE. (Sees that his son-in-law hesitates to obey him.) "I beg your forgiveness." Ah!
> GEORGE DANDIN. I beg your forgiveness.
> MONSIEUR DE SOTENVILLE. "For the nasty thoughts I had about you."
> GEORGE DANDIN. "For the nasty thoughts I had about you."]

The accusation and the debasement seek to distinguish Dandin from all the other participants, to make him a thing apart, even while he is not. Thus the groundwork for sacrifice is laid.

Two other aspects of this scene, in certain ways very close to the play's penultimate scene, stand out. First, it is here that Dandin "enrage de bon coeur d'avoir tort, lorsque j'ai raison," so that at this early moment, the difference between right and wrong already begins to dim, while the inability of language to express this difference becomes increasingly evident. Secondly, and no less importantly, Dandin's repetition of Sotenville's words has an effect contrary to the one desired. Rather than accentuating the difference between Dandin and his judge, this scene makes them sound alike; they say the same words and are equally foolish. Moreover, in the brief six-line scene that follows, Dandin, despite his humiliation, refuses to consider himself guilty and believes that he may eventually succeed in proving his innocence to the judges he has chosen: "Allons, il s'agit seulement de désabuser le père et la mère, et je pourrai trouver peut-être quelque moyen d'y réussir" (1.7) [Now the only thing to do is open her parents' eyes, and perhaps I'll be able to find some way of doing that]. Nothing has changed at the end of the first act. On the contrary, the situation has returned to square one.

In the play's penultimate scene, Dandin will once again be mortified, but this time he accepts his unhappy fate: "Ah! je le quitte maintenant, et ne n'y vois plus de remède" (3.8)[11] [Ah! I give up, I no longer see any possible solution]. Whereas the first act centered on the resolution of a point of honor between Dandin and Clitandre, at stake here is the play's fundamental crisis, the relationship between Dandin and his wife, which has destroyed all order in the family. Angélique tells her father that the dilemma is beyond resolution: "vous verrez que ce sera dès demain à recommencer" [you'll see that as early as tomorrow it will just begin all over again], but Monsieur de Sotenville insists, "Nous y donnerons ordre" [We'll get things in order]. He commands his son-in-law: "Allons, mettez-vous à genoux" (3.7) [Go ahead, on your knees]. Dandin's kneeling calls to mind the ceremony of the *amende honorable*, which has both legal and religious connotations.[12] From the beginning of this scene, Dandin is portrayed as a victim. Angélique accuses him of adultery, and he is not permitted to defend himself. He calls heaven as his witness: "J'atteste le Ciel que j'étais dans la maison" [I call Heaven to witness that I was in the house], and kneeling down proclaims: "Ô Ciel! Que faut-il dire?" (3.7). [O, Heaven! What must I say?]. According to his fate, George Dandin becomes the victim in a sacrificial rite.

Dandin is no more reprehensible than the other characters but is chosen as a victim, a scapegoat, to be sacrificed for the sake of order in the family. If he does not literally die in the rite, he does suggest that he will end his life by drowning himself. In the first act, Monsieur de Sotenville had criticized him for his behavior toward Clitandre and prepared the way for Dandin to become a sacrificial victim: "Vous méritez, mon gendre, qu'on vous dise ces choses-là; et votre procédé met tout le monde contre vous" (1.6) [Son-in-law, you deserve to have these things said to you, and your conduct sets everyone against you]. But the choice of Dandin as victim is not motivated by his guilt, for all the characters are in one way or another guilty. As René Girard explains:

> Pour qu'une espèce ou une catégorie déterminée de créatures vivantes (humaine ou animale) apparaisse comme sacrifiable, il faut qu'on lui découvre une ressemblance aussi frappante que possible avec les catégories (humaines) non sacrifiables, sans que la distinction perde sa netteté, sans qu'aucune confusion soit jamais possible.[13]

> [For a species or a specific category of creatures (human or animal) to appear to be appropriate victims of sacrifice, as striking a resemblance as possible with those (human) categories that cannot be sacrificed must be found in it; but this must be done without any loss of sharpness in the distinction between the category that can be sacrificed and the one that cannot, or with any possible confusion between the two.]

Dandin resembles the other characters, but the demands he makes upon them separate him from their community. They therefore unite against him.

This somber denouement follows logically upon the rest of *George Dandin*. The characters' harshness and cruelty toward each other darken its comedy. Both Angélique and Dandin threaten suicide. The wife's behavior and the husband's violent reactions sow disorder in the family, as Bourdaloue and Rousseau understood. Only the sacrificial rite at the play's conclusion can restore order, but to assure its permanent restoration, the victim would truly have to be sacrificed. He would have to be destroyed. In his last monologue, George Dandin recognizes that he has been defeated—"lorsqu'on a, comme moi, épousé une méchante femme, le meilleur parti qu'on puisse prendre, c'est de s'aller jeter dans l'eau la tête la première" (3.8) [when one has, as I have, married a wicked woman, the best thing one can do is throw oneself headfirst into a body of water]—but it is far from certain that he will kill himself. The sacrifice manqué gives the denouement a flavor of dark comedy. Order is restored, but only momentarily. Nothing has really changed. Angélique herself foresees that everything will soon start all over again.

7

"J'ai découvert que mon père est mon rival": Love, Greed, and Rivalry in *L'Avare*

AVARICE SERVES A DUAL FUNCTION IN *L'AVARE*: IT DEFINES HARPAGON'S character and betokens a contagion that touches every aspect of his family's existence. From the moment he steps on stage, he is obsessed with money. His first words order La Flèche, his son's valet, to leave immediately, lest the servant spy on him in the privacy of his own home and discover the whereabouts of his hidden treasure. The play ends with Harpagon eagerly awaiting the moment when he can see once again "ma chère cassette" (5.6) [my dear money-box].[1] By this time, his treasure has become the old man's only friend, "mon support, ma consolation, ma joie" (4.7) [my support, my consolation, my joy]. Harpagon's conviction that deprived of his money, he can no longer carry on anchors the play's comic vision in a darker realm not unlike that of *George Dandin*. Indeed, the miser is arguably as unhappy before the theft of his ten thousand écus as he is after it. He frets constantly about the danger of having so much money around the house (1.4). Burying his money in the garden puts it out of sight but not out of mind, for he is terrified that others may guess his secret. Were the true extent of his wealth to become known, he would fear for his life: "un de ces jours on me viendra chez moi couper la gorge, dans la pensée que je suis tout cousu de pistoles" (1.4) [one of these days they'll come and cut my throat in my own house in the belief that I'm made of gold pieces]. Harpagon's greed has turned his life into a nightmare.

It has also contaminated the social and moral order of his household. Ironically, Harpagon comes to a point when he tells the Commissaire investigating the theft of his box that if the crime "demeure impuni, les choses les plus sacrées ne sont plus en sûreté" (5.1) [remains unpunished, the most sacred things are no longer safe]. He fails to grasp that punishing the culprit will make no difference, but he is not wrong about "les choses les plus sacrées."

They have been tainted. As Louis Lacour says in his edition of *L'A-vare*, "il nous semble assister à la décadence d'une famille"[2] [we seem to be witnessing a family's decline]. Harpagon no longer fulfills the most elementary obligations of a father, preferring his money even to the life of his daughter. Elise's revelation that she had been saved from drowning by Valère, whom Harpagon believes to be guilty of the theft, elicits from her father his nastiest line: "Tout cela n'est rien; et il valait bien mieux pour moi qu'il te laissât noyer que de faire ce qu'il a fait" (5.4) [All that is nothing; and it would have been much better for me if he had let you drown than do what he's done]. Paternal love has been banished from the repertoire of Harpagon's feelings. Paternal authority fares no better. Harpagon's children refuse to obey him, lie to him, and plot against their father's tyranny. Harpagon mistreats his servants, who, in turn, wish their master no good. To defend themselves against him, members of the household adopt certain of his worst flaws. And all of this leaves the family on the brink of turmoil.

Rousseau's brief critique of *L'Avare* continues his emphasis on this tendency toward the disintegration of a family order: "C'est un grand vice d'être avare et de prêter à usure; mais n'en est-ce pas un plus grand encore à un fils de voler son père, de lui manquer de respect, de lui faire mille insultans reproches, et, quand ce père irrité lui donne sa malédiction, de répondre d'un air goguenard, qu'il n'a que faire de ses dons?"[3] [It is a great vice to be greedy and to loan at usurious rates; but isn't it an even greater one for a son to rob his father, not to respect him, and to reproach him in a thousand insulting ways, and when the father, thus provoked, curses the son, to respond jeeringly that he'll have nothing to do with his father's gifts?]. Although he makes no attempt to justify the rapacious Harpagon, the more dangerous transgression, in his eyes, is the abrogation of filial duty. The machinations of a miser represent a limited threat. He might, at worst, make his children miserable until he mends his ways or dies. However, when the child maltreats his father, the very order on which family relations rest is called into question. The contours of the relationship between father and son become hazy in *L'Avare*, as Harpagon discredits himself and Cléante increasingly takes liberties with his father. Rousseau focuses on the dissolution of the special bond between father and son, because this is a crisis fundamental to the play's action and indicative of the chaos that threatens the family.

Desire for riches invades every quarter of life in this household, bringing with it confusion and disorder. The discourse of love itself, usually free from such concerns, has been contaminated directly and indirectly by money. The first impediment to her love for Valère that Elise mentions is "l'emportement d'un père" [a father's anger], but her real reservation is that Valère will have a change of heart, a "froideur criminelle dont ceux de votre sexe *payent* le plus souvent les témoignages trop ardents d'une innocente amour" (1.1; emphasis added) [criminal coolness with which those of your sex most often repay any too ardent proof of an innocent love]. To his assurance that he, Valère, is different, Elise replies that all men sing the same tune: "Tous les hommes sont semblables par les paroles; et ce n'est que les actions qui les découvrent différents" (1.1) [Men are all alike in their words; and it is only their actions that show them to be different]. Distinguishing one man from another may not be as simple as it would seem. Similarities have, perhaps, more force—and are more troubling—than difference. As for Valère's behavior, his own description of it makes one understand the young woman's hesitation. In order to be close to his beloved, Valère has insinuated himself into Harpagon's household by assuming the role of a servant. Such a ploy may be justified in the name of love, but Valère has gone further than is prudent, hoping to seduce the father along with his daughter. His tactic is at best hypocritical, even though his adversary is a despicable old miser. Valère draws Elise's attention to the fact that he is merely pretending to be something that he is not: "Vous voyez comme je m'y prends . . . sous quel masque de sympathie et de rapports de sentiments je me déguise pour lui plaire, et quel personnage je joue tous les jours avec lui" (1.1) [You see how I am going about it . . . what a mask of sympathy and conformity of feelings I disguise myself under to please him, and what a part I play with him every day]. The goal, to "acquérir sa [Harpagon's] tendresse" (1.1) [win his affection], is couched in terms of acquisition. Valère gloats over having succeeded famously in deceiving his future father-in-law: "J'y fais des progrès admirables" (1.1) [I am making admirable progress in this]. His self-satisfaction derives in part from his sense that he is acting on principle, but the principle reflects a singular cynicism: "et j'éprouve que pour gagner les hommes, il n'est point de meilleure voie que de se parer à leurs yeux de leurs inclinations, que de donner dans leurs maximes, encenser leurs défauts, et applaudir à ce qu'ils font" (1.1) [and I find that to win men, there is no better way than to adorn oneself before their eyes with their inclinations, fall in with their maxims, praise their defects, and applaud whatever they do]. Whether or not this role is played well matters little to him. All men are taken in by flattery. It cannot be helped if, in the process, "La sincérité souffre un peu au métier que je fais" [Sincerity suffers a bit in the trade I am plying]. A bit? In any event, Valère enunciates a maxim not unrelated to Elise's conviction that all men are alike: "mais quand on a besoin des hommes, il faut bien s'ajuster à eux; et puisqu'on ne saurait les gagner que par-là, ce n'est pas la faute de ceux qui flattent, mais de ceux qui veulent être flattés" (1.1) [but when you need men, you simply have to adjust to them; and since that's the only way to win them over, it's not the fault of those who flatter, but of those who want to be flattered]. Refusing all responsibility for his dishonest behavior, he sweeps away a major difference between flatterer and flattered. Real guilt lies with the victim of flattery rather than with its perpetrator. On at least one level, that of culpability, the difference between trickster and dupe is reversed. The two may not be identical, but a barrier separating them has broken down. As differences crumble, the distinction between the noble, magnanimous Valère, who saves Elise's life by risking his own, and the wily pretender may well be called into doubt. At the very least, Valère demonstrates that he is neither honesty and goodness incarnate nor an absolute scoundrel. Verbs often associated with financial dealings, such as "gagner" [win] and "acquérir" [win], signal the impact of money and greed on human relations in Harpagon's family, as Elise, at the end of this scene, implores Valère to do his best to "gagner l'appui de mon frère" (1.1) [win my brother's support].

Money impinges more directly on Cléante's love for Mariane. The young girl lives with her sick mother in a state of near penury. Cléante would like to lighten her burden by discreetly providing for the family's financial needs: "Figurez-vous, ma soeur, quelle joie ce peut être que de relever la fortune d'une personne que l'on aime" (1.2) [Just imagine, sister, what a joy it can be to restore the fortunes of a person we love]. Only Harpagon's stinginess prevents his son from fulfilling this desire. His tightfistedness leaves Cléante "dans l'impuissance de goûter cette joie, et de faire éclater à cette belle aucun témoignage de mon amour" (1.2) [powerless to taste this joy and to display to this beauty any token of my love]. The juxtaposition of the words "impuissance" and "joie" suggests the strength of Cléante's feelings toward a father who "s'oppose à nos désirs" (1.2) [must oppose our desires].

Curiously, Cléante articulates only one way of conveying his love, and that is through the giving of money. The choice of a monetary gift to express devotion is hardly unique in Molière's theater. Dom Garcie de Navarre would have liked to bestow upon Done Elvire just such a present; Alceste harbors the same dream;

and Orgon is so generous to Tartuffe that the impostor returns half of what he receives without, apparently, noticing the loss. In light of this, one may well suppose that Cléante, who, after all, is not the most high-minded of men, might, like those characters and his own father, use money as a means of acquiring power. Without evidence in the play, the suspicion cannot be proven, but such a motive on his part is not beyond the realm of possibility. In any case, money and love are, for better or for worse, inextricably linked in Cléante's mind.

The power of wealth overwhelms Harpagon's imagination; he can think of little else. Knowing full well that Mariane is not rich, he allows, somewhat vaguely, that "si l'on n'y trouve pas tout le bien qu'on souhaite, on peut tâcher de regagner cela sur autre chose" (1.4) [if she doesn't bring as much money as one would like, one can try to make it up in other ways]. He nonetheless hopes to extract a dowry from the mother of his intended. The contradiction is a glaring one but gives no pause to the miser, who insistently questions the "femme d'intrigue" [a woman who lives by her wits], Frosine, about whether she has explained that "il fallait . . . qu'elle [Mariane's mother] se saignât pour une occasion comme celle-ci" (2.5) [she had to . . . bleed herself, for an occasion like this one]. That he would pursue a woman without visible wealth in itself shows the depth of his feelings for her. Still, he cannot conceive of a marriage that will not make him a richer man. For his children's marriages, money determines who the spouse will be. Elise is to wed Anselme, "dont on vante les grands biens" (1.4) [who's said to be very wealthy] and who "s'engage à la prendre sans dot" (1.5) [undertakes to take her without dowry]. Cléante will become the husband of a widow, presumably rich. No value, no institution—love, marriage, family—is sacred where financial gain seems possible. Harpagon's obsessive desire for wealth undercuts the very institutions and beliefs on which his existence is built.

The breakdown of order is vividly represented by frequent recourse to physical violence as a replacement for rational discourse. No sooner has he appeared on stage than Harpagon threatens La Flèche with a sound thrashing because the valet asks logical questions: "Tu fais le raisonneur. Je te baillerai de ce raisonnement-ci par les oreilles" (1.3) [A reasoner, are you? I'll give you a piece of that reasoning about your ears]. Jacques receives a beating for telling his master the truth (3.1) and, at the play's conclusion, risks being hanged for having lied about the theft of the money box. Truth and falsehood incite the same reaction, violence. Poor Jacques also comes in for a beating by Valère, who, in his treatment of the servant, behaves exactly like Harpagon. When Cléante refuses to bow to parental authority by giving up Mariane, Harpagon again reacts with a violent threat: "Je te ferai bien me connaître, avec de bons coups de bâton" (4.3) [I'll make you respect me all right—with a good stick!]. Only the rod guarantees his power over his son. He regularly resorts to violence as he tries to shore up a crumbling order. After losing his treasure, he will go so far as to prescribe violent acts against himself as a means of uncovering the truth about the theft. Truth itself, apparently, cannot exist without the exercise of violence. The dilemma confronting Harpagon is that violence engenders greater violence and, ultimately, chaos, rather than an order that he can dominate from his position as head of the family. As the action of the play unfolds, turmoil overtakes Harpagon's household.

The old miser, Euclio, in Plautus's *Aulularia*, the primary source of *L'Avare*, shares Harpagon's obsession with a large fortune. Both have found for their daughters a suitor who does not insist on a dowry; both are unnecessarily suspicious of anyone who might conceivably rob them; both treat others, especially servants, rudely. Molière found in Plautus the idea for some of the best comic bits of his play. Harpagon's first encounter with La Flèche (1.3), the miser's famous monologue (4.7), and the extended misunderstanding between Harpagon and Valère over the theft (5.3) all have specific counterparts in the Latin play.[4] Molière has turned to Plautus with great profit. However, having found the givens of his plot in the Roman tradition, he proceeds to create a work that is in every way more radical than his model.[5] Although the protagonists of the two plays suffer from the same malady, Euclio realizes that money is the cause of his woes and would almost prefer to be done with his riches rather than continue to be burdened by them. Nor does he allow money to destroy the good order of his household. Plautus's conception of the comic hero clearly leaves open the possibility of redemption from his madness. Euclio's obsession is less destructive than Harpagon's because it does not overpower every other value in his life. The single-mindedness of Harpagon, by contrast, is absolute.

This mania, whose intensity makes it so typical of Molière's theater, must be viewed in the context of another, more crucial, addition to the plot of Plautus's play. Harpagon, unlike Euclio, is in love, and he loves the same woman as his son. The rivalry between father and son has a powerful impact upon affairs of the purse as well as affairs of the heart. What Molière has done by changing

Plautus in this way is to shift the entire focus of his play away from the emphasis on a predetermined character trait that alone explains a character's dilemma. If only Euclio can be less greedy, overcome a flaw in his personality, all will once again be well. Lyconides will marry Phaedria, and Euclio will be freed from the suffering caused by his wealth. Although the text of the *Aulularia* is not complete, it is clear from the second argument that this is precisely what happens:

> Auro formidat Euclio, abstrudit foris.
> Re omni inspecta compressoris servolus.
> Id surpit. illic Euclioni rem refert.
> Ab eo donatur auro, uxore et filio.[6]

Such a resolution in *L'Avare*, or in any Molière play, for that matter, would be virtually unthinkable. Good Moliéresque maniac that he is, Harpagon leaves the stage as he had stepped onto it, obsessed with his chest full of money. His final act is to have Anselme pay the Commissaire, which frees Harpagon to "voir ma chère cassette" (5.6) [see my dear money-box]. The miser remains unaltered, but turmoil does not ensue. In fact, a measure of order is restored to the household.

In *L'Avare*, the knot to be undone by the comic denouement is not, as in Plautus's play, simply greed. Rather, greed is the sign of a deeper malaise. Already a wealthy man, Harpagon has no ostensible reason to worry about his money. That he cannot put aside thoughts of it even for a moment indicates how thoroughly he identifies with it. Through his accumulated wealth and through it alone, is he able to relate to the world in which he lives. Miserliness seeps into his every sentiment: "En un mot, il aime l'argent, plus que réputation, qu'honneur et que vertu" (2.4) [In a word, he loves money, more than reputation, honor, and virtue]. It envelops his humanity. He is, as La Flèche says, "de tous les humains l'humain le moins humain" (2.4) [of all humans the least human human]. The servant does not exaggerate. Harpagon's conception of himself depends upon his wealth. He is attached to his "chère cassette" in the same way as Monsieur Jourdain is to social status or Argan, the "malade imaginaire," to illness. To protect it, he keeps the money box buried in the garden. To dig it up, to have it at hand, would change nothing. But the possession of money suffices to provide him with a means of asserting his dominance over others.

As the father of Cléante and Elise, Harpagon has a large say in deciding whom they will marry. Money solidifies his paternal authority by eliminating any uncertainty about an otherwise difficult decision. Valère prevaricates in his response to Harpagon's famous "sans dot": "Vous avez raison: voilà qui décide tout, cela s'entend. . . . Ah! il n'y a pas de réplique à cela . . . Il est vrai: cela ferme la bouche à tout, *sans dot*" (1.5) [You're right. That decides the whole thing . . . Ah! There's no answer to that . . . That's true; that stops every mouth: *without dowry*]. Harpagon believes every word of this. Rather than complicating the issue, financial considerations make good sense of it. Both power and right are on Harpagon's side. Cléante experiences his father as a tyrant and swears to his sister that unless things change, "nous le quitterons là tous deux et nous affranchirons de cette tyrannie où nous tient si longtemps son avarice insupportable" (1.2) [we shall both leave him and free ourselves from this tyranny in which his insupportable avarice has held us for so long]. Greed is at the heart of Harpagon's imperious control over the lives of his children. Greed also sets him apart from everyone else in the play. It makes him different, and he must defend himself against attack on every side: "Je ne veux point avoir sans cesse devant moi un espion de mes affaires, un traître, dont les yeux maudits assiègent toutes mes actions" (1.3) [I don't want to have eternally before me a spy on my affairs, a traitor, whose cursed eyes besiege all my actions]. The military image of a siege translates perfectly the configuration of Harpagon's relations with others: they against me, a fortress of strength. As he himself puts it, even his children have joined the ranks of the enemy: "Cela est étrange, que mes propres enfants me trahissent et deviennent mes ennemis!" (1.4) [It's a strange thing that my own children betray me and become my enemies!]. By cunning or by force, the enemy must be defeated, brought under control, made subservient to a more powerful master.

Harpagon's strategy is a simple one, easily recognizable to readers of Molière. He will marry his children to well-heeled mates from whom the family will, hopefully, benefit, and keep Mariane for himself, pinching his pennies all the while. Needless to say, Cléante and his sister have ideas of their own about the future. In a certain sense, Harpagon is right to see his children as his enemies, for they become rivals with him in a struggle over their own destiny. Elise takes badly the news of her father's intention that she marry Anselme. Going so far as to threaten suicide if forced to marry, she flatly rejects Harpagon's design. The dialogue between father and daughter is a model of imitative belligerence. Elise and Harpagon speak the same language, use the same words. All that

distinguishes the words of one from the words of the other is an
occasional direct negation of what has just preceded or will shortly
follow. Harpagon's obstinacy is met by the obstinacy of his daughter, her tartness by his irony:

ELISE. Je vous demande pardon, mon père.
HARPAGON. Je vous demande pardon, ma fille.
ELISE. Je suis très humble servante au Seigneur Anselme; mais avec
    votre permission, je ne l'épouserai point.
HARPAGON. Je suis votre très humble valet; mais, avec votre permission,
    vous l'épouserez dès ce soir.
ELISE. Dès ce soir?
HARPAGON. Dès ce soir.
ELISE. Cela ne sera pas, mon père.
HARPAGON. Cela sera, ma fille.
ELISE. Non.
HARPAGON. Si.
ELISE. Non, vous dis-je.
HARPAGON. Si, vous dis-je.
ELISE. C'est une chose où vous ne me réduirez point.
HARPAGON. C'est une chose où je te réduirai.
ELISE. Je me tuerai plutôt que d'épouser un tel mari.
HARPAGON. Tu ne te tueras point, et tu l'épouseras. (1.4)

[ELISE. (with another curtsy) I beg your pardon, father.
HARPAGON. (mimicking the curtsy) I beg your pardon, daughter.
ELISE. (with another curtsy) I am Seigneur Anselme's very humble ser-
    vant; but with your permission, I won't marry him.
HARPAGON. (mimicking the curtsy) I am your very humble valet; but
    with your permission, you will marry him this evening.
ELISE. This evening?
HARPAGON. This evening.
ELISE. (with another curtsy) That shall not be, father.
HARPAGON. (mimicking the curtsy) That shall be, daughter.
ELISE. No.
HARPAGON. Yes.
ELISE. No, I tell you.
HARPAGON. Yes, I tell you.
ELISE. That's something you shall not force me to.
HARPAGON. That's something I shall force you to.
ELISE. I'll kill myself rather than marry such a husband.
HARPAGON. You shall not kill yourself, and you shall marry him.][7]

Having two interlocutors contradict each other with much the
same words, a stock comic technique, is more than a clever way of
eliciting laughter. That both parties to the disagreement use the

same language identifies them with each other. Each contradicts the other in the hope of having his—or her—own way. In this particular instance, Elise's position is clearly more sympathetic than Harpagon's, although one might expect—and Rousseau would hope—that the daughter would treat her father with more respect. Harpagon's behavior and Elise's response to it endanger the good order of the household by suggesting that there is a similar basis for parental authority and a child's disobedience. The duel ends in a draw, the father's authority challenged and no resolution of the quarrel in sight. Assuming opposite stances, Elise and Harpagon behave similarly. Their only recourse is a third party.

Valère's situation as Harpagon's trusted servant and secret lover of Elise makes him at once an "ideal" choice as judge—father and daughter agree on his probity!—and the person least likely to resolve the dispute. How like the Sotenvilles! Without even knowing the subject of the quarrel, Valère declares Harpagon in the right: "vous ne sauriez avoir tort, et vous êtes toute raison" (1.5) [You couldn't be wrong, and you are reason itself]. As soon as the old man leaves the room, Valère explains to Elise that favoring Harpagon has been nothing but a ploy. Valère is on Elise's side. Despite his double talk, he knows very well where his sympathy lies. So does the audience. At this early point in the play, it is neither necessary nor desirable that the conflict be resolved. Valère's duplicity, however, merely hides the fact that there is no rational resolution possible to the dilemma created by Harpagon's rivalry with his children. This unhappy truth will be apparent as Harpagon takes on his son.

Cléante explicitly and cynically recognizes his father's authority over him at the beginning of his first conversation with his sister: "je sais que je dépends d'un père, et que le nom de fils me soumet à ses volontés" [I know that I am dependent on a father, and that the name of son subjects me to his will]. But let there be no mistake about it, Cléante says this only "afin que vous ne vous donniez pas la peine de me le dire" (1.2) [so that you won't take the trouble to tell it to me]. What he wants, in truth, is to check Harpagon's power. He sees his father as an obstacle to success and will shortly learn that Harpagon is also his rival for the affection of Mariane. The two distinguishing comic features of Harpagon, his inappropriate love for Mariane and his preoccupation with money, place him in rivalry with his son. It is this rivalry and its ramifications that motivate much of the action in the play. Molière remains consistent in his depiction of rivalry: it leads again, in *L'Avare*, directly to the disintegration of a family order founded on differences among members of the household.

The scene in which Cléante realizes that Maître Simon has arranged for him to borrow money at usurious rates from none other than his own father is reminiscent of the debate between Harpagon and Elise. Using the same comic device, Molière puts similar words into the mouths of his characters. This time, however, the similarity of the two characters is emphasized as each accuses the other of criminal behavior. Rather than contradicting each other, father and son see each other as mirror images of themselves. The dialogue blurs the distinction between usury and profligate borrowing:

> HARPAGON. Comment, pendard? c'est toi qui t'abandonnes à ces coupables extrémités?
> CLÉANTE. Comment, mon père? c'est vous qui vous portez à ces honteuses actions?
> HARPAGON. C'est toi qui te veux ruiner par des emprunts si condamnables?
> CLÉANTE. C'est vous qui cherchez à vous enrichir par des usures si criminelles?
> HARPAGON. Oses-tu bien, après cela, paraître devant moi?
> CLÉANTE. Osez-vous bien, après cela, vous présenter aux yeux du monde? (2.2)

> [HARPAGON. What, you scoundrel? It's you who abandon yourself to these guilty extremities?
> CLÉANTE. What, father? It's you who lend yourself to these shameful actions?
> HARPAGON. It's you who are trying to ruin yourself by such disgraceful borrowings?
> CLÉANTE. It's you who are trying to enrich yourself by such criminal usury?
> HARPAGON. Do you really dare appear before me thus?
> CLÉANTE. Do you really dare show your face to the world after this?]

The difference between borrower and lender, like that between flatterer and flattered, disappears as Harpagon and Cléante are reduced to the same level.[8] When Cléante asks which of them is guiltier, Harpagon responds by ordering his son to leave, for there seems to be no clear-cut answer to that query.

When he invites Mariane to his house and introduces her to his family, Harpagon is unaware that she and Cléante love each other and hears as an impertinence his son's open opposition to Mariane's becoming "ma belle-mère" (3.7) [my stepmother]. Since

Mariane understands what Cléante means, she praises his honest expression of his feelings. His candor takes a curious turn as the young suitor declares his love: "souffrez, Madame, que je me mette ici à la place de mon père, et que je vous avoue que je n'ai rien vu dans le monde de si charmant que vous" (3.7) [allow me, Madame, to put myself in my father's place and admit to you that I have seen nothing in the world as charming as you]. To Harpagon's objection, Cléante retorts that "C'est un compliment que je fais pour vous à Madame" (3.7) [It's a compliment I'm paying for you to Madame]. In order to vie with his father, Cléante replaces him. Their struggle for Mariane's hand results in the son's speaking and standing in for the father. Harpagon resents this: "Mon Dieu! j'ai une langue pour m'expliquer moi-même, et je n'ai pas besoin d'un procureur comme vous" (3.7) [My Lord! I've a tongue to explain myself with, and I don't need an advocate like you]. He must assert himself to avoid being eliminated altogether. The barrier between father and son, which should protect the role of each, is momentarily lowered in this scene—momentarily and dangerously. For Cléante does not stop at speaking for his father. He presents to Mariane a diamond ring he has taken from Harpagon's finger. Although beside himself at the thought of the expense of this gift, the miser can do nothing to reclaim it without compromising his love. Cléante wants Mariane to have the ring and forces it on her. Harpagon wants the opposite but dares not contravene his son's "generosity." The obstinacy of the father and son and their desire for the same woman paradoxically unites the two and compels them to act in the same way. Rivalry, which should separate them, does the contrary. The comic effect of the scene derives in part from Harpagon's impotence when faced with a rivalry that levels differences. In their dispute over money, Cléante and Harpagon behave similarly. Now, where love is involved, Cléante slips into the role assumed by his father.

When it finally occurs to him that his son might also love Mariane, Harpagon tricks Cléante into admitting his passion and then orders him to give up his pursuit of her. The son must marry the woman his father has chosen for him. In other words, Harpagon wants both to defeat Cléante and make him obedient to his will. Nowhere is Harpagon's desire for power better articulated. Cléante's will, however, is no less strong. He refuses to acquiesce. On the contrary, the young man embraces rivalry with his father and the terrible struggle it implies: "je vous déclare, moi, que je ne quitterai point la passion que j'ai pour Mariane, qu'il n'y a point d'extrémité où je ne m'abandonne pour vous disputer sa conquête"

(4.3) [*I* declare to *you* that I will never give up my passion for Mariane, that I will go to any extreme to dispute your conquest of her]. Recognizing the deadlock at which he has arrived with Cléante, Harpagon exploits the difference that constitutes the order bolstering his whole existence: "Ne suis-je pas ton père? et ne me dois-tu pas respect!" (4.3) [Am I not your father? And don't you owe me respect?]. Cléante's response is devastating in its confirmation that rivalry has erased even this difference: "Ce ne sont point ici des choses où les enfants soient obligés de déférer aux pères, et l'amour ne connaît personne" (4.3) [These are not matters in which children are obliged to defer to fathers; and love is no respecter of persons]. Love does not distinguish between father and son. Harpagon's threat to beat his son, his readiness to yield to violence, illustrates the irrational, chaotic state into which rivalry has cast his family.[9]

Once again, a third person is called upon to adjudicate the dispute. This time, Maître Jacques will be the judge. As in *George Dandin*, the role of justice in *L'Avare* is to prevent the onslaught of chaos by maintaining an order based on difference. By deciding for one or the other party, justice makes a distinction between the two. Harpagon's repeated choice of his servants as mediators indicates how badly he wants to control events. It also undermines the potential efficacy of the system of justice, for it is equally unlikely that his servants would rule against him as it is that Harpagon would accept a judgment against himself rendered by a servant. The structure of the scene in which Harpagon and Cléante appear before Maître Jacques shows why rivalry saps the power of justice to maintain differences. Harpagon and Cléante argue virtually identical cases. Both love a woman whom they want to marry, each is prevented from doing so by the importunities of the other. Harpagon thinks it wrong that Cléante will not obey him. Cléante accuses his father of a love inappropriate for a person of his advanced age. As if to underline their identity, Maître Jacques answers Harpagon and Cléante with the same words. To Harpagon's complaints about his son, he declares: "Ah! il a tort" [Oh! He's wrong]; to Cléante's about his father, perhaps a bit more emphatically but not significantly, "Il a tort assurément" [He is certainly wrong]. Both are also told, "Vous avez raison" (4.4) [You're right]. For Maître Jacques, Harpagon and Cléante are identical in their stubbornness, and he treats them similarly. His would-be "resolution" to the dilemma is no less artificial or more satisfactory than had been the miser's peremptory dismissal of his son after their quarrel about money or Valère's unwillingness to side openly with

Elise against Harpagon. At the same time that he tells each man the other is wrong, he assures each that the other has capitulated. Harpagon is overjoyed to learn that his son will obey him, and Cléante believes that his father will let him marry Mariane. When, in the course of their reconciliation, they discover the truth, the father curses the son, who answers with the phrase that incurred Rousseau's wrath:

> HARPAGON. Et je te donne ma malédiction.
> CLÉANTE. Je n'ai que faire de vos dons. (4.5)

> [HARPAGON. And I give you my curse.
> CLÉANTE. I have no use for your gifts.]

The face of justice in these scenes is altogether farcical. Maître Jacques is hardly a worthy judge of any cause, let alone one that concerns his master. On the other hand, the task of the real representative of justice, when he appears later in the play, will be no easier nor will he meet with any greater success.

As the difference between the antagonists becomes increasingly problematic, justice loses its capacity to function decisively. Harpagon thinks of nothing but hoarding money and is properly accused of avarice by his family and servants. He, in turn, condemns them for going to the opposite extreme with their spendthrift ways. Money, in L'Avare, is a preoccupation shared by characters of every stripe. Their attitudes toward it divide them into two groups: Harpagon and the others. In the final analysis, it is impossible to say that right is on the side of one or the other. Rivalry between Harpagon and members of his family has them all behaving in the same way, albeit in the name of opposing principles. The Commissaire, called by Harpagon to unravel the mystery of the theft of the strongbox, makes no headway because Harpagon can give him no clues. Harpagon believes that everyone is guilty. To the reasonable question "Qui soupçonnez-vous de ce vol?" [Whom do you suspect of this theft?] his response is categorical: "Tout le monde" (5.1) [Everyone]. Justice itself is ensnared in the net that Harpagon casts, losing its special, and necessary, quality of disengagement and impartiality. Should the culprit not be found, Harpagon will lump justice together with all the other guilty parties: "et si l'on ne me fait retrouver mon argent, je demanderai justice de la justice" (5.1) [and if they don't get my money back, I'll demand justice of justice itself]. It is in the context of this leveling of all differences that Harpagon's famous monologue must be read.

Outraged and maddened by the loss of his precious money box, Harpagon bemoans his fate. The tone and substance of his monologue, based on a similar speech of Euclio, accent the depth of the crisis triggered by the theft. Without realizing it, Harpagon lays bare the truth of his situation. Money has meant far more to him than the financial security that comes with wealth. Life is worth living only if he can recover his money. Along with his "cassette," the miser has lost a firm grasp on himself. No longer can this most egotistical of creatures be certain of his identity: "Mon esprit est troublé, et j'ignore où je suis, qui je suis, et ce que je fais" (4.7) [My mind is troubled, and I don't know where I am, who I am, or what I'm doing]. The most telling manifestation of his alienation is his total inability to distinguish between various groups of people. Friends and enemies, servants and family, all dissolve into one single category: thief. Since all are identical, all are to be treated in the same way. Indeed, Harpagon does not even spare himself: "Je veux aller querir la justice, et faire donner la question à toute la maison: à servantes, à valets, à fils, à fille, et à moi aussi" (4.7) [I'm going to fetch the law, and have everyone in my house put to the torture: maidservants, valets, son, daughter, and myself too]. The miser's identification, his self, is lost in the undifferentiated mass of humanity subsumed under the name "voleur" [thief]. His tirade pushes to the limit a tendency to suspect everyone, to deny distinctions that make it possible for society to function. Even the audience is included in his suspicions. Crazed, he stares at them and realizes that everyone is laughing at him: "Ils me regardent tous, et se mettent à rire" (4.7) [They're all looking at me and laughing]. Harpagon has always been distinguished by his wealth and the sense of power it has brought him. Now, all is lost. His enemies—and all are enemies—mock him. In a particularly dramatic metaphor, he reaches out for the arm of a suspected culprit only to discover he has seized his own arm. Despite the claim that this scene is exaggerated,[10] it constitutes a powerful comic representation of a crisis that is the natural outcome of imitative rivalry. He who would be superior to others descends to the same level as those he intended to dominate and, in the process, loses his own identity.

This is a kind of death, and Harpagon links the theft of his money to his own demise. The opening words of his monologue, "Au voleur! au voleur!" [Stop, thief! Stop, thief!], are counterbalanced by "à l'assassin! au meurtrier!" (4.7) [Assassin! Murderer!]. In the next lines, he equates being robbed with being "perdu" [ruined], being "assassiné" [assassinated] and having his throat slit.

More references to death than to the robbery occur in the first lines of Harpagon's speech, and the miser's last words are a threat of multiple executions followed by his suicide: "Je veux faire pendre tout le monde; et si je ne retrouve mon argent, je me pendrai moi-même après" (4.7) [I'll have everybody hanged; and if I don't find my money, I'll hang myself afterward]. Thus, the monologue begins and ends with death. Addressing his lost money, Harpagon gives vent to his despair: "sans toi, il m'est impossible de vivre. C'en est fait; je n'en puis plus; je me meurs, je suis mort, je suis enterré" (4.7) [without you, it's impossible for me to live. It's all over, I can't go on; I'm dying, I'm dead, I'm buried]. He looks for a savior to bring him back to life: "N'y a-t-il personne qui veuille me ressusciter, en me rendant mon cher argent, ou en m'apprenant qui l'a pris?" (4.7) [Isn't there anyone who will bring me back to life by giving me back my dear money, or by telling me who took it?]. Although the comic impact of Harpagon's obsession with death is undeniable, the presence of the spectre of death throughout the play makes it a powerful image.[11]

More than one character is touched by death. In the first scene of the play, Elise evokes the day she might have drowned had not Valère saved her from the fury of the waves. Mariane and her mother, who never appears on stage, are haunted by the presumed death of the girl's father. Valère and Mariane had, as children, been saved from death in a shipwreck. And Harpagon is terrified at the prospect of his death. His monologue in act 4, with its repetition and intensification of much that he says elsewhere, is the culminating point of his fear. One of the reasons he resents Cléante's extravagant spending is that it might encourage people to think of Harpagon as a rich man, and that, in turn, will endanger his life: "les dépenses que vous faites seront cause qu'un de ces jours on me viendra chez moi couper la gorge, dans la pensée que je suis tout cousu de pistoles" (1.4) [the expenses you incur, will be the reason why one of these days they'll come and cut my throat in my own house in the belief that I'm made of gold pieces]. His prediction is now fulfilled: "On m'a coupé la gorge" (4.7) [they've cut my throat]. Earlier, Harpagon would have liked to have the inventor of "ces grands hauts-de-chausses" [these big breeches] hanged for an invention that can serve to hide stolen goods (1.3). Now, the once-powerful master will hang himself after having others hanged for the crime. Like his money chest, which he had "enterré dans mon jardin" (1.4) [bur(ied) in my garden], Harpagon is himself interred: "je suis enterré" (4.7).

Avarice is a fortification that Harpagon erects to protect himself against the unknown and, ultimately, against death. As La Flèche explains to Frosine, the very sight of a borrower, who might ask him to part with money, strikes Harpagon "par son endroit mortel" (2.4) [in his vulnerable spot]. Money is the miser's only defense against his own demise. Therefore, he cannot take lightly the threat of losing it. Money alone gives substance to an existence otherwise lacking solid, visible underpinnings. Harpagon needs money for the same reason that Pascal's hunter needs the hare. Piling it up diverts his attention from his own emptiness. Riches serve him well as a basis for creating an identity different from that of others, and on this difference can be founded his conviction that he is superior to them. Molière, of course, knows as well as Pascal that even though Harpagon's wealth may be real, the superiority that he would construct upon it is imaginary, always likely to crumble. And try as he may, Harpagon cannot suppress the truth. He lives in constant fear of being robbed. The least suggestion that he might lose money brings him face to face with the possibility of his own annihilation. When La Merluche runs on stage and accidentally knocks him down, the miser is certain that his creditors have paid the lackey to do him in: "Ah! je suis mort" [Oh! I'm dead], he cries as he falls (3.9). Robbery, for him, is the equivalent of murder.[12] Harpagon believes that he can avoid death by barricading himself behind his wealth. Madness—probably—but that conviction helps explain his aberrant behavior.

Furthermore, the rivalry in which he engages with such fervor runs the risk of ending with the death, real or symbolic, of at least one of the combatants. To rob Harpagon of his money is to steal his identity, and, as he himself says, there is no reason to go on living without his money. Likewise, were he to lose the struggle of wills with his son, his identity as a superior being would be crushed. Cléante is not unaware of the mortal dimension of his battle with his father. No wonder the avarice of a father, he tells La Flèche, can reduce a son to wishing his father dead (2.1). Harpagon does not realize that he is himself the father in question when Maître Simon tells him that his perspective creditor "s'obligera, si vous voulez, que son père mourra avant qu'il soit huit mois" [will guarantee, if you want, that his father will die in the next eight months]. Unintentional irony permeates Harpagon's insouciant response: "C'est quelque chose que cela" (2.2) [Well, that's something]. But Cléante is not the only person who looks forward to Harpagon's death. Jokingly commenting on Harpagon's youthfulness, Frosine assures the miser that he will live to a ripe old age:

"Il faudra vous assommer, vous dis-je; et vous mettrez en terre et vos enfants, et les enfants de vos enfants" (2.5) [They'll have to kill you, I tell you; and you'll bury your children and your children's children]. In retrospect, her joke becomes less droll when later she explains to Mariane that it would be "impertinent" of Harpagon not to die within three months of their marriage and thus leave his wife a rich widow (3.4). What Frosine's comment suggests is that death awaits the old miser whether he wins or loses his struggle with Cléante for the hand of Mariane. Their rivalry, it would seem, inevitably degenerates into annihilation and death.

Shortly after discovering the theft of his money, Harpagon learns from Valère that Elise has agreed to marry her young suitor. The miserly father has now lost both his money and his daughter. He does not trust his servants, his son has turned against him, and justice has no power to reestablish order: "Voici un étrange embarras" [Here's a fine kettle of fish], says Frosine (5.4), understanding the case. Harpagon's household is on the brink of chaos. Figuratively, at least, Harpagon is threatened with death: "On m'assassine dans le bien, on m'assassine dans l'honneur" (5.5) [I'm being assassinated in my property, I'm being assassinated in my honor]. Anselme, to whom he says these words, will restore a measure of order. For he turns out to be the long lost father of Mariane and Valère, the "late" Dom Thomas d'Alburcy, whose family believed he had been killed at sea while seeking exile from Naples and who, convinced that his family has perished, has come to France and assumed a new identity. Before the revelation, he is on the point of seeking consolation in a new family with Elise as his wife. With encouragement from Anselme, a different kind of father, and the promise from Cléante that Harpagon's money will be returned, the miser consents to the marriage of his son to Mariane and his daughter to Valère. Defeated in love by the force of events, he clings all the more fiercely to his greed, insisting that Anselme give his children money for their weddings, underwrite the expenses of the weddings, buy him a new suit for the ceremony, and provide the Commissaire's salary.

At first blush, this conclusion to the play is no more than a deus ex machina.[13] Only by an authorial ploy does a semblance of order return. Nevertheless, the comic denouement of L'Avare follows logically from everything preceding it. The restoration of order at the end of the play is literally snatched from the clutches of death. Without Dom Thomas, there is no foreseeable resolution of the crisis unless Harpagon dies. Keeping out of the path of death has been at the root of the way in which Harpagon has organized life.

To trick death, the ultimate destruction of the will, has been the miser's goal, and by avoiding it, he has made sense of a meaningless existence and averted a confrontation with the absence of meaning. The resurrection of Dom Thomas does the same thing.

The resolution provided by Anselme is by no means a final one, and this is the significance of the end of *L'Avare*. If the "étrange embarras" can be eliminated only by the return to life of a man believed to have long been dead, it is apparent that this "embarras" is resistant to all but the most powerful of remedies. Death will, in the end, overcome attempts to conquer it. As in other plays of Molière, the monomaniac remains unrepentant and unreformed. A crisis of order in the household brought about by Harpagon's rivalry with his son has been narrowly averted. That his avarice has remained untouched by the momentary return to order leaves the permanent risk of a new and equally devastating crisis. *L'Avare* is among the more somber of Molière's plays. Not the least of reasons for this are the serious implications of the play's conclusion and its relentless pursuit of the destructiveness of rivalry between a father and his son.

8

Impossible Desire: Becoming a Mamamouchi
in *Le Bourgeois gentilhomme*

MOLIÈRE'S FIRST BIOGRAPHER, GRIMAREST, TELLS A STORY THAT HAS become legendary about the opening performance of *Le Bourgeois gentilhomme* at Chambord.[1] The tale is probably aprocryphal but is not, for that, any the less revealing.[2] At the supper following the performance, the king apparently did not compliment Molière on the play, with the inevitable result that the courtiers proceeded to level against it all manner of harsh criticisms. The court was up in arms against Molière, who was so chagrined that he refused to appear in public. Several days later, the play was mounted again, and this time Louis was lavish in his praise: "vous n'avez encore rien fait qui m'ait plus diverti," he told Molière, "et votre pièce est excellente"[3] [You have yet to do anything that entertained me more, and your play is excellent]. The reaction of the court was instantaneous; it was also the precise opposite of what it had initially been. As if by magic, Molière was transformed from a writer over the hill into "cet homme . . . inimitable"[4] [this inimitable man]. The play was also a great success in Paris, where "chaque Bourgeois y croyoit trouver son voisin peint au naturel; il ne se lassoit pas d'aller voir ce portrait"[5] [every bourgeois thought he saw his neighbor painted lifelike in it and did not tire of going to view the portrait].

There may not be a grain of truth in Grimarest's story, but one cannot fail to appreciate its congruence with the subject of *Le Bourgeois gentilhomme*. In describing the courtiers' reactions, Grimarest evokes a closed world whose inhabitants model their thoughts and actions on what they imagine is the king's will. They are themselves devoid of opinions, tastes, or desires that can be called their own. The only difference between Monsieur Jourdain and Grimarest's courtiers is that they need not ask whether "les gens de qualité" [people of quality] would approve of their behavior.[6] They already know this. Without such knowledge, they would be paralyzed. The

court of Louis XIV resembles that of the lion in La Fontaine's fable
"Les Obsèques de la lionne" (book 8, fable 14):

> Je définis la cour un pays où les gens,
> Tristes, gais, prêts à tout, à tout indifférents,
> Sont ce qu'il plaît au Prince, ou s'ils ne peuvent l'être,
>   Tâchent au moins de le paraître,
> Peuple caméléon, peuple singe du maître;
> On dirait qu'un esprit anime mille corps;
> C'est bien là que les gens sont de simples ressorts.
>
> (vv. 17–23)[7]

> [What is the Court? A Country where
> the people all are gay, severe,
> alert, inert—or what the Prince
> would have them be; or else evince
> such evidence as may convince
> him. They are their Master's apes, chameleonic
> strictly regimented, catatonic!]

A play that displeases the king automatically draws the condemnation of his court. Should he change his mind, his courtiers will me-
chanically, like "de simples ressorts," follow suit. The courtiers
have no autonomy, and since all share the same desires, rivalry
among them is as inevitable as among Molière's characters.

   In Paris, Grimarest's bourgeois act out their own version of the
drama. They have no king to provide infallible guidance and find
Monsieur Jourdain's antics funny. All agree, however, that he reminds them of other bourgeois they know. Their unanimity on this
point explains the play's success at the box office. Parisian bourgeois head to the theater en masse in order to enjoy the spectacle
of bourgeois other than themselves being mocked. At the court, it
was the rush to embrace the king's supposed opinion that led the
courtiers to behave alike. In town, the urge not to see oneself in
Jourdain has the same effect. The bourgeois join Molière's audience and feel vastly superior to his laughable protagonist. Individual distinctions among the bourgeois, as among the courtiers,
diminish. As if to suggest that Molière understood this phenomenon, Grimarest recounts that the king also withheld judgment
about Les Femmes savantes, telling the playwright what he thought
only after the second performance of the play. This time, "Molière
n'en demandoit pas davantage, assuré que ce qui plaisoit au Roi,
étoit bien reçu des connoisseurs, et assujetissoit les autres. Ainsi il
donna sa pièce à Paris avec confiance le 11ᵉ de Mai 1672"[8] [Molière

asked for nothing more, certain that what was pleasing to the king would be well received by the connoisseurs and that others would feel compelled to like it as well. Thus he confidently put on his play in Paris on 11 May 1672].

Monsieur Jourdain's single-mindedness about becoming a *gentilhomme*, combined with his conviction that this will be achieved by imitating those whom he calls "les gens de qualité," corresponds to the servility of the courtiers to the king in Grimarest's anecdote. Just as they have no independent opinion of what makes a play good or bad, Jourdain has not the faintest idea of his own about how to be a *gentilhomme*. The courtiers want their king's approval; Jourdain seeks the recognition of society. Thus he dons outlandish new clothes and instructs his lackeys: "Suivez-moi, que j'aille un peu montrer mon habit par la ville" (3.1) [Follow me while I go and show off my coat a bit around town]. Being a *gentilhomme* will distinguish him from his social class and from his family, but the distinction will have no meaning unless others see his change of station and, by their respect, confirm it. Monsieur Jourdain is, of course, overjoyed to learn that the count Dorante has spoken of him in the king's chambers. But he remains blind to the other characters in the play, who, not unlike Grimarest's bourgeois, delight in the valet Covielle's making a fool of the would-be *gentilhomme*. They all attend and enjoy immensely the initiation rite that elevates him to the august rank of Mamamouchi. The ceremony, however, implicates everyone. Even the caustic Madame Jourdain is obliged to join in the fantasy put on for her husband, who, as Covielle predicts, plays his role to perfection.

The close parallel between Grimarest's little story, in its description of character and situation, and *Le Bourgeois gentilhomme* must be read in the context of the times. Moralists and memorialists of the period confirm the absolute authority of the king and the fawning submission of his court to Louis's will. The desire of the bourgeoisie to rise in the social hierarchy was actually encouraged by a king profoundly mistrustful of the nobility and forever in need of the money that only rich bourgeois could provide. Monsieur Jourdain represents an exaggerated version of a type not uncommon in seventeenth-century France. Bourgeois and courtier alike found him so funny because they recognized in him characters well known to them. Grimarest's story and Molière's play depict a social reality of the period.

Molière emphasizes Monsieur Jourdain's desire to become a *gentilhomme* and does so to the exclusion of personal traits that might give the character more depth. Critics tend to agree on the defi-

ciencies of the play's plot. Antoine Adam calls it "la plus inconsis-
tante des intrigues" [the most loose of plots] and says that the play
itself is "bâtie à la diable"⁹ [built in a harum-scarum kind of way].
To Judd Hubert, "*Le Bourgeois gentilhomme* seems loosely con-
structed and, at times, almost thrown together."¹⁰ Gérard Defaux
disagrees with the line of criticism that sees the play as slight, as a
mere buffoonery, but concedes that it has generally been dismissed
as lacking the dramatic heft of comedies like *Le Misanthrope*, *Tartuffe*, and *Dom Juan*.¹¹ The characters in the play are thinly drawn,
without the complexity of motivation and behavior of an Alceste, a
Tartuffe, or an Orgon. For all that, this *comédie-ballet* continues to
attract audiences who appreciate its farcical elements and its spec-
tacular effects, particularly the Turkish ceremony which, in the
opinion of Antoine Adam, is the play's raison d'être.¹² Ironically,
these same components may, as Judd Hubert notes, stand in the
way of literary analysis:

> *Le Bourgeois gentilhomme* is undoubtedly excellent theater, with its farci-
> cal scenes, its music, its dancing. But just for this reason, it would seem
> to lend itself less readily to stylistic analysis than more strictly literary
> works such as *Le Misanthrope*. Moreover, it hardly seems to provide crit-
> ics with suitable material for deep psychological analysis or moral pro-
> nouncements.¹³

The main characters in *Le Bourgeois gentilhomme* are very simple;
some might say simpleminded. Character development is sketchy
at best. Monsieur Jourdain has one goal and one only, to become a
gentilhomme. Even his amorous interest in Dorimène stems
uniquely from his desire for social status.¹⁴ Although Jourdain, like
Orgon and the imaginary invalid, Argan, wants his daughter to
marry a man who will further her father's ends, he is far less tyrannical than they and finally assents to Lucile's marriage to Cléonte.¹⁵
His mania makes him happy and droll; it is not marked by the ill
will toward family so common among Molière's monomaniacs. Madame Jourdain is sharp-tongued and sour, her good sense tem-
pered by acerbity. Whatever Monsieur Jourdain wants she
opposes. Her objections, though always rational, are hardly more
thoughtful than her husband's madness. Dorimène, a kindly but
bemused spectator, is unable to perceive the true nature of her
lover, Dorante, who misleads both Jourdain and her. From a moral
perspective, it is difficult to assess which is worse, Jourdain's folly
or Dorante's knavery. Lucile and Cléonte are a pair of youthful
lovers whose fidelity to each other is too easily shaken. Fortunately,

the stock Molière servants, Nicole and Covielle, are there to put things aright.

In essence, *Le Bourgeois gentilhomme* exhibits the most fundamental elements of Molière's comic vision and presents them in their starkest form. The comedy is unfettered by complexities in characters' motivations or by intricacies of plot. Monsieur Jourdain resembles Molière's other great comic figures in his desire to distinguish himself from others, in his need to have them validate his difference, and in his will to exercise control over his family. However, the play's title suggests his desire for distinction is pushed so far beyond the realm of possibility that it can only be laughable. An imaginary invalid, a religious hypocrite, or an educated fool, are all conceivable. For a seventeenth-century audience, a foolish bourgeois who is also a *gentilhomme* is not. Jourdain's pretension is too outrageous not to evoke laughter and ridicule. Nor is his desire for social elevation mitigated by factors like Harpagon's fixation on death or Alceste's love for Célimène. Jules Brody concisely characterizes what separates tragedy from comedy: "Si la tragédie traite du problème de l'individu aux prises avec un monde qui s'oppose de manière intolérable à son voeu de bonheur, la comédie, à son tour, s'intéresse au problème que présentent au monde les exigences intolérables d'un individu"[16] [If tragedy deals with the problem of the individual at grips with a world that stands intolerably in opposition to his wish for happiness, comedy, in its turn, takes up the problem that intolerable demands of an individual present to the world]. Monsieur Jourdain is, in this regard, a prototypical comic figure.[17] Nevertheless, given Molière's continued emphasis on the subject, it is not surprising that even in this more lighthearted *comédie-ballet*, the plot revolves around rivalry and its ability to level differences.

Monsieur Jourdain's desire to rise into the ranks of the nobility and to have a noble mistress makes him the unwitting rival of Dorante, who hopes to marry Dorimène. So mindless and free of deep-seated nastiness is the old bourgeois that this rivalry does not eventuate in turmoil. Jourdain and Dorante remain the best of friends throughout the play. The rich bourgeois supplies the funds that permit Dorante to live in the high style of a courtier and, in return, is able to luxuriate in the flattery and empty gestures that make him feel important. Nicole may find Monsieur Jourdain's costume enormously funny, but Dorante assures him that "Vous avez tout à fait bon air avec cet habit, et nous n'avons point de jeunes gens à la cour qui sont mieux faits que vous" (3.4) [You look very smart in that coat, and we have no young men at the court who are better turned out than you are]. And who but Dorante could bring Jourdain's name to the attention of the court in the king's presence, as he claims to have done (3.4)? Other rivalries in the play will erupt into violence, but Jourdain does not even realize that Dorante is his rival. As Madame Jourdain tells her husband, "Allez, vous êtes une vraie dupe" (3.4) [Go on, you're a real dupe].

What the unspoken rivalry between Monsieur Jourdain and Dorante does bring to the fore is the similarity of the two characters. Though at opposite ends of the social hierarchy—a bourgeois and a *gentilhomme*—Jourdain and Dorante think in the same way. Dorante's perverse trickery matches Jourdain's uncomprehending foolishness, and the two men reveal that beneath the surface of appearances, they are alike. Both, for example, lay out huge sums to indulge their fancy for sartorial splendor. Much of the money that Dorante borrows from his friend goes to pay his "plumassier" [plume-seller], his "tailleur" [tailor], and his "marchand" (3.4)[18] [clothier]. Both are money-conscious, not to say money-mad. Jourdain keeps track of the exact sum owed him by Dorante, who seems to think of nothing but securing the next loan. When Dorante asks how high his debt has risen, Monsieur Jourdain first reviews each loan individually, then:

> MONSIEUR JOURDAIN. Somme totale, quinze mille huit cents livres.
> DORANTE. Somme totale est juste: quinze mille huit cents livres. Mettez encore deux cents pistoles que vous m'allez donner, cela fera justement dix-huit mille francs, que je vous payerai au premier jour. (3.4)

> [MONSIEUR JOURDAIN. Sum total, fifteen thousand eight hundred francs.
> DORANTE. Sum total is correct: fifteen thousand eight hundred francs. Now, add another two hundred pistoles that you're going to give me, that will make precisely eighteen thousand francs, which I'll pay you the first chance I get.]

As for women, bourgeois and *gentilhomme* agree that a lady's heart is not won, but bought:

> DORANTE. Vous avez pris le bon biais pour toucher son coeur: les femmes aiment surtout les dépenses qu'on fait pour elles; et vos fréquentes sérénades, et vos bouquets continuels, . . . le diamant qu'elle a reçu de votre part, et le cadeau que vous lui préparez, tout cela lui parle bien mieux en faveur de votre amour que toutes les paroles que vous auriez pu lui dire vous-même.
> MONSIEUR JOURDAIN. Il n'y a point de dépenses que je ne fisse, si par-

là je pouvais trouver le chemin de son coeur. Une femme de qualité a pour moi des charmes ravissants, et c'est un honneur que j'achèterais au prix de toute chose. (3.6)

[DORANTE. You took the right approach to touch her heart. Above all else women like the expenditures people make for them; and your frequent serenades and continual bouquets, . . . the diamond she has received on your behalf, and the party you are preparing for her— all this speaks to her far better in favor of your love than any words you might have said to her yourself.
MONSIEUR JOURDAIN. There are no expenditures I would not make if thereby I could find the way to her heart. A woman of quality has ravishing charms for me, and it's an honor I would buy at any price.]

On these subjects, at least, the striking coincidence of attitude makes distinctions between bourgeois and nobility moot.

When Dorimène comes to Monsieur Jourdain's for dinner, Dorante succeeds in making her believe that it is he, not the bourgeois, who is her host. She wears a diamond ring purchased for her by Monsieur Jourdain but given to her by Dorante. Rather than competing openly with his rival, Dorante pretends to collaborate in Jourdain's pursuit of the marquise:

Pour moi, je ne regarde rien, quand il faut servir un ami; et lorsque vous me fîtes confidence de l'ardeur que vous avez prise pour cette marquise agréable chez qui j'avais commerce, vous vîtes que d'abord je m'offris de moi-même à servir votre amour. (3.6)

[For my part, I don't worry about anything when a friend needs a service; and when you confided to me the passion you had formed for this charming marquise whom I knew, you saw that right away I freely offered myself to serve your love.]

For his part, Jourdain is in awe of Dorante and wants nothing more than to "vous rendre mes petits services" (3.4) [(be) at your service]. Neither character appreciates the role that the other plays in his relationship with Dorimène. While they court the same woman, with the same ring, at the same dinner table, the only thing that distinguishes Monsieur Jourdain and Dorante from each other is that one of them, Dorante, knows the truth. Were that truth to be forgotten, even for a moment, the situation would move from the comic to the chaotic, with the two men courting the same woman in the same way. Like Molière's other plays, *Le Bourgeois gentilhomme* reveals how rivalry functions to erode differences between rivals, but in this instance, a violent encounter is avoided.

Molière's comic vision assures that the audience will find Jourdain laughable, not pitiable, wicked, tyrannical, or threatening.

The play opens on a scene of ever-so-polite rivalry between the Maître à Danser and the Maître de Musique. Progressively, a counterpoint develops between the ludicrous actions of the protagonist and the increasingly intense rivalry among Jourdain's teachers. Tension builds to an explosion in the third scene of the second act, where the Maître de Philosophie, overcome by a paroxysm of rage, throws himself at his rivals, who beat him up. Although the play's first two acts are riotously funny, some critics have found fault with them. Antoine Adam contends that the real action of the play does not begin until the third act, while the first two are little more than a sequence of loosely strung *lazzi*.[19] On the other hand, these acts are so successful as comedy that it is worthwhile to reexamine them in the context of the whole play. The first two acts of *Tartuffe* draw a powerful portrait of the hypocrite from what other characters say about him. The opening acts of *Le Bourgeois gentilhomme* do the same thing for Jourdain by putting on display the character's escapades, which are played out within the frame of his teachers' rivalries. Those rivalries will have echoes in the rest of the play and must not, therefore, be ignored.

The Maître de Musique and the Maître à Danser, along with their colleagues in fencing and philosophy, have been hired to teach Jourdain how to become a *gentilhomme*. They are all four demanding taskmasters, and each is convinced that his particular discipline is essential. The curtain rises on a conversation between the Maître à Danser and the Maître de Musique, who more or less calmly disagree about the best kind of student. The more refined Maître à Danser regrets having to "se produire à des sots" (1.1) [display ourselves to fools]. His ideal student values the finer points of the art of dance and applauds his teacher's graceful efforts. For the Maître de Musique, positive student evaluations are fine, but "il y faut mêler du solide" (1.1) [you have to mix in something solid]. The ideal pupil praises "avec les mains" [with the open hand], and Monsieur Jourdain's virtue is his "discernement dans sa bourse; ses louanges sont monnayées" (1.1) [discernment in his purse; he praises in cash]. Both teachers have other students, but the great advantage of Monsieur Jourdain is that "il nous donne moyen de nous faire connaître dans le monde; et il payera pour les autres ce que les autres loueront pour lui" (1.1) [he's giving us a chance to make ourselves known in society; and on behalf of the others he will pay for what the others will praise for him].

As the lessons begin, competition between the music teacher and the dance instructor intensifies. Their arts are, they continue to believe, complementary, but each is at pains to demonstrate that without his discipline the very course of world events would be altered. In their dialogue, Molière accents the parallel forms that their claims take:

> MAÎTRE DE MUSIQUE. Il n'y a rien qui soit si utile dans un État que la musique.
> MAÎTRE À DANSER. Il n'y a rien qui soit si nécessaire aux hommes que la danse.
> MAÎTRE DE MUSIQUE. Sans la musique, un État ne peut subsister.
> MAÎTRE À DANSER. Sans la danse, un homme ne saurait rien faire.
> MAÎTRE DE MUSIQUE. Tous les désordres, toutes les guerres qu'on voit dans le monde n'arrivent que pour n'apprendre pas la musique.
> MAÎTRE À DANSER. Tous les malheurs des hommes, tous les revers funestes . . . tout cela n'est venu que faute de savoir danser. (1.2)

> [MUSIC MASTER. There's nothing so useful in a state as music.
> DANCING MASTER. There's nothing so necessary to men as the dance.
> MUSIC MASTER. Without music a state cannot subsist.
> DANCING MASTER. Without the dance a man couldn't do anything.
> MUSIC MASTER. All the disorders, all the wars we see in the world come only from not learning music.
> DANCING MASTER. All the misfortunes of men, all the deadly disasters . . . all these have come just from not knowing how to dance.]

The two teachers conclude that wars could be prevented and governments better managed if everyone knew how to dance and could appreciate music. As befits the arts they represent, the Maître à Danser and the Maître de Musique keep their rivalry strictly within the bounds of decorum. It is easy for Jourdain, this time, to agree with both: "vous avez raison tous deux" (1.2) [That's true, you're both right]. In other words, he treats them just as they have behaved, identically. The calm of their low-key rivalry will, however, soon be shattered.

The Maître d'Armes is neither so correct nor so placid as his colleagues. Fencing, he asserts, is a science not to be compared with dance and music. By affirming its superiority, he heightens the rivalry among the three teachers, and a violent fight almost breaks out. Only the arrival of the Maître de Philosophie keeps the three from coming to blows. He, of all people, should be able to resolve their dispute reasonably, to "mettre la paix entre ces personnes-ci" [make peace between these people], as Jourdain asks him to do (2.3). Having explained that a wise man must always hold himself above insults flung at him by others, the philosopher takes umbrage at the self-aggrandizing talk of his colleagues and enters the fray himself. Personal invective flies and a brawl ensues.[20] Afraid of damaging his new chamber robe, Monsieur Jourdain retires from the scene: "Oh! battez-vous tant qu'il vous plaira" (2.3) [Oh, fight all you please!]. In these opening scenes, rivalry forms a magnetic field, its attraction ineluctable. Every member of this little faculty wants to be the best and force others to accept his superiority. What separates them is what also draws them together, their rivalry.

No substantial difference exists between Monsieur Jourdain and his teachers. He can withdraw from their quarrel because they are neither his models nor his rivals. It is not by chance that Molière opens his play with a great "scholarly debate." The rivalry among the teachers is the same as the various rivalries among other characters woven into the rest of the play. The first two acts of *Le Bourgeois gentilhomme* alert the audience to a pattern of behavior that is at the heart of the play.

The lovers' quarrel in the third act, which has been criticized for some of the same reasons as the introductory acts, originates in Cléonte's competitive desire to break with Lucile before she can abandon him.[21] He tells his valet, Covielle, that honor demands preparedness for Lucile's eventual infidelity: "Je veux faire autant de pas qu'elle au changement où je la vois courir, et ne lui laisser pas toute la gloire de me quitter" (3.9) [I mean to keep step with her in this change toward which I see her hurrying, and not let her have all the glory of leaving me]. Covielle is in love with Jourdain's servant, Nicole, but in imitation of his master, turns away from her. In this scene, all four shift easily from one role to its opposite, from rejected lover to the lover who spurns a partner. As the scene begins, Lucile and Nicole want to explain to Cléonte and Covielle that the presence of Lucile's aunt had, in an encounter earlier in the day, kept the young women from talking to their lovers. The men refuse to engage in the conversation, and Cléonte repeats to Lucile what he had told Covielle: "je veux être le premier à rompre avec vous, et . . . vous n'aurez pas l'avantage de me chasser" (3.10) [I mean to be the first to break with you . . . you shall not have the advantage of sending me away]. Now it is the turn of the women to stop speaking, and the men plead for an explanation. Then, in a second abrupt transition, Cléonte and Covielle threaten to die of their unrequited love and once again fall silent, while the young women try to make themselves understood.

Whether Cléonte loves Lucile or she him has nothing to do, in this scene, with their responses to one another. Their conflict is as automatic as Monsieur Jourdain's reliance on *les gens de qualité*. Cléonte repels Lucile's entreaties, and she repels his. They vie with one another to be contrary, and their servants do likewise. The determining factor in the behavior of the four young lovers is not what each wants, but rather what each perceives the other as wanting. Both partners in each of the couples alternate between begging for the other's love and turning away from it. Cléonte and Covielle speak in interchangeable expressions. Lucile's "Qu'est-ce donc, Cléonte?" [Why, what is it, Cléonte?] is echoed by her servant's "Qu'as-tu donc, Covielle?" [What's wrong with you, Covielle?]. The mistress asks her lover "Etes-vous muet, Cléonte?" [Are you struck dumb, Cléonte?] and the servant imitates her: "As-tu perdu la parole, Covielle?" [Have you lost your tongue, Covielle?]. With Lucile's explanation, harmony returns at scene's end, and Covielle reverts to the language of his social class: "Qu'on est aisément amadoué par ces diantres d'animaux-là [women]" (3.10) [How easily we get softened up by these confounded creatures!].

In *Le Bourgeois gentilhomme*, more brilliantly than in other Molière plays, the leveling effect of rivalry wreaks havoc on language, which loses its capacity to constitute meaning on which reality is founded. Words become commodities to be bought and sold,[22] and their value is determined by their purchasers and sellers, not by the words' intrinsic meanings. When the tailor's assistants call Monsieur Jourdain "mon gentilhomme" [the gentleman], "Monseigneur" [My Lord], and, finally, "Votre Grandeur" [Your Eminence], he tips them more handsomely with every new salutation (2.5). These titles, ridiculously inappropriate for a person of Jourdain's rank, fool no one.[23] Jourdain is prepared to pay for "Votre Grandeur," and the tailor's assistant is more than happy to oblige with whatever title. Similarly, by lending Dorante money not likely to be repaid, Monsieur Jourdain purchases the count's kind words to the king and the privilege of being "son cher ami" (3.3) [his dear friend].

Despite Madame Jourdain's certainty that she does not need an interpreter in order to speak with the Grand Turk's son (5.6), having one might well have proven useful to her earlier in the play. From his philosopher, her husband has learned the difference between poetry and prose: "tout ce qui n'est point prose est vers; et tout ce qui n'est point vers est prose" (2.4) [whatever isn't prose is verse, and whatever isn't verse is prose]. Shortly afterwards, by way of demonstrating his intellectual superiority and her idiocy, Monsieur Jourdain asks his wife what she is speaking (3.3). The correct answer is, of course, "de la prose," but Madame Jourdain cannot know this. The meaning of the word is intact, but the way Jourdain uses the word obscures that meaning. For his wife, words have distinct meanings that can define those who speak them. She reproaches her husband for rejecting Cléonte's proposal to marry Lucile, on the basis that the young man is not a *gentilhomme*: "Et votre père n'était-il pas marchand aussi bien que le mien?" (3.12) [And wasn't your father a tradesman just like mine?]. Monsieur Jourdain is rankled by this suggestion about his modest background, and Covielle, disguised as a Turkish friend of Jourdain's late father, empties the word "marchand" of its meaning:

Lui marchand! C'est pure médisance, il ne l'a jamais été. Tout ce qu'il faisait, c'est qu'il était fort obligeant, fort officieux; et comme il se connaissait fort bien en étoffes, il en allait choisir de tous les côtés, les faisait apporter chez lui, et en donnait à ses amis pour de l'argent. (4.3)

[He, a merchant? That's sheer calumny; he never was. All he did was that he was very obliging, very helpful; and since he was a real connoisseur of cloth, he went around and picked it out everywhere, had it brought to his house, and gave it to his friends for money.]

Language has been destabilized, just as what remains of reality begins to disappear in the fog of the Turkish ceremony.

From the moment that Covielle appears in disguise, Jourdain must adjust to a totally meaningless language. It is not a foreign language whose rules he does not know, but one quite literally devoid of meaning. Without an interpreter, Jourdain cannot express himself, even for a purpose as basic as introducing Dorante to the Grand Turk's son (5.4). The interpreter does not translate the "Turkish" spoken by the disguised characters. He invents French sentences that will satisfy Jourdain. The bourgeois's loss of the ability to use language independently corresponds to his loss of self. His desire to become a *gentilhomme* has brought him to the point of absolute dependency upon others. Others must communicate to him the meaning of the social status he acquires—the rank of Mamamouchi, "c'est-à-dire, en notre langue, Paladin" (4.3) [that is to say, in our language, a paladin]. It has no meaning in itself.

The Turkish ceremony and its language encompass not only Jourdain but all the players involved in the ploy to trick him. None of them understand the language any better than Jourdain. All are as dependent as he upon the outcome of Covielle's "bourle" (3.13) [hoax] to attain their ends. How else could Covielle and Nicole be permitted to marry? How else can Dorante continue to hide from Dorimène the truth about his dishonest behavior, and hope for her to marry him? Under what other circumstances would Monsieur Jourdain consent to the marriage of Lucile and Cléonte, for which both of them and Madame Jourdain long? When Covielle tells Madame Jourdain "que tout ceci n'est fait que pour nous ajuster aux visions de votre mari, que nous l'abusons sous ce déguisement, et que c'est Cléonte lui-même qui est le fils du Grand Turc" (5.6) [that all this is being done just to fall in with your husband's visions, that we're fooling him in this disguise, and that it's Cléonte himself who's the son of the Grand Turk], his explanation must be read literally. Jourdain is being duped, but in order to trick him, Covielle and the others have no choice but to accommodate themselves to his folly, to "nous ajuster aux visions de votre mari." Even the intractable Madame Jourdain, when she realizes what is happening, gives in: "Ah! comme cela, je me rends" (5.6) [Ah! In that case, I give in]. His wife's surrender elicits one of Jourdain's funniest lines: "Ah! voilà tout le monde raisonnable" (5.6) [Ah! Now everybody's reasonable]. Clearly, everyone is not "raisonnable," but Jourdain's assessment indicates that all participate in his madness. In that, they are all identical, and similar to him.

The conclusion of Le Bourgeois gentilhomme shows how Jourdain's desire and the ensuing rivalry reduce differences among competing characters and uncover their sameness. Responding to Monsieur Jourdain's fear that Lucile will be too headstrong to accept marriage with the Grand Turk's son, Covielle reassures him: "il se rencontre ici une aventure merveilleuse, c'est que le fils du Grand Turc ressemble à ce Cléonte, à peu de chose près . . . et l'amour qu'elle a pour l'un pourra passer aisément à l'autre" (4.3) [there's a wonderful coincidence here, that the son of the Grand Turk bears a very close resemblance to this Cléonte . . . and her love for the one may pass easily to the other]. Covielle might well have told the gullible old man that the Grand Turk's son is so handsome that Lucile cannot but love him. Despite the risk of giving away his trick, he insists rather upon the resemblance, in this case real, between the French and "Turkish" Cléontes. The function of the Turkish ceremony is to foster resemblance where difference once ruled. André Gide, an avid reader of Molière, saw this when he spoke of "cette 'érosion des contours' que j'admire tant dans Le Bourgeois, Le Malade, ou L'Avare"[24] [this "wearing away of the contours" that I admire so much in Le Bourgeois, Le Malade, or L'Avare].

Comedy's tendency to reveal the commonality of opposites is typical of Molière's plays. What sets Le Bourgeois gentilhomme apart is that the sower of discord, responsible for the breakdown of differences, suffers no loss. Nor, in real terms, is an earlier good order reconstituted at play's end. Monsieur Jourdain has his way by the creation of an imaginary order in which everyone is happy. His rivalry with Dorante emerges again as the bourgeois reacts to the count's intention to marry Dorimène. It is quelled by a lie, namely, that the marriage has been concocted to trick Madame Jourdain. The Turkish festivities are a *divertissement* in the etymological and the Pascalean sense that they divert attention from the truth. Jourdain is duped but believes it is he who is duping his wife and daughter. The three couples participate in deceiving Monsieur Jourdain but must play along with his madness as well. The family's problems are resolved, but only for as long as the Turkish fantasy lasts. That no permanent restitution of order is possible in the wake of what is wrought by desire and rivalry continues to be one of the important lessons of Molière's theater.

The curtain falls, as it must, before the arrival of the notary, who, as an officer of the law, would represent hard reality. His normal stock-in-trade is the kind of distinctions that have been broken down by the imaginary. What the imaginary has made possible— Monsieur Jourdain's new social rank and the three marriages—can occur only because everyone has been drawn into the imagination's net, and the notary's appearance would break the spell. Monsieur Jourdain's family, servants, and friends all laugh heartily at his foolishness, but they cannot separate themselves completely from it. Even while laughing, they are forced, collectively, to play according to Jourdain's rules.

Le Bourgeois gentilhomme is a comedy about comedy. By calling upon fantasy, Molière shows how rivalry, once unleashed, implicates everyone, diminishing the distance between the mocked and those who mock them. Here, as in other comedies, there is a happy ending. In *Le Bourgeois gentilhomme*, however, Molière makes explicit what in other plays is an underlying conclusion: the resolution of the dilemma created by Monsieur Jourdain's behavior can last only as long as the fantasy lasts, which cannot be for long.

9

Philosophers and Fools:
The World of *Les Femmes savantes*

THE COLLAPSE OF DIFFERENCE AND THE THREAT OF CHAOS THAT FOL-
lows upon it come to the fore during a ridiculous verbal duel situ-
ated in the precise middle of *Les Femmes savantes*, Molière's penultimate comedy. Like his earlier counterpart, Tartuffe, Trissotin does
not appear on stage until the third act of the play,[1] and Molière
has prepared his audience to greet the ludicrous "bel esprit" with
unrestrained skepticism. Philaminte's "héros d'esprit" [intellectual
hero] (Translation by author), Clitandre complains, "m'inspire au
fond de l'âme un dominant chagrin" (1.3.230, 246) [repels me
from the very bottom of my soul].[2] Ostensibly addressing his sister,
Bélise, but intending that his wife, Philaminte, overhear what he
has to say, Chrysale echoes Clitandre's sentiments:

> Je n'aime point céans tous vos gens à latin,
> Et principalement ce Monsieur Trissotin:
> C'est lui qui dans des vers vous a tympanisées;
> Tous les propos qu'il tient sont des billevesées.
>
> (2.7.609–12)

> [And I could do without your Latin-speaking gang,
> And in particular that Monsieur Trissotin.
> He's made a fool of you in public with his verse,
> And everything he says is nonsense, if not worse.]

Trissotin has insinuated himself into the household by playing
upon the foolish desire of Chrysale's wife, daughter, and sister to
adopt the ways of those whom they consider "learned." Trissotin
has become their model.

His dear friend, Vadius, is cut from the same cloth. Superficially
learned—"Il sait du grec, ma soeur!" (3.3.943) [Oh, sister . . . The
gentleman speaks Greek!]—and always ready to display his knowledge, Vadius wants nothing more than to be introduced into Phi-

laminte's salon, where he will find an eager audience for his "petits vers pour de jeunes amants" (3.3.967) [little verses all about young love]. When Vadius is announced by the footman, Trissotin assures Philaminte of his friend's worthiness. Purportedly lettered and highly cultivated, Vadius "peut tenir son coin parmi de beaux esprits" (3.3.939)[3] [holds his own among the finest minds in town]. The tennis metaphor turns out to be prophetic, for Vadius will suddenly become Trissotin's bitter rival in a battle of verbal thrusts that each parries and returns to the other. Neither Trissotin nor Vadius is secure in the certainty of his own worth. Each relies upon others for knowledge that his poetic work and, therefore, its creator have merit. They derive their sense of themselves from others, even though Vadius can imagine nothing more foolish than "un auteur qui partout va gueuser des encens" (3.3.960) [Brash writers of that sort, fishing for compliments]. Their friendship stands upon an instinctive understanding of the other's need for recognition. Even before their feud over the "Sonnet à la Princesse Uranie sur sa fièvre" [Sonnet to Princess Uranie on her Fever], Molière suggests a rivalry between Vadius and Trissotin, as they try to outdo each other with flattery:

> Trissotin. Est-il rien d'amoureux comme vos chansonnettes?
> Vadius. Peut-on rien voir d'égal aux sonnets que vous faites?
> Trissotin. Rien qui soit plus charmant que vos petits rondeaux?
> Vadius. Rien de si plein d'esprit que tous vos madrigaux?
>
> (3.3.977–80)

> [Trissotin. Is there anything so charming as your canzonets?
> Vadius. Would it be possible to match your sonnets?
> Trissotin. What could be more delightful than your sweet roundels?
> Vadius. What could be wittier than your dear madrigals?]

The repetition of "rien" is an ironic commentary on the ultimate value of all this praise and hints at the nullity of those who proffer and receive it. Trissotin and Vadius simultaneously imitate and vie with each other in their mutual admiration. The syntax of their language is imitative, its substance competitive:

> Trissotin. Si la France pouvait connaître votre prix . . .
> Vadius. Si le siècle rendait justice aux beaux esprits. . . .
>
> (3.3.983–84)

> [Trissotin. If only France appreciated what you're worth . . .
> Vadius. If only intellect were valued on this earth . . .]

The scene turns ugly when Vadius, unaware that the sonnet advising Princess Uranie to drown her fever in a bath is Trissotin's, condemns its author. The quarrel between the two *beaux esprits* shows the reverse side of their emulative friendship. Vadius now mocks rather than lauds Trissotin sonneteer. For his part, Trissotin, who has just told his friend that "aux ballades surtout vous êtes admirable" (3.3.981) [Your *ballades* are innovative, and so *au fait*], declares: "la ballade, à mon goût, est une chose fade" (3.3.1006) [The *ballade* in my view is scarcely avant-garde]. An audience familiar with Molière will hardly be taken aback when, from this reversal, two characters locating themselves at opposite poles assume a striking sameness. Using like arguments both defensively and offensively, the two rivals become mirror images of each other. When Vadius unwittingly criticizes his friend's sonnet, Trissotin characteristically calls upon the opinion of others in his own defense: "Beaucoup de gens pourtant le trouvent admirable" [But people who have heard it say it's very fine]. Vadius retorts: "Cela n'empêche pas qu'il ne soit misérable" (3.3.993–94) [That doesn't stop it being a total waste of time]. Vadius has composed a ballad and wants to read it to the assembled company. He responds to Trissotin's disparaging appraisal of the ballad form just as Trissotin had responded to him: "La ballade pourtant charme beaucoup de gens" (3.3.1008) [Yet it's a form of verse that some appreciate]. Trissotin's riposte is predictable: "Cela n'empêche pas qu'elle ne me déplaise" (3.3.1009) [The fact remains that I can't stand this type of verse]. The dispute rapidly degenerates into a match of name-calling in which verbal repetition at the beginning of each round and the symmetry of the versification call attention to the identical nature of the rivals:

> TRISSOTIN. Allez, petit grimaud, barbouilleur de papier.
> VADIUS. Allez, rimeur de balle, opprobre du métier.
> TRISSOTIN. Allez, fripier d'écrits, impudent plagiaire.
> VADIUS. Allez, cuistre. . . .
>
> (3.3.1015–18)

> [TRISSOTIN. Be off, you pompous twit, you scribbling featherbrain!
> VADIUS. Be off, you cheapskate poet, you put our craft to shame!
> TRISSOTIN. Be off, you copycat, you pushy plagiarist!
> VADIUS. Be off, you wretched hack . . .]

Philaminte's attempt to resolve the quarrel fails, as does Vadius's appeal to the authority of Boileau, who, more than anyone else, ought to be able to discern the better poet: "Oui, oui, je te renvoie à l'auteur des *Satires*" [You took a drubbing in the *Satires* of Boileau]. "Je t'y renvoie aussi," Trissotin snaps back (3.3.1026–27) [He mocks at you as well]. Vadius and Trissotin are similar at the outset. Their altercation makes them indistinguishable. Neither can assert himself without denigrating the other. Each thinks badly of the other, and they castigate each other with identical language. Trissotin's sonnet and Vadius's ballad seem quite beside the point. The real contention is a personal one between two characters who only know how to affirm themselves by dominating the other:

> Vadius. Ma plume t'apprendra quel homme je puis être.
> Trissotin. Et la mienne saura te faire voir ton maître.
>
> (3.3.1041–42)

> [Vadius. My pen will show you whom you're fighting, never fear.
> Trissotin. And you will learn from mine just who's the master here.]

By subjugating Vadius, Trissotin hopes to give meaning to his own vacuous existence. Vadius, likewise, believes that to defeat Trissotin will make him a man. But their mutual lack of substance merely renders them empty imitations of each other. As so often in Molière's plays, each character sees the truth of the other while remaining blind to his own. Trissotin understands Vadius's inability to distinguish between himself and his friend. Vadius accuses Trissotin of the same flaw:

> Trissotin. Vous donnez sottement vos qualités aux autres.
> Vadius. Fort impertinemment vous me jetez les vôtres.
>
> (3.3.1013–14)

> [Trissotin]. If you think I'm like you, you must be ignorant.
> Vadius. And if you think the same, then you're impertinent.]

All the two rivals can do is hurl insults back and forth. Not one of their barbs carries the day, because none is more than a dull reflection of the taunt motivating it.

Despite its foolishness, the dispute of the *beaux esprits* typifies what happens when differences break down. Vadius and Trissotin want the same thing, to be different from others. One recalls Alceste's succinct but potentially threatening "Je veux qu'on me distingue" (1.1.63) [I want to be distinguished from the rest]. That and the concomitant desire for superiority make them identical. The emergence of this sameness brings in its wake disruption and disorder. The writer of sonnets and the writer of ballads are brothers under the skin, albeit, like their predecessors, Orgon and Tartuffe, enemy brothers. No resolution to their quarrel appears possible: it is to be continued "chez Barbin," at the publisher's, where, one can only assume, the endless bickering will be taken up again (3.3.1044). Molière dispenses with the problem posed in this scene by having Vadius, an episodic character, leave the stage, never to reappear. This simple solution, which averts rivalry's disruptive force without effectively dissipating it, will not serve should a similar conflict erupt among the play's major characters.

As in *Le Tartuffe*, two teams are aligned against each other in *Les Femmes savantes*, but here they are symmetrical. Each has five players: Chrysale, Henriette, Clitandre, Ariste, and Martine will take on Philaminte, Armande, Trissotin, Bélise, and Vadius.[4] Chrysale and his adherents stand irrevocably opposed to the *femmes savantes* and their "learned" models. The *savantes* would have members of Chrysale's household reject the worldly, the carnal, in favor of the life of the mind—or their version of it. In their ideal world, love does not lead to concupiscence. Nor, perish the thought, does anyone ever break the linguistic rules of the noted grammarian Vaugelas. To guarantee Trissotin's presence in the household and impart to her hopelessly materialistic daughter, Henriette, a sense of life's higher values, Philaminte plans to marry her off to the "bel esprit." Her other daughter, Armande, who is enamored of Henriette's lover, Clitandre, supports Philaminte in this project. Henriette and her father, Chrysale, adamantly oppose this scheme. Chrysale takes an equally dim view of his wife's preciosity. When Philaminte wants to fire her servant, Martine, for abuse of the French language, Chrysale resists:

> Qu'importe qu'elle manque aux lois de Vaugelas,
> Pourvu qu'à la cuisine elle ne manque pas?
> . . . .
> Je vis de bonne soupe, et non de beau langage.
> Vaugelas n'apprend point à bien faire un potage.
> (2.7.525–26, 531–32)

> [Who cares if she never studied Vaugelas?
> Her cooking's where she needs a varied repertoire.
> . . . .
> I live off tasty soup, not off a learned book
> And Vaugelas's grammar book can't teach a girl to cook.]

With his "Je vis de bonne soupe," Chrysale situates himself on the side of the material and represents the solid good sense of a staunch bourgeois.

The symmetrical oppositions among the characters extend well beyond the hilarious division over Vaugelas and French grammar. Chrysale and Philaminte are pitted against each other in a struggle for mastery of the household. More than the matter of correct usage or the marriage of their daughter, the question of who will lay down the law preoccupies them. Their daughters compete for Clitandre. Both want to marry him, and that, more than the issue of marriage as a way of life, is at the root of their struggle. And, finally, Clitandre and Trissotin are rivals for the hand of Henriette. The distribution of characters and, indeed, the entire action of the play are organized around these fierce rivalries. They form the dynamic core of *Les Femmes savantes*. Not unexpectedly in the light of Molière's other plays, these rivalries lead to entrenched divisions among the characters and reduce the players to interchangeable faces. As they fight for superiority over each other, Chrysale and Philaminte, Henriette and Armande, Clitandre and Trissotin appear more and more alike. Theirs is a pitched battle not of alterities but of similarities, and it threatens the order of their world.

Unlike Vadius and Trissotin, Clitandre and Trissotin, in the early scenes of the play, seem pointedly different. The former, as he himself puts it, has a "coeur . . . né sincère" (1.3.215) [heart born sincere] that burns for Henriette with a "sincère flamme" (1.4.275) [sincere love] (Translation by author). Although he had first loved Armande with what he calls "une flamme immortelle" (1.2.139) [feelings . . . unshakeable], Clitandre now wants to marry Henriette. To win her hand, he will have to charm the girl's mother, a difficult task. For Clitandre disapproves of both Philaminte's pretensions to learning and the company she keeps. He tells Henriette:

> Je respecte beaucoup Madame votre mère;
> Mais je ne puis du tout approuver sa chimère,
> Et me rendre l'écho des choses qu'elle dit,
> Aux encens qu'elle donne à son héros d'esprit.
>
> (1.3.227–230)

> [I do believe your mother's worthy of respect,
> But self-deception's quite a character defect.
> I find I can't agree with most of what she says,
> For instance in the compliments she always pays
> To Monsieur Trissotin.]

Without realizing that Trissotin is about to become his rival, Clitandre paints a derisive portrait of the pedant. To avoid discussing Trissotin with Philaminte, he asks Henriette's aunt, Bélise, to intervene for him.

Bélise is a minor character on the side of the *savantes* who seconds Philaminte's worshipful attitude toward Trissotin. She lives on the fringes of the play's central action. However, she possesses one characteristic that makes her both very funny and crucial to an understanding of the play: she is convinced that all men, without distinction, are in love with her. In her humorous, nonsensical way, Bélise is the first to suggest that differences between characters may be of less moment than similarities. When Clitandre approaches her with the tale of his love, Bélise immediately assumes that she is herself its object: "Ah! tout beau, gardez-vous de m'ouvrir trop votre âme: / Si je vous ai su mettre au rang de mes amants, / Contentez-vous des yeux pour vos seuls truchements" (1.4.276–78) [Hold on! Don't tell me what you feel! For I'm above / All that. I know that you're my suitor, like the rest—/ Keep silent!—Your two eyes alone may try their best / To plead your cause]. As she later explains to Ariste, it is precisely by such "muets truchements" that she recognizes the love of Dorante, Damis, Cléonte, and Lycidas for her (2.3.384). It goes without saying that none of them, who, in any case, do not appear in the play, has declared his love to Bélise. How often Molière sends the reader back to his earlier works, not only by his repetition of structural patterns but also by his duplication of names! Just after Philaminte reveals to Henriette her plan to have the girl marry Trissotin, Bélise releases the "bel esprit" from her imagined hold on him:

> Je vous entends: vos yeux demandent mon aveu,
> Pour engager ailleurs un coeur que je possède.
> Allez, je le veux bien. A ce noeud je vous cède:
> C'est un hymen qui fait votre établissement.
>
> (3.4.1076–79)

> [That look speaks volumes. Yes, you're still my supplicant.
> Can you be marrying another, when you're mine?
> Go on—I give you up most gladly. I resign.
> If you marry my niece, your future is secure.]

Bélise believes that all men are equally susceptible to her charms, even though none seems to be. She simply does not distinguish among individuals in matters of love. To her, they are all alike. Chrysale and Ariste dismiss her as mad: "Notre soeur est folle, oui"

(2.4.397) [Our sister's raving mad]. Her madness, however, takes the same form as the rivalry of characters who believe themselves to be far more perspicacious than Bélise.

Clitandre, who also finds Bélise mad—"Diantre soit de la folle avec ses visions" (1.4.325) [The woman's mad. To hell with her illusions!]—is sure of his superiority to Trissotin. But the differences between them begin to vanish as soon as the two become rivals. Like his cohorts, Clitandre makes a display of his lack of refinement and his inability to imagine love without its physical component:

> Pour moi, par un malheur, je m'aperçois, Madame,
> Que j'ai, ne vous déplaise, un corps tout comme une âme;
> Je sens qu'il y tient trop, pour le laisser à part;
> De ces détachements je ne connais point l'art:
> Le Ciel m'a dénié cette philosophie,
> Et mon âme et mon corps marchent de compagnie.
>
> (4.2.1213–18)

> [Unfortunately, though, I'm not the same as you:
> I don't just have a soul, I've got a body too.
> It means too much to me, I won't cast it aside:
> I don't possess the art of being rarefied.
> The good Lord has denied me your philosophy;
> My body and my soul keep perfect company.]

Armande's brand of love, free of what she calls "les sales désirs" (4.2.1208) [filth] and he the "commerce des sens" (4.2.1222) [sensuality], holds little attraction for him: "Je suis un peu grossier, comme vous m'accusez; / J'aime avec tout moi-même, et l'amour qu'on me donne / En veut, je le confesse, à toute la personne" (4.2.1224–26) [And you're right to say that I'm a trifle crude. / I love with all of me, and not just with my soul; / My love's directed at my mistress as a whole]. This distinguishes Clitandre from the likes of Trissotin, or so he thinks. But Henriette will discover a Trissotin far from innocent of physical instincts when she asks that he forsake her for one of the many women who appear in his poetry and for whom he expresses such "amoureuse ardeur" (5.1.1523) [protestations]. All that, he responds, amounts to nothing but words: "C'est mon esprit qui parle, et ce n'est pas mon coeur. / D'elles on ne me voit amoureux qu'en poète; / Mais j'aime tout de bon l'adorable Henriette" (5.1.1524–26) [My intellect speaks in my poems, not my heart. / Expressing love for them is purely etiquette. / My real affection's for my darling Henriette]. Henriette takes offense at the declaration of love, probably reading in the words "tout de bon" more than they literally say but just what Trissotin has in mind. At the very least, she interprets his attempts to win her hand in marriage as a violent gesture and must wonder just how different Trissotin and Clitandre are, after all.

Upon being told of Philaminte's scheme to marry Henriette to Trissotin, Clitandre first reacts not to the rivalry but rather to the unworthiness of his rival, whom he thinks beneath him (4.2.1249–52). When the rivals meet, they taunt each other with reciprocal verbal attacks that make them sound very much alike. Philaminte introduces Clitandre as a man who "fait profession de chérir l'ignorance" (4.3.1273) [values ignorance], and this sets off a round of sparring not unlike the earlier battle between Trissotin and Vadius. The struggle has a strong undercurrent of violence. Philaminte and Trissotin refer to it as a "combat" (4.3.1319, 1325); Clitandre calls his rival "un si rude assaillant" (4.3.1315) [such a mighty foe]. The argument centers on whether a "savant" or an "ignorant" is more likely to be a "sot." Clitandre holds that "un sot savant est sot plus qu'un sot ignorant" [An untaught fool is bad, a learned fool is worse], while Trissotin argues that this is impossible because "ignorant et sot sont termes synonymes" (4.3.1296, 1298) [Most people tend to link up "ignorant" with "fool"]. What the two fail to recognize, of course, is that each uses the very same epithet to describe the other.

The more heated the battle becomes, the more difficult it is to distinguish between the characters. If they remain on opposite sides, they nonetheless speak the same language:

> TRISSOTIN. Il faut que l'ignorance ait pour vous de grands charmes,
>   Puisque pour elle ainsi vous prenez tant les armes.
> CLITANDRE. Si pour moi l'ignorance a des charmes bien grands,
>   C'est depuis qu'à mes yeux s'offrent certains savants.
> TRISSOTIN. Ces savants-là peuvent, à les connaître,
>   Valoir certaines gens que nous voyons paraître.
>
> (4.3.1305–10)

> [TRISSOTIN. Sheer ignorance to you must have enormous charms:
>   You're fighting for it, and we see you take up arms.
> CLITANDRE. I do find ignorance's charms congenial
>   Since I have witnessed pedants in tutorial.
> TRISSOTIN. Those pedants, when you get to know them, are as good
>   As certain gentlemen who haunt the neighbourhood.]

Nothing separates the "certains savants" from the "certaines gens" in their desire for superiority. When, accusing Clitandre of defending the court's myopic perspective, Trissotin assails it as a center of ignorance (4.3.1325–30), he seems to have gone too far. With the force of social hierarchy on his side, Clitandre should now be able to end the dispute in his own favor. However, social superiority does no more to quell this fight than Boileau had done to put an end to Trissotin's struggle with Vadius. Clitandre and Trissotin are locked in a disruptive rivalry that knows no issue.

In the play's first scene, Armande, representing the views of the clan of learned women, is horrified that her sister, Henriette, would consider marriage. The word itself disgusts her: "Sur quelle sale vue il traîne la pensée?" (1.1.12) [It makes me think strange thoughts, too shaming to explain!]. Committing oneself to "un idole d'époux et des marmots d'enfants" [your lord and master, and a brat or two] is best left to crude, common folk (1.1.30–31). Henriette finds nothing distasteful in either the word or the institution. Armande may reject marriage for herself, but Henriette will not. After all, "Le Ciel, dont nous voyons que l'ordre est tout-puissant, / Pour différents emplois nous fabrique en naissant" (1.1.53–54) [We all know God controls the Heavens and the earth, / We know he's destined us for different roles from birth]. Order is, in this view, founded upon difference and the harmonious accommodation of differences among individuals in an integrated social fabric. Both Henriette and Armande make a great show of the traits that distinguish them. Like her lover, Henriette affects ignorance. Her sister uses the word "bas" to describe Henriette's thoughts and behavior: "Mon Dieu, que votre esprit est d'un étage bas!" (1.1.26) [Good grief! How common!]. Armande would have Henriette forgo the "bas amusements" (1.1.32) of marriage:

> A de plus hauts objets élevez vos desirs,
> Songez à prendre un goût des plus nobles plaisirs,
> Et traitant de mépris les sens et la matière,
> A l'esprit comme nous donnez-vous toute entière.
>
> (1.1.33–36)

> [But you should live your whole life on a higher plane,
> And opt for nobler joys. Look here, let me explain:
> You should give up the senses, scorn base things like that,
> And use your brain, don't waste your time in idle chat.]

What distinguishes the *femmes savantes* is their more elevated, superior desires.

Yet Henriette, at first so willing to accept her sister's characterization of her, rejects it where her choice of lovers is concerned:

"Manque-t-il [Clitandre] de mérite? est-ce un choix qui soit bas?" (1.1.90) [Is he lacking in merit? Would choosing him be a lowly choice?] (Translation by author). She remains as proud in love as is her sister in matters of the mind. By her refusal to give in to Clitandre's insistence on marriage and its bed, Armande has lost him to Henriette. But when she sees no hope of his changing, she offers herself to him, thus collapsing a difference between herself and her sister:

> Puisque, pour vous réduire à des ardeurs fidèles,
> Il faut des noeuds de chair, des chaînes corporelles,
> Si ma mère le veut, je résous mon esprit
> À consentir pour vous à ce dont il s'agit.
>
> (4.2.1237–40)

> [If your fidelity can't otherwise by won,
> Except by fleshly bonds and claims, let it be done.
> If mother will agree, then I'll take on the task—
> And I'll resign myself to do the things you ask.]

Armande had earlier seen the rejection of marriage as a means of asserting superiority:

> Loin d'être aux lois d'un homme en esclave asservie,
> Mariez-vous, ma soeur, à la philosophie,
> Qui nous monte au-dessus de tout le genre humain,
> Et donne à la raison l'empire souverain.
>
> (1.1.43–46)

> [Don't be a husband's slave—reject the marriage vow—
> Instead take up philosophy, and do it now.
> You'll see, you'll rise above the common human race.
> Philosophers alone put reason in its place.]

To be different is to be superior, to be master rather than slave. But Henriette's more earthly desires make her just as imperious as her sister. When Clitandre explains to her his loathing for Trissotin, her response reveals that love's tyranny is no less total than that of "la philosophie":

> Vous devez vous forcer à quelque complaisance.
> Un amant fait sa cour où s'attache son coeur,
> Il veut de tout le monde y gagner la faveur;

Et pour n'avoir personne à sa flamme contraire,
Jusqu'au chien du logis il s'efforce de plaire.

(1.3.240–44)

[You've got to be polite. It means you'll have the nous
To play a part. You lovers have to do your bit,
Gain favour in the household, try to score a hit,
Check everyone's included in your dialogue—
And even make advances to the family dog.]

Not surprisingly, Clitandre uses similar words to describe the two sisters. Armande's eyes have been cruel to him, they "régnaient sur mon âme en superbes tyrans" (1.2.142) [ruled over my heart, and tortured me with pride]. Unable to bear up under their tyranny, he sought "Des vainqueurs plus humains et de moins rudes chaînes" [a kinder love, and chains less hard to bear], and now no power on earth "me puisse à mes fers arracher" (1.1.144, 150) [will ever make us part]. These are standard images in the language of preciosity, but there are others Clitandre could have chosen were not Henriette, like her sister, a "chaîne," however "moins rude." The sisters do not suspect how alike they are. In the third act of the play, they taunt each other with virtually the same words and the same dictum. Dismayed to learn of her mother's plan for her future, Henriette is reminded by her sister: "Cependant, bien qu'ici nos goûts soient différents, / Nous devons obéir, ma soeur, à nos parents" (3.5.1095–96) [Well, even if our views on marriage aren't the same, / Obedience to our parents has to be our aim]. As if to underscore the shared identity she would rather deny, Henriette, when she knows that Chrysale wants her to marry Clitandre, gibes her sister: "Il nous faut obéir, ma soeur, à nos parents" (3.5.1104) [Obedience to our parents, sister, is our aim]. Again, Molière uses parallel speech to emphasize the likeness of rivals, undercutting their apparent differences.

Antoine Adam, although highly critical of *Les Femmes savantes*, has understood the centrality of the role of Philaminte: "dès qu'il s'agit seulement de savoir si Philaminte réussira à dominer son mari et à faire le mariage de sa fille, la pièce remonte, l'intérêt se tend, le rythme s'accélère"[5] [As soon as the matter at hand is knowing whether Philaminte will succeed in dominating her husband and arranging her daughter's marriage, the play revives, interest intensifies, and the pace picks up]. The play's truly dangerous rivalry arises between Philaminte and Chrysale. Upon the resolution of their dispute rest the futures of Henriette, Armande, and their suitors, as well as the order of the divided family.[6] The struggle between husband and wife originates less in their disagreement about a suitable mate for Henriette or Chrysale's unwillingness to accept his wife's "learning" than in a will to power equally puissant on both sides. Chrysale, encouraged by Ariste and Henriette, decides no longer to allow his wife to reign over his household. He will stand his ground and organize his struggle around the issue of his daughter's marriage. But Philaminte is not easily dismissed. Speaking to Armande, she proceeds forcefully to the crux of the matter:

> Je lui [Henriette] montrerai bien aux lois de qui des deux
> Les droits de la raison soumettent tous ses voeux.
> Et qui doit gouverner, ou sa mère ou son père,
> Ou l'esprit ou le corps, la forme ou la matière.
>
> (4.1.1127–30)

> [Her father or her mother—who must take control?
> Is it form or matter, body or pure soul?
> She can't make such a choice alone—she needs a guide.
> I'll show her which of us has reason on her side.]

Earlier, Ariste goads Chrysale with the accusation that Philaminte has absolute power ("un pouvoir absolu") and lords it over him (2.9.661, 678), and in her first encounter with Chrysale, Philaminte displays her will to dominate by insisting her maid, Martine, be fired for infractions against the rules of Vaugelas. To Chrysale's objections, she retorts: "Je ne veux point d'obstacle aux désirs que je montre" (2.6.440) [I'm mistress here. Don't think you can take *me* to task]. Her desire, like her tone, is absolute. "Il faut qu'absolument mon désir s'exécute" [I've got to be obeyed], she later tells Chrysale, demanding that her daughter marry Trissotin (5.3.1674). Desire defines Philaminte's character. She repeatedly uses the words "je veux." About Martine, she declares: "Je veux qu'elle sorte" (2.6.431) [She must go, right now]; about Henriette's marriage to Trissotin: "Je l'ai dit, je le veux" (5.3.1676) [And that's an order]. The object of her desire is more often than not determined by the status of her rivalry with others. Martine's dismissal has less to do with Martine than with her mistress's wish to be superior to men by becoming an arbiter of grammatical conventions. The fulfillment of Philaminte's desire would distinguish her from others, but to no permanent avail, since rivalry continually and effectively devalues her superiority by bringing her to the same level as those whom she wants to dominate.

For all his apparently good instincts concerning the well-being of his daughter and the choice of a proper husband for her, Chrysale is, like Orgon, essentially absorbed throughout the play by the issue of his mastery over the household. He will become progressively more adamant about this—as adamant as his wife—so that from the end of the fourth act on, the text is replete with his frequent pronouncements on the subject:

> Ah! je leur ferai voir si, pour donner la loi,
> Il est dans ma maison d'autre maître que moi.
>
> (4.5.1443–44)

> Je n'aurais pas l'esprit d'être maître chez moi?
>
> (5.2.1580)

> Ma volonté céans doit être en tout suivie.
>
> (5.2.1586)

> Le Ciel me donne un plein pouvoir sur vous [Henriette].
>
> (5.2.1591)

> [I tell you, I've the right to choose my daughter's spouse;
> It's time I showed them who's the master in this house.
>
> I don't have the nous, / At my age, to be master here, in my own house?
>
> Look, I take the decisions, you do what I say.
>
> And I'll dispose of you as I think best.]

At first he seems to think he has the upper hand and accepts Clitandre as his daughter's fiancé without consulting Philaminte: "Je réponds de ma femme, et prends sur moi l'affaire" (2.4.412) [I'll answer for my wife: the matter's up to me]. Shortly after this, he learns better. When he cannot prevail upon his wife not to dismiss Martine, the seeds of battle are sown. His brother, Ariste, coaches him in the ways of mastery, explaining that Chrysale himself is to blame for allowing Philaminte to lead him around "en bête par le nez" (2.9.682) [like a donkey, by the nose]. Ariste intends by his advice to stir Chrysale's desire:

> Quoi? vous ne pouvez pas, voyant comme on vous nomme,
> Vous résoudre une fois à vouloir être un homme?

A faire condescendre une femme à vos voeux,
Et prendre assez de coeur pour dire un: "Je le veux"?

(2.9.683–86)

[Yes, you've become a laughing stock. Can't you decide
To stand up like a man, not run away and hide?
To make that woman realize she must obey,
And have the guts to say: "I'll run the place my way"?]

He incites in his brother the will to power. Chrysale must resolve to "*vouloir* être un homme," and boldly to state, "je le veux." Inspired by Ariste and society's image of manliness, he must want the subjugation of Philaminte. Like Vadius, Chrysale will be a man only when he has proven himself to others. He immediately decides to take on his wife when Ariste menaces him with that most seventeenth-century of threats, ridicule: "Et votre lâcheté mérite qu'on en rie" (2.9.696) [Your cowardly behaviour's nothing but a joke]. Ridicule reflects the sharply negative opinion of others. Chrysale, like so many of Molière's characters, depends upon opinion for recognition of his superiority.

From this point on, Chrysale's insistence that Henriette marry the man she loves is directed solely against his wife: "Et je lui [Philaminte] veux faire aujourd'hui connaître / Que ma fille est ma fille, et que j'en suis le maître / Pour lui prendre un mari qui soit selon mes voeux" (2.9.703–5) [All that must stop, today. I'll have her know / My daughter's mine to give, and what I say must go. / The husband that she gets must be the man I choose]. Chrysale could be merciless with his daughter were her will to conflict with his. He is bent upon proving to his audience—in this case, Ariste— that he is a man and therefore deserving of the approval of others: "Et je m'en vais être homme à la barbe des gens" (2.9.710) [No matter how she rails, I'll show her I'm a man]. Without that, he is nothing. Moreover, he who would be master is subject to him whose approval he seeks. Ariste responds to his brother's resolution with the highly suggestive "Vous voilà raisonnable, *et comme je vous veux*" (2.9.706; emphasis added) [At last you're talking sense, I see you share my views]. However resolute, in his struggle with his wife, Chrysale can never win once and for all. At the end of the play, he does have his way, for Henriette will marry Clitandre, but Philaminte, who has been won over on this single point, is hardly reformed. She remains faithful to her "philosophie." This portends the renewal of rivalry between her and her husband. Chrysale longs for mastery but is unlikely to attain it.

The more forcefully he expresses his desire, the more intense and destructive his rivalry with Philaminte becomes. His assurances to Henriette that Clitandre is the man "dont je veux que vous soyez la femme" (3.6.1102) [whose wife I want you to be] (Translation by author) provides him with a means of dominating Philaminte: "Et dès ce soir je veux, / Pour la contrecarrer, vous marier vous deux" (4.5.1435–36) [Tonight, I know what I must do: / I'll show her who's the boss, by marrying you two]. To keep Martine as his maid will accomplish the same goal: "Je veux, je veux apprendre à vivre à votre mère, / Et, pour la mieux braver, voilà, malgré ses dents, / Martine que j'amène, et rétablis céans" (5.2.1566–68) [It's time I showed your mother who's the master now. / Though she may show her teeth, to demonstrate who's boss / I've brought Martine back home. I want to make her cross]. Chrysale's every act is colored by his rivalry with "ma femme à mes désirs rebelle" (5.2.1597) [my wife, who rebels against my desires] (Translation by author). His perception of her as the obstacle to his mastery is, of course, correct, for Philaminte's desire is no different from his: "Nous verrons qui sur elle [Henriette] aura plus de pouvoir, / Et si je la saurai réduire à son devoir"(4.4.1415–16) [Well, we'll see which of us can have the stronger hold, / And I'll make sure the hussy does as she is told]. Husband and wife seek the same elusive power over others. Each believes that if the other can be mastered, success will be at hand. Unfortunately, there is a price to pay for this mutual obstinacy. Although he blames Philaminte, Chrysale clearly sees the disorder it wreaks upon his family. He tells his wife that she should be less concerned with scientific investigation of the moon than with her household "où nous voyons aller tout sens dessus dessous" (2.7.570) [Where everything is topsy-turvy, goodness knows]. The natural order of things has, once again in Molière's work, been turned upside down: "Raisonner est l'emploi de toute ma maison, / Et le raisonnement en bannit la raison" (2.7.597–98) [The staff's commitment to their learning's quite immense, / But so much reasoning has banished common sense].

The struggle ends in the presence of a representative of the law, the notary—the one who could not appear in *Le Bourgeois gentilhomme*—who has been summoned for Henriette's betrothal. But even the majesty and power of the law, which is the foundation of a well-ordered society, prove impotent to resolve the conflict generated by the rivalry of Chrysale and Philaminte. The cries of rivals shouting contrary things with an identical voice drown out the notary's call for a reasonable decision:

PHILAMINTE. Mettez, mettez, Monsieur, Trissotin pour mon gendre.
CHRYSALE. Pour mon gendre, mettez, mettez, Monsieur, Clitandre.
LE NOTAIRE. Mettez-vous donc d'accord, et d'un jugement mûr
   Voyez à convenir entre vous du futur.
PHILAMINTE. Suivez, suivez, Monsieur, le choix où je m'arrête.
CHRYSALE. Faites, faites, Monsieur, les choses à ma tête.

(5.3.1625–30)

[PHILAMINTE. Just write down Monsieur Trissotin, for he's my choice.
CHRYSALE. Write down Monsieur Clitandre: he has a father's voice.
LAWYER. Agree between yourselves, I can't do any more.
   You must decide which one's to be the son-in-law.
PHILAMINTE. Monsieur, do as I ask, I've said how it's to be.
CHRYSALE. Monsieur, do as I ask, you can depend on me.]

Chaos is imminent, for the law cannot maintain order in the face of such radical discord. As in Molière's earlier plays, the characters' persistence in their follies engenders the disintegration of order, carrying them to the brink of turmoil. Philaminte and Chrysale, the *femmes savantes* and their adversaries, bear equal responsibility for the disarray. The law is powerless to distinguish between the just and the unjust. Although reasons can be mounted for taking either side in the case, the overwhelming similarity of the litigants outweighs the arguments.

   The notary plays a very small role in *Les Femmes savantes* and arrives at a moment when the idea of a civil law with the power to decide between right and wrong has already been dangerously compromised. Both the *savantes* and their opponents rely heavily upon all manner of laws to justify their positions or, more frequently, to impose their will on others. From the outset, Armande exhorts her sister against servitude to the "lois d'un homme" in favor of submission to the laws of "la philosophie" (1.1.43, 44–48) and invokes the parental law according to which parents choose their children's mates (1.2.165–66). To Philaminte's preoccupation with the laws of grammar (2.6.466, 2.7.517), Chrysale responds that he could care less about the "lois de Vaugelas" (2.7.525). Only one law matters to him, the one he lays down for others to follow (4.5.1443–44). Philaminte, of course, has her own laws for others to obey, especially Henriette (4.1.1127–28). Characters speak of a bewildering variety of "lois" no fewer than fifteen times in *Les Femmes savantes* and quite often by way of trying to bring others to heel. That laws are exploited in so many different domains and figure so prominently in every aspect of rivalry effectively undermines their power to function properly.

In the presence of all but Vadius, who has long since disappeared from the scene, Ariste plays a trick on Chrysale and Philaminte. He sends to each of them a letter announcing financial ruin. The family is apparently bankrupt. Predictably, Trissotin bows out of his upcoming marriage to Henriette, and Philaminte realizes, to her disgust, that he had all along been interested only in money. Armande's understanding of the outcome, namely, the marriage of Clitandre and Henriette, provides the key to the mechanism that resolves the family's dilemma with a question to her mother: "Ainsi donc à leurs voeux vous me sacrifiez?" (5.4.1770) [You plan to sacrifice me to their happiness?]. Philaminte does not disagree that a sacrifice has taken place, but "Ce ne sera point vous que je leur sacrifie" (5.4.1771) [It will not be you whom I sacrifice to them] (Translation by author). The sacrificial victim is Trissotin, and an ideal victim he is. The elimination of Trissotin from the household represents a real loss for Philaminte and a substantial victory for her husband. It does not, however, threaten Philaminte in a way that would make her strike back at Chrysale and start the chain of violent repartee all over again. Trissotin belongs to the clan of the *savantes* without being so integral a part of it that his disappearance will call its existence into doubt. His sacrifice ends the struggle that is the occasion for the rivalries, though the rivalries will surely continue. For a brief moment, members of Chrysale's family can exhibit their differences without setting in motion the implacable process of violent rivalry. After Trissotin's last words, Clitandre offers himself to Henriette, and his fortune to her family, putting aside his disapproval of Philaminte: "Je m'attache, Madame, à tout votre destin" (5.4.1730) [I'll help you out. Whatever happens, I'll be true]. With his rival gone, Clitandre can preserve both his distinction from the *femmes savantes* and the good order of the household that he hopes to enter. It has repeatedly been said that Molière's great characters are monomaniacal and incapable of reform. Analysis of his earlier plays bears this out, and *Les Femmes savantes* again confirms it. In a very real sense, nothing substantial has changed at the end of the play. The last of the *savantes* to speak, Bélise warns that Clitandre may come to regret his marriage: "Qu'il prenne garde au moins que je suis dans son coeur" (5.4.1774) [Clitandre, don't forget your heart is ever mine]. Chrysale's is the last word, a command to the notary that his authority be recognized. By her philosophic acceptance of defeat, Philaminte demonstrates her fidelity to the principle of mind over matter that she has espoused from the beginning. The expulsion of Trissotin works no magic on the rivals. It does, however, neutralize the destructive power of their rivalry. At the end of the fifth act, disorder is warded off by the reintegration of difference into the fabric of the family's life. As Molière attests over and over again, where rivalry reigns, order can never be permanent. The sacrifice of Trissotin keeps anarchy at bay—but not forever. The happy ending of *Les Femmes savantes* is the final prelude to a new confrontation with chaos, this time inspired by Argan's imaginary maladies.

10

Doctors and Actors: The Victory of Comedy in *Le Malade imaginaire*

Of all Molière's plays, the one most favored by André Gide was *Le Malade imaginaire*: "c'est elle qui me paraît la plus neuve, la plus hardie, la plus belle—et de beaucoup"[1] [it is the one that seems to me the newest, the boldest, the finest—and by far]. What moved Gide in this chef d'oeuvre is the prose of an author who has arrived at the summit of his art. And yet, Molière uses this magnificent prose in the service of a plot that at times surprises an audience familiar with his theater by its lack of originality. Numerous critics have pointed out the similarities between *Le Malade imaginaire* and other Molière plays. As Antoine Adam says, *Tartuffe*, *L'Avare*, *Le Bourgeois gentilhomme*, and *Les Femmes savantes* all put on stage a parent, usually a father, who selects for his daughter a husband who fulfills parental needs rather than those of his future wife.[2] For Gérard Defaux, "*Le Malade imaginaire* ressemble étrangement, et d'une façon presque gênante" [*Le Malade imaginaire* resembles strangely and in an almost embarrassing way] these same plays.[3] Robert Garapon and John Cairncross emphasize the links between *Le Malade imaginaire* and *Tartuffe*.[4] Patrick Dandrey calls Argan "ce nouvel Orgon"[5] [this new Orgon]. Financial considerations having made it advantageous for the actors in Molière's troupe to put off its publication in France (they had the sole right to perform the work until it appeared in print), his last play was first published in 1674 by Daniel Elzevir in Amsterdam.[6] In this edition, whose lack of fidelity to Molière's text is noteworthy, there is an extremely interesting mistake: Argan's name appears as Orgon. The Elzevir edition seems to be a transcription of the text done by someone who had attended a performance of *Le Malade imaginaire* and had tried to reconstitute the play from memory. It is not difficult to understand why a spectator who had seen *Tartuffe* might make such an error.

In both plays, Molière presents a myopic, obsessive character taken in, one by false piety and the other by medicine. Haunted by the desire to be seen by others as "divinely absolute,"[7] Orgon does his best to integrate Tartuffe into his family. No less tormented by his health than Orgon by his soul, Argan responds in similar fashion, surrounding himself with doctors. The two servants, Dorine and Toinette, make fun of their masters. Each of them takes charge of the life of a daughter ill treated by a father whose egotism could thwart her love. Neither Cléante nor Béralde can overcome the madness of these monomaniacs with solid good sense, because in the final analysis, Orgon and Argan are not just a pair of simpletons tricked by a couple of rogues more clever than they, but rather willing victims, characters whose passivity in the face of fraud obscures their real aggressiveness. What Lionel Gossman says of Alceste—"'Je veux' is never far from his lips"[8]—is equally true for these two patresfamilias. The scene in which Orgon tries to convince his daughter to accept Tartuffe as her husband is structurally identical to that in which Argan announces that he has chosen Thomas Diafoirus for Angélique. As long as they think that their fathers' ideas coincide with their own, the daughters swear obedience. Their submissiveness vanishes once they discover their fathers' true intentions. When Mariane explains to her father that she would be lying to say that she loves Tartuffe, Orgon replies stridently: "Mais je veux que cela soit une vérité" (2.1.451) [I want it to be true]. Argan responds similarly to Toinette's protestation that Angélique "n'est point faite pour être Madame Diafoirus": "Et je veux, moi, que cela soit" (1.5)[9] [she's not cut out to be Madame Diafoirus / And I want that to be]. Although the father has, by virtue of his paternity, a certain power over his daughter, that does not suffice. His often repeated "Je veux" is a measure of the intensity of his desire for power. He insists "je veux qu'elle exécute la parole que j'ai donnée" (1.5) [I want her to carry out the promise I've given]. If the servant thinks him incapable of anything so cruel as locking his daughter up in a convent for the rest of her life, she is mistaken: "Ouais! voici qui est plaisant: je ne mettrai pas ma fille dans un couvent, si je veux? (1.5) [Well now! That's a good one! I won't put my daughter in a convent if I want to?]. Flying into a rage at the intervention of Toinette, who speaks of her master's natural goodness, Argan is reminiscent of the Orgon who does not want to be loved (2.2.545): "Je ne suis pas bon, et je suis méchant quand je veux" (1.5) [I am not good, I'm bad when I want to be]. By emphasizing their desire for a power that, as heads of households they already possess, the two men make plain their profound lack of confidence in themselves.[10]

Argan's project to assume an identity that distinguishes him from others and makes of him a superior being originates in his inferiority complex, as his affectation itself, sickness, suggests. Although his illnesses are imaginary, he does suffer from them, and they debilitate him psychologically. He is totally lacking in self-assurance. His certainty that he is sick lifts the veil on his secret vision of himself as inferior. Convinced, albeit wrongly, that his wife, Béline, loves him, he still finds it hard to believe that she could love a man like him: "Voilà une femme qui m'aime . . . cela n'est pas croyable" (2.6) [There's a woman who loves me so . . . It's incredible]. His insecurity is magnified by Béline and Angélique, who resist him, which they would not dare to do were he firmly in command of his household. With so little self-esteem, he hopes to win for himself a place of dominance and superiority in the small world of his family by manipulating the external manifestation of his inner weakness, his imagined ill health.

To consolidate his own superiority, Argan sets out to prove his difference from others. The familial order he has in mind would be based on a hierarchical system of differences with Argan on the highest rung of the ladder. However, his dependence on others constitutes a major impediment to the realization of his vision. No sooner does Argan appear on stage than his desire to be seen by others becomes clear. He is infuriated that his family has abandoned him: "Il n'y a personne: j'ai beau dire, on me laisse toujours seul; il n'y a pas moyen de les arrêter ici" (1.1) [There's nobody here. No matter what I say, they always leave me alone; there's no way to keep them here]. He demands the undivided attention of those around him, and when his servants do not immediately respond to his ring, begins to scream abusively, enraged that they would leave "un pauvre malade tout seul" (1.1) [a poor invalid all alone like this]. Like Pascal's miserable human being, Argan cannot endure solitude, which leaves him bereft of an identity that only others can grant. Contemplating his illness in solitude reduces it to a mere affliction, but in the presence of others, his bad health gives meaning and value to an otherwise purposeless existence. In short, his ill health is his path to distinction.

As so often in Molière's theater, wealth too plays a significant role in the attempts of this rich bourgeois to rise above others. Le Malade imaginaire opens with a comic monologue in which Argan divides his vigilance between money and the medications his pharmacist, Monsieur Fleurant, inflicts upon him.[11] Noticing the high price of one of his treatments, he exclaims: "Ah! Monsieur Fleurant, tout doux, s'il vous plaît; si vous en usez comme cela, on ne voudra plus être malade" (1.1) [Ah! Monsieur Fleurant, gently, if you please; if you treat people like that, they won't want to be sick any more]. Good health cannot be bought, nor does Argan really want to buy it, but surrounding himself with doctors and all their medical paraphernalia has little to do with being cured of illness. For their part, the doctors themselves do not deny their preoccupation with money. Toinette ironically supports Monsieur Diafoirus's complaint that people of high social rank expect their doctors to cure them. "Cela est plaisant," she remarks, "et ils sont bien impertinents de vouloir que vous autres messieurs les guérissiez: vous n'êtes point auprès d'eux pour cela; vous n'y êtes que pour recevoir vos pensions, et leur ordonner des remèdes; c'est à eux à guérir s'ils peuvent" (2.5) [That's a funny one, and they are mighty presumptuous to insist that you gentlemen cure them; you're not there for that; you're there only to receive your fees and prescribe remedies for them; it's up to them to be cured if they can]. Diafoirus responds with a simple "cela est vrai" [That's true]. Obviously, as long as his money holds out, Argan can count on the doctors. Money, moreover, unlike health, is a material, substantial commodity. Argan wants to accumulate it in order to give his life a solidity it lacks. The fortune that Thomas Diafoirus will inherit impresses him as much as the medical skill of his future son-in-law: "Monsieur Diafoirus n'a que ce fils-là pour tout héritier; et, de plus, Monsieur Purgon . . . lui donne tout son bien, en faveur de ce mariage; et Monsieur Purgon est un homme qui a huit mille bonnes livres de rente" (1.5) [Monsieur Diafoirus has only that son for his sole heir, and what's more, Monsieur Purgon . . . will leave him his entire estate in view of this marriage; and Monsieur Purgon is a man who has a good eight thousand francs a year of income]. In the third act, Purgon will break with his patient, and Argan's punishment begins with the loss of what Purgon had promised Diafoirus: "pour finir toute liaison avec vous, voilà la donation que je faisais à mon neveu, en faveur du mariage" (3.5) [to end all dealings with you, here is the donation I was making to my nephew in favor of the marriage]. Money, like the presence of the doctors who take care of him, is a tangible sign of Argan's superiority. Purgon understands instinctively how tightly bound in his patient's mind are money and medicine. To have value, distinctiveness, whether financial or medical, requires recognition by others. Insofar as they serve the same end, Argan confuses in his mind a band of doctors and the great sums of money that permit him to buy their services.

To center his family's attention on himself is for Argan a way to establish his mastery, which, as will become apparent, is his great-est desire. His tone when speaking to his daughter parallels Or-gon's rough treatment of Mariane. Both fathers have the same objective, domination. They want to bring into their families a son-in-law they choose, and they see their demands for their daugh-ters' acquiescence as proof of their own power. Obedience, which ought to be inspired by filial affection, is instead a mark of submis-sion to the tyrannical desire of the father. These overbearing par-ents care little about being loved; they want to rule, absolutely and unchallenged. Like a typical Molière character, Argan reveals his desire without taking full cognizance of the truth he utters. To call himself "maître" when speaking to Toinette in the first act of the play may be little more than a convention of language indicative of their roles.[12] The response that Argan gives later to a question posed by his brother is not:

> BÉRALDE. D'où vient, mon frère, qu'ayant le bien que vous avez, et n'ayant d'enfants qu'une fille . . . que vous parlez de la mettre dans un couvent?
> ARGAN. D'où vient, mon frère, que je suis maître dans ma famille pour faire ce que bon me semble? (3.3)

> [BÉRALDE. How does it happen, brother, that with the money you have, and no children but one daughter . . . that you're talking about put-ting her into a convent?
> ARGAN. How does it happen, brother, that I am master in my family to do what seems good to me?]

Argan could not express his will to power more explicitly.

Medicine and its practitioners open for him the road to suprem-acy. By playing them against the healthy—that is to say, against others in general—Argan means to establish the difference be-tween himself and them so as to institute within the family an order in which he can reign as absolute master. Sickness is a disorder, but, paradoxically, Argan uses it to create order. The role of in-valid seems perfectly adaptable to his quest for an identity that will signify his mastery over his household. Without behaving inhu-manely, after all, the others cannot ignore the plaints of a sick man, especially a sick man who might at any moment die. He must be listened to, cared for, cosseted, and, finally, obeyed. Such is his thinking, in any case. Illness permits Argan to impose his will on his family and to feel assured of his own existence. By distinguish-ing him from others, it furnishes him with a clearly defined iden-tity.

Argan does not stray far from the path already beaten by many characters in Molière's earlier plays.[13] His poor health has the same usefulness that contempt for society's codes of behavior had for Dom Juan, virtue for Alceste, social pretensions for Monsieur Jourdain, or pedantry for Philaminte. All of these characters enlist their obsessions in the struggle to gain superiority over others. The greatest obstacle to their desire for power comes from the hollowness of the human heart, as Pascal has it. They feel the emptiness keenly. Argan can no more find happiness within himself than can other Molière characters. He must search it out elsewhere, as they do, in others' eyes and words. Argan's mania, however, is distinct from theirs in its total inability to bring happiness of any kind. Harpagon can tell himself he will perhaps be happy when he has more money. Nor is it beyond the realm of possibility to think that Monsieur Jourdain might find a degree of contentment were he to attain a higher social rank, and the virtue that Alceste claims to crave has value in itself. Being sick, on the other hand, is unlikely to result in anything positive. Thus, in this, his last play, Molière shows more explicitly and definitively than in his earlier works that his characters' obsessions are but pretexts to hide a profound desire for self-affirmation through the domination of others.

In the final analysis, personal superiority in Molière's plays is almost always built upon nothing more substantial than the recognition others grant. If characters are to experience the feeling of superiority so necessary to their sense of self, others must affirm it by their recognition. The natural resistance of those others both fascinates and intrigues. It also creates rivalry between characters that is the source of a disorder threatening their world.[14] Orgon competes for control with the members of his family and even, toward the end of the play, with Tartuffe himself. Dom Juan, though superior to the likes of Pierrot, becomes the peasant's rival. In *Le Misanthrope*, Alceste vies with others in the domains of love, virtue, literature, and the law. To avoid the disorder that stems from rivalry, the character guilty of introducing it must be neutralized. Someone must be sacrificed; someone must serve as the scapegoat.[15]

In *Le Malade imaginaire*, the illness on which Argan counts to distinguish himself compels him to live a life of contradiction, as Toinette's description of her master suggests: "Il marche, dort, mange, et boit tout comme les autres; mais cela n'empêche pas qu'il ne soit fort malade" (2.2) [He walks, sleeps, eats, and drinks just like anyone else; but that doesn't keep him from being very sick]. He is sick, but he is not sick. Although his sickness makes him different from everyone else, he behaves "tout comme les autres." Not surprisingly, therefore, Toinette must remind Argan, as he leaves the stage, that he is sick and cannot "marcher sans bâton" (3.1) [walk without a stick]. Béralde, in the same act, turns his brother's supposed illness against him. The proof that Argan is, in fact, a quite healthy specimen "c'est qu'avec tous les soins que vous avez pris, vous n'avez pas pu parvenir encore à gâter la bonté de votre tempérament, et que vous n'êtes point crevé de toutes les médecines qu'on vous a fait prendre" (3.3) [is that with all the cares you have taken you haven't yet succeeded in ruining the sound-ness of your system, and that you haven't burst with all the medi-cines they've had you take]. Argan can do whatever he wants to distinguish himself from others, he always ends by resembling them. His treatments have an effect antithetical to that intended: they demonstrate the good health that he shares with those to whom he would be superior through bad health. The difference between Argan and the other members of his family is not accentu-ated. It is erased.

Medicine and doctors actually prevent the imaginary invalid from accomplishing what he sets out to do. If medicine can give Argan a kind of prestige, it also has the contrary quality of blurring distinctions. Before the Diafoiruses, father and son, leave his house, Argan asks them to tell him "un peu comment je suis" (2.6) [how I am]. Thomas's diagnosis is peremptory: his future father-in-law has "le pouls d'un homme qui ne se porte point bien" [the pulse of a man who is not well], a sign of an "intempérie dans le *parenchyme splénique*, c'est-à-dire la rate" (2.6) [an intemperance in the splenic parenchyma, that is to say the spleen]. The dialogue that follows shows how medicine, which in Argan's eyes should make him different, acts instead to level difference:

ARGAN. Non: Monsieur Purgon dit que c'est mon foie qui est malade.
MONSIEUR DIAFOIRUS. Eh! oui: qui dit *parenchyme*, dit l'un et l'autre, à cause de l'étroite sympathie qu'ils ont ensemble. . . . Il vous ordonne sans doute de manger force rôti?
ARGAN. Non, rien que du bouilli.
MONSIEUR DIAFOIRUS. Eh! oui: rôti, bouilli, même chose. (2.6)

[ARGAN. No. Monsieur Purgon says it's my liver that's sick.
MONSIEUR DIAFOIRUS. Oh, yes! If anyone says *parenchyma*, he says both, because of the close sympathy they have with each other . . . No doubt he orders you to eat a lot of roast meat?
ARGAN. No, nothing but boiled.
MONSIEUR DIAFOIRUS. Oh, yes! Roast, boiled, all the same thing.]

By repeating the words "Eh! Oui" before each negation of a self-evident distinction, Molière comically underscores medicine's refusal to distinguish even between completely different things. Argan says "non" and the doctor says "oui," but medicine's "oui" only confirms the doctors' tendency to obscure differences. When Toinette disguises herself as a doctor, she picks up on this characteristic of medicine by attributing all of Argan's symptoms—whether those associated with his liver or his spleen, his eyes or his stomach—to his lung (3.10). The laughter in this scene is the laughter of a writer who fully understands his protagonist's turn of mind, who wants comic doctors to cure rather than encourage their patient and to cure not with medicine but with ridicule.

The rivalry so typical of Argan's way of relating to others extends to his relations with his doctors. From his first monologue, Argan, although intimidated by the doctors and their allies, the apothecaries, nevertheless threatens Fleurant with the loss of a profitable patient. Argan wants the doctors to recognize his individual worth, but the individuality he hopes to acquire by the agency of medicine is denied from the moment he finds himself in their company. When Monsieur Diafoirus comes to introduce his son to Argan, a dialogue of the deaf ensues between the imaginary invalid and Thomas's father:

> ARGAN. Je reçois, Monsieur . . .
> MONSIEUR DIAFOIRUS. Nous venons ici, Monsieur . . .
> ARGAN. Avec beaucoup de joie . . .
> MONSIEUR DIAFOIRUS. Mon fils Thomas, et moi. . . . (2.5)

> [ARGAN. Sir, I receive . . .
> MONSIEUR DIAFOIRUS. We come here, sir . . .
> ARGAN. With great joy . . .
> MONSIEUR DIAFOIRUS. My son Thomas and I . . .]

Stage directions for the scene suggest that Argan loses his individuality as his voice and that of Monsieur Diafoirus blend together in cacophony: "Ils parlent tous deux en même temps, s'interrompent et confondent" (2.5)[16] [They both speak at the same time, interrupting each other]. Their entangled speeches make it difficult, if not impossible, to sort out what they are trying to say. Each hopes to impress the other by his politeness, but they end up merging in a single gush of babble into one ridiculous entity.

In his attitude toward his family, Argan sounds very much like Purgon. Before understanding that he intends to marry her off to

Thomas Diafoirus, Angélique tries to please her father, and Argan allows that "Je suis bien aise d'avoir une fille si obéissante" (1.5) [I'm very glad to have such an obedient daughter]. In point of fact, he exacts this obedience from her. Purgon is no different. He expects his patients to submit to the will of their doctor and refuses to continue to care for Argan, "[p]uisque vous vous êtes soustrait de l'obéisssance que l'on doit à son médecin" (3.5) [(s)ince you absconded from the obedience that a man owes to his doctor]. Purgon and his patient, identical in their desire for control, often speak the same language. When Béralde proposes that his brother stop dwelling on his own condition and distract himself with Molière's comedy, Argan damns the author as "un bon impertinent" [a really impertinent fellow] and imagines himself in the role of an avenging doctor who would extract the appropriate punishment for Molière's insolence: "si j'étais que des médecins, je me vengerais de son impertinence; et quand il sera malade, je le laisserait mourir sans secours. . . . et je lui dirais: 'Crève, crève! cela t'apprendra une autre fois à te jouer à la Faculté'" (3.3) [If I were a doctor, I'd take revenge on his impertinence; and when he's sick, I'd let him die without any help. . . . and I'd say to him: "Croak! Croak! That'll teach you another time to make fun of the Faculty of Medicine!"]. Not long after, Purgon, in his turn, denounces Argan with a condemnation identical to the attack of the imaginary invalid against Molière. Argan identifies with his doctor in order to be different from those who challenge medicine, but contrary to his expectations—though clearly not to the expectations of those who, unlike him, appreciate Molière—his individuality evaporates in that identification.[17]

Without knowing it, Argan undergoes an identity crisis, causing the good order of his family to unravel. His madness prevents the natural course of events. Nothing could be more in conformity with nature than Angélique's love for Cléante, which cannot progress normally toward marriage, as it ought. Argan's passion for medicine and for doctors places an immovable obstacle in love's path. According to Béralde, confidence in medicine is misplaced, even in the face of illness: "Il ne faut que demeurer en repos. La nature, d'elle-même, quand nous la laissons faire, se tire doucement du désordre où elle est tombée" (3.3) [All you have to do is rest. Nature, by herself, when we let her be, gently makes her way out of the disorder into which she has fallen]. Order is a beneficent law of nature applicable to life in general as to matters of health. Yet all of Argan's actions run counter to it. He sows turmoil in his family, which falls into a dysfunctional state. One of his daughters is obliged to feign death to protect herself against her father, and venality weighs on the whole household. Béline, the doctors, and even, from time to time, Argan himself show as much or more interest in money as in the well-being of the family. Disorder smolders just below the surface and moral deterioration testifies to it.

In play after play, Molière demonstrates that despite the flaws of characters who almost never cast off their imperfections, order can be restored, if only temporarily and within the strict confines of the play's conclusion. The vital principle of comedy followed here is, as Jacques Guicharnaud puts it, "le triomphe nécessaire de l'ordre sur la corruption assuré par des moyens non héroïques"[18] [the necessary triumph of order over corruption ensured by non-heroic means]. In short, order triumphs in the very midst of corruption, but for that to happen, the perpetrator of disorder must be rendered ineffective. Thus, George Dandin is sacrificed in an atmosphere of cruelty and violence; an unrepentant Dom Juan descends into hell; and Tartuffe is escorted to prison. Violence counters violence to reestablish order without the characters' having to change in a fundamental way. For Monsieur Jourdain, Molière chooses an equally efficacious though less harsh and more comic method of expulsion,[19] but the result is the same, the chosen victim is ousted, if only in the imagination, from the community he has disrupted. In *Le Malade imaginaire*, with an eye no doubt on the scapegoat mechanism that had served so well against disorder in his earlier plays, Molière has Argan's family call upon comedy itself to cure the invalid of his imagined illness by administering to him an inoculation, a weakened, less active dose of the very illness from which he suffers.

In Harold Knutson's view, Béline is "the true scapegoat of *Le Malade imaginaire*."[20] By her expression of joy and avarice at the sight of her supposedly dead husband, she lowers herself to the level of a frightful shrew. She leaves the stage debased, her power in the house nullified. Argan realizes at last that his wife's corrupt character justifies Béralde's negative opinion of her. Her defeat changes nothing essential, even temporarily, in the circumstances of the family. Argan remains as attached as ever to his obsession, and his daughter still refuses to obey him. If the goal of the scapegoat's expulsion is to restore order to the family, Béline as sacrificial victim fails. Eliminating her might rid the family of avarice, but that is not the major illness from which it suffers.

The character who ought logically be the object of an exorcism is Argan. Indeed, Purgon does condemn him to death for not having

followed the prescribed regimen of enemas. The mere pronounce-
ment has its effect on a terrified Argan who cries out, "Ah, mon
Dieu! je suis mort" (3.6) [Oh, good Lord! I'm a dead man]. When
Toinette assumes the role of a "médecin passager" [traveling doc-
tor], who seeks out only "des maladies d'importance" (3.10) [im-
portant illnesses], she ends her visit to the imaginary invalid by
suggesting that her new patient have one of his arms cut off and
one eye put out so as not to limit nourishment to the other one,
its rival for food. This satirical prescription for improving Argan's
health resonates with the ritual mutilation of a scapegoat or *sparagmos* and also reminds the audience, however comically, that rivalry
leads inevitably to violence.[21] Medicine, with which Argan has always collaborated, becomes a ferocious adversary. Molière has already shown the close resemblance between Argan and Purgon; he
now puts on display the violence that typically follows upon rivalry
in so much of his work. In these scenes, he places in full view the
violence inherent in the scapegoat mechanism. Ridicule is his in-
strument, but the laughter he provokes has meaningful implications for his audience. If, in some of his earlier works, the violence
of an exorcism put an end to the violence between rivals, in his
last play, Molière looks to another way—comedy—to exorcise the
demon and reestablish order.

The malady from which Argan suffers is, according to Béralde,
"la maladie des médecins" (3.4) [the malady of doctors], and its
cure is a vaccination composed of the same virus. Argan will be im-
munized against doctors by becoming a doctor himself: "Voilà le
vrai moyen de vous guérir bientôt; il n'y a point de maladie si osée,
que de se jouer à la personne d'un médecin" (3.14) [That's the real
way to get well soon; and there is no illness so daring as to trifle
with the person of a doctor]. This treatment is less painful but
structurally similar to the banishment of a scapegoat. René Girard
compares vaccination and Purgon's enemas with certain rites of
purification, including that of the *pharmakos* punished:

L'opération bénéfique est toujours conçue sur le mode de l'invasion
repoussée, de l'intrus maléfique chassé hors de la place. . . . L'intervention médicale consiste à inoculer "un peu" de la maladie, exactement
comme les rites qui injectent "un peu" de violence dans le corps social
pour le rendre capable de résister à la violence.[22]

[The benefic operation is always conceived of as a kind of invasion re-
pelled, an evil intruder chased away. . . . Medical intervention consists
of inoculating with "a little" of the illness to be cured, just like those

rites that inject "a little" violence into the social body in order to make
it capable of resisting violence.]

Laughter replaces violence as the constitutive element in the vaccine that restores Argan's health and acts to reestablish order in
the family. Although Argan "fasse le premier personnage" [play(s)
the leading part] in the curative *divertissement* (3.14), everybody is
inoculated in the little comedy in which all play a role: "Nous y
pouvons aussi prendre chacun un personnage, et nous donner
ainsi la comédie les uns aux autres" (3.14) [We can also each of us
take a part, and thus put on a comedy for one another]. Without
everyone's participation, there can be no recovery of order. Disorder is a social illness; its cure must be social as well. Comedy, "une
cérémonie burlesque d'un homme qu'on fait médecin en récit,
chant, et danse" (3.14) [a burlesque, with recitative, song, and
dance, of the conferral of the degree of Doctor of Medicine on a
candidate (a Bachelor) by the Faculty], is a regulated disorder that
drives out real disorder. Disguised as a doctor, Argan becomes, for
just a moment and under tightly controlled circumstances, the
doctor who had previously been his master and rival, and this
without wreaking the chaos that such a loss of identity usually
holds in store.

    Comedy's role in the resolution of Argan's identity crisis cannot
be exaggerated. The love of Angélique and Cléante wins out in the
end, but comedy as much as love, Philip R. Berk remarks, is "responsible for defeating the professional schemes of the doctors to
subjugate Argan and Argan's own tyrannical fiction of ill health."[23]
Molière sees in his comic art the capacity that sacrificial rites once
had. When Argan refuses to go to a Molière play, Béralde arranges
to make his brother an actor in another comedy. Béralde must be
taken seriously when he says that in his play, everyone, rather than
duping Argan, will "s'accommoder à ses fantaisies" (3.14) [(be) ac-
commodating ourselves to his fancies]. To cure his brother, Béralde seizes upon those "fantaisies" and manipulates them
skillfully. He understands that Argan's imaginary illness has a quite
real dimension. Argan may not be physically ill, but his desire to
be different and superior to others and his identification with doctors are not for that any the less destructive. Society must protect
itself against Argan's sickness despite its imaginary character, and
comedy is the vaccine of choice.

    The imagination, which Pascal calls "cette maîtresse d'erreur et
de fausseté" (fragment 82) [this mistress of error and falsehood], is

at the root of much of the action in Molière's last play.[24] Critics have often commented that Argan does not change, even after having discovered his wife's perversity and the essential goodness of the daughter who disobeys him. He retains his belief in medicine and orders Cléante to become a doctor before marrying Angélique. Nor does his attachment to money lessen. Béralde understands this as he reassures his brother that becoming a doctor "ne vous coûtera rien" (3.14) [It won't cost you a thing]. The power of Argan's imaginary illness calls to mind Pascal's texts on the imagination, "[c]ette superbe puissance, ennemie de la raison qui se plaît à la contrôler et à la dominer" (fragment 82)[25] [this haughty power, the enemy of reason, that takes pleasure in controlling and dominating reason]. Doctors, who have grasped this truth, derive their power from a costume that speaks to the imagination of their patients. Pascal calls the mask that doctors wear "cette montre si authentique" (fragment 82).[26] His tone in this passage is at once ironic and serious, for even though the doctors' power is based only on appearances, people need doctors. Pascal condemns the contrivances of the imagination while recognizing that human beings cannot live without the imaginary. They must somehow escape the feeling of their own emptiness, whose most striking and disturbing image is death. Argan's illness is a diversion that permits him to close his eyes to his greatest fear, death.[27]

Le Malade imaginaire begins and ends with death. At the conclusion of his long opening monologue, Argan exposes his real fear in a desperate, comic cry: "ah, mon Dieu! ils me laisseront ici mourir" (1.1)[28] [oh, good Lord! They're going to leave me here to die]. Death is mentioned in the play more than sixty times,[29] and the final word uttered on stage is a salutation in macaronic Latin to the newly initiated doctor: "Et seignet et tuat!" (Troisième Intermède) [Et bleedet et killat!]. The use of words like "tuat" and "occidendi" in the play's conclusion and the hasty departure of Toinette in her doctor's outfit to attend "une grande consultation qui se doit faire pour un homme qui mourut hier" (3.10) [a big consultation to be held for a man who died yesterday] tie the practice of medicine to death. To consult a doctor is to play with death. Béralde does not question Purgon's good faith. On the contrary, he explains to his brother, "c'est un homme tout médecin, depuis la tête jusqu'aux pieds; un homme qui croit à ses règles plus qu'à toutes les démonstrations des mathématiques, et qui croirait du crime à les vouloir examiner . . . c'est de la meilleure foi du monde qu'il vous expédiera" (3.3) [he's a man who's all doctor, from head to foot, a man who believes in his rules more than all the demonstrations of math-

ematics, and who would think it a crime to want to examine them
. . . it's in the best faith in the world that he'll expedite you]. The
doctor's role is to help his patient die more easily, more surely, in
a better state of health. Argan is no less terrified by death than Pascal's human beings, but his fear comes out in an obsessive, comic
way. Death hangs over and haunts him. Louison, his younger
daughter, pretends to be dead to escape her father's whipping,
and Purgon pronounces a death sentence upon him.[30] Twice in
succession, Argan encounters death by imitating it. In these two
scenes, death is, for a very short time, brought to heel. To fake
death is a way of reassuring oneself against its power. It goes without saying, though, that the Argan who rises from his "death bed"
remains fearful of death. He redirects his thoughts away from it by
his continued insistence on bringing a doctor into his family.
Death, of course, stays on the prowl no matter what Argan does.[31]

By playing with death, Argan tries to neutralize it, which explains his lack of fear when he plays dead. Comedy domesticates
noxious forces by integrating them into quotidian life, rendering
them commonplace. A small dose of medicine cures the sickness of
medicine for a short time and "a little bit" of death has the same
passing effect upon the fear of dying. What Molière portrays in *Le
Malade imaginaire* is the necessarily temporary character of such a
cure. Argan's secret desire not to die is utterly fanciful. By forget-
ting that Orgon does not really change, it might be possible to
imagine that the order restored by Tartuffe's expulsion could endure, but Argan's "cure," given the nature of his illness, must be
ephemeral. It is impossible to escape death. At the end of *Le Malade
imaginaire*, as in most comedy, order is restored, but this time it is
necessarily and explicitly short-lived. The fixity represented by a
permanent order that Argan seeks cannot be realized. Pascal experiences the impossibility of finding "une assiette ferme, et une dernière base constante" (fragment 72) [a firm, stable position and an
ultimate, unchanging foundation] as a source of anguish.[32] Molière, who contemplates the same truth at the moment of his death,
makes of it a subject of comedy. The search for some stable, fixed
order animates much of the theater of Molière, who shares with
Pascal a sense of the impossibility of permanence. The great genius
of *Le Malade imaginaire* is to strip away all illusions and speak this
sad truth with a laughter devoid of bitterness.

Notes

INTRODUCTION

1. Antoine Adam, *Histoire de la littérature française au XVIIe siècle*, 5 vols. (Paris: del Duca, 1948–56), 5:105. Hereafter cited as *Histoire*.

2. Paul Hazard, *La crise de la conscience européenne 1680–1715*, 3 vols. (Paris: Boivin, 1935), 1:265. The source of the translations of passages from Hazard's work is Paul Hazard, *The European Mind (1680–1715)*, trans. J. Lewis May (London: Hollis & Carter, 1953).

3. Ibid., 1:265.

4. Ibid., 1:283.

5. Jacques Bénigne Bossuet, *Maximes et réflexions sur la comédie*, in *Oeuvres complètes*, ed. F. Lachat (Paris: Louis Vivès, 1875), 27:27.

6. Larry Riggs, "Intimations of Post-Structuralism: Subversion of the Classicist Subject in *Les Femmes savantes* and *Le Tartuffe*," *Literature, Interpretation, Theory* 2 (1990): 62.

7. Ibid.

8. Larry Riggs, "Reason's Text as Palimpsest: Sensuality Subverts 'Sense' in Molière's *Les Femmes savantes*," *Papers on French Seventeenth Century Literature* 28 (2001): 99, 96.

9. Larry Riggs, "Molière, Paranoia, and the Presence of Absence," *Cahiers du Dix-Septième* 6 (1992): 205.

10. Paul Bénichou, *Morales du grand siècle* (Paris: Gallimard, 1948), 159.

11. Ibid., 160.

CHAPTER 1. LOVE AND RIVALRY

1. Speaking of Molière's earliest works, Joseph Pineau refers to jealousy as an aspect of "ce qui ne tardera pas à s'épanouir dans les oeuvres de leur auteur" (*Le Théâtre de Molière: une dynamique de la liberté* [Paris: Minard, 2000], 12) [what will not be long in blossoming in their author's work].

2. In his edition of Molière, Georges Couton enumerates the lines from *Dom Garcie de Navarre* that reappear in 4.2 and 4.3 of *Le Misanthrope*. (Molière, *Oeuvres complètes*, ed. Georges Couton, 2 vols. [Paris: Gallimard, 1971], 2:1342). All further references to material from this edition, other than Molière's plays, will be indicated by the letters *OC*, followed by volume and page numbers. References for citations from this edition will appear in the text. Marcel Gutwirth gives a complete list of the borrowings from *Dom Garcie de Navarre* ("*Dom Garcie de Navarre* et *Le Misanthrope*: de la comédie héroïque au comique du héros," *PMLA* 83 [1968]: 125 n. 16).

3. The source of translations of passages from *Le Misanthrope* is Molière, *The Misanthrope, Tartuffe, and Other Plays*, trans. Maya Slater (Oxford: Oxford University Press, 2001). Reprinted by permission of Oxford University Press.

4. All translations of lines from *Dom Garcie de Navarre* are by the author.

5. In a telling essay on the rage of Molière's characters, Louise Horowitz asserts: "And power—who's got it—is what Molière's theater is about" ("Life in the Slow Lane: Molière's Marginal Men," *Papers on French Seventeenth Century Literature* 16 [1989]: 74).

6. Alceste's "coeur" is like everything else about him. As Lionel Gossman says, "'Je veux' is never far from his lips" (*Men and Masks* [Baltimore: Johns Hopkins University Press, 1963], 67). According to Jules Brody, "Alceste aspires to the exclusive possession of Célimène, who is sought after by all men" ("*Dom Juan* and *Le Misanthrope*, or the Esthetics of Individualism in Molière," *PMLA* 84 [1969]: 574) (Hereafter cited as "*Dom Juan* and *Le Misanthrope*").

7. Marcel Gutwirth dismisses those critics for whom these lines reveal Alceste as a great egotist and characterizes what he says here as little more than the utopian dream of all couples in love from time immemorial ("Visages d'Alceste," *Oeuvres et critiques* 6 [1981]: 84). These lines, however, are not the only ones in which Alceste displays such self-centeredness.

8. Analyzing this same passage, Lionel Gossman notes that "the language he [Alceste] speaks is the language of power, not the language of love" (*Men and Masks*, 74).

9. Descartes makes the distinction in *Les Passions de l'âme*: "Et on mesprise un homme qui est jaloux de sa femme, pource que c'est un tesmoignage qu'il ne l'ayme pas de la bonne sorte. . . . Je dis qu'il ne l'ayme de la bonne sorte: car s'il avoit une vraye Amour pour elle, il n'auroit aucune inclination à s'en defier" (*Les Passions de l'âme*, ed. Geneviève Rodis-Lewis [Paris: Librairie Philosophique J. Vrin, 1955], 189) [And we hold in contempt a man who is jealous of his wife, because this is an indication that he does not love her in the right way. . . . I say that he does not love her in the right way, because if he had a true love for her, he would not be inclined to distrust her].

10. Célimène also tells Alceste that "vous ne m'aimez pas comme il faut que l'on aime" (4.3.1421) [you don't care for me as you should].

11. René Girard, "Perilous Balance: A Comic Hypothesis," in *"To Double Business Bound": Essays on Literature, Myth, Mimesis and Anthropology* (Baltimore: Johns Hopkins University Press, 1978), 129. In the same essay, Girard contends that "Molière's laughter is anti-Cartesian, because it reveals as false the pretensions of Descartes's *cogito*" (133).

12. *Men and Masks*, 73–79.

13. Not only are Célimène and Arsinoé like each other in their indirect approach. They also resemble Alceste in his criticism of Oronte's sonnet (Brody, "*Dom Juan* and *Le Misanthrope*," 572).

14. Arsinoé begins her attack with "Hier j'étais chez des gens de vertu singulière, / Où sur vous du discours on tourna la matière" (3.4.885–86) [Some people I met yesterday, all most upright, / Began to talk of you, and were less than polite]. Célimène follows with the claim of a similar experience: "En un lieu l'autre jour, où je faisais visite, / Je trouvai quelques gens d'un très rare mérite" (3.4.921–22) [The other day, as I was visiting somewhere, / I met some very worthy people gathered there] who "Firent tomber sur vous, Madame, l'entretien" (3.4.924) [And then, Madame, the conversation turned to you].

15. The only difference between this passage and the conclusion of Céli-

mène's speech (3.4.957–60) is in their first lines. Célimène begins: "Madame, je vous crois aussi trop raisonnable" (3.4.957) [Madame, I know for sure you're much too sensible].

16. René Jasinski puts it this way: "Ainsi les deux caractères s'éclairent l'un par l'autre dans leurs plus secrètes profondeurs. D'où la portée de la prodigieuse scène où ils s'affrontent. La coquette et la prude y échangent leurs vérités" (*Molière et* Le Misanthrope [Paris: Nizet, 1970], 218–19) [Thus these two characters shed light on each other's innermost depths. Whence the impact of the wonderful scene in which they insult each other. The coquette and the prude exchange truths in that scene]. According to Roxanne Lalande, "Arsinoé's thinly veiled attack and Célimène's hostile reply are symmetrically inverted reflections of one another" (*Intruders in the Play World: The Dynamics of Gender in Molière's Comedies* [Madison: Fairleigh Dickinson University Press, 1996], 161).

17. *Molière et* Le Misanthrope, 219.

18. Jean Jacques Rousseau, *Lettre à Mr. d'Alembert sur les spectacles*, ed. M. Fuchs (Lille: Giard; Geneva: Droz, 1948), 48. Page references for citations from this work will appear in the text. Translations of citations from Rousseau are by the author.

19. That play too begins with a heated discussion between two men, the brothers Ariste and Sganarelle, about the extent to which individuals should accommodate themselves to society. Their difference of opinion is more frivolous; it centers on clothing rather than virtue. Ariste, clearly the wiser of the brothers, takes a stand close to Philinte's:

> Mais je tiens qu'il est mal, sur quoi que l'on se fonde,
> Du fuir obstinément ce que suit tout le monde,
> Et qu'il vaut mieux souffrir d'être au nombre des fous,
> Que du sage parti se voir seul contre tous.

(1.1.51–54)

> [But I maintain no reason makes it right
> To shun accepted ways from stubborn spite;
> And we may better join the foolish crowd
> Than cling to wisdom, lonely though unbowed.]

This translation is from Molière, Tartuffe *and Other Plays by Molière*, trans. Donald M. Frame (New York: New American Library, 1967).

20. Marie-Odile Sweetser, "Théâtre du monde et monde du théâtre: *Le Misanthrope*," *Le Moliériste* 3 (1996–97): 70.

21. Marie-Odile Sweetser points out that Alceste and Célimène resemble other characters: "Si Alceste et Célimène diffèrent des autres par leur idéal, ils leur ressemblent étrangement par leurs instincts et par leur conduite" ("Structures et signification du *Misanthrope*," *French Review* 49 [1976]: 512) [If Alceste and Célimène differ from others in their sense of the ideal, in their instincts and their behavior, they strangely resemble others].

22. Pierre Force, *Molière ou le prix des choses: morale, économie et comédie* (Paris: Nathan, 1994), 164.

23. A number of critics have recognized this identity. Citing the same lines, Max Vernet attributes the resemblance of Alceste and Oronte to the strategy Célimène employs with them (*Molière: côté jardin, côté cour* [Paris: Nizet, 1991], 224). Jacques Guicharnaud refers to "le parallélisme entre l'attitude d'Oronte et celle d'Alceste, chacun ayant les mêmes exigences que l'autre" (*Molière: une aventure*

théâtrale [Paris: Gallimard, 1963], 465) [the parallelism between the attitude of Oronte and that of Alceste, each making the same demands as the other]. Lionel Gossman speaks of "the underlying similarity of Alceste and Oronte" (*Men and Masks*, 89), and for Larry Riggs, "Oronte . . . is not merely Alceste's rival for Célimène: he is his *double*" ("Another Purloined Letter: Text Transparency, and Transcendence in *Le Misanthrope*," *French Review* 66 [1992]: 33).

24. Célimène also reminds one of Dom Juan when she asks Alceste, "Des amants que je fais me rendez-vous coupable? / Puis-je empêcher les gens de me trouver aimable?" (2.1.462) [Is it my fault if people fall in love with me? / Am I responsible? It's not that I agree / To welcome them]. Like the don with Monsieur Dimanche, she invites Arsinoé to have a seat (3.4.878). Jacques Guicharnaud compares Alceste and Oronte to Charlotte and Mathurine trying unsuccessfully to force Dom Juan to say which of them he will marry (*Molière: une aventure théâtrale*, 466).

25. *Men and Masks*, 78.

26. Jules Brody maintains that the characters in *Le Misanthrope* resemble each other more in what they desire than those in any of Molière's other plays. Alceste is just like everyone else—except Philinte and Eliante, in Brody's view—in his "pursuit of preference" ("*Dom Juan* and *Le Misanthrope*," 570).

Chapter 2. Power and Identity

1. See Jacques Truchet's short but useful biographical note on Donneau de Visé in Jacques Scherer and Jacques Truchet, eds., *Théâtre du XVIIᵉ siècle*, 2 vols. (Paris: Gallimard, 1975–86), 2:1561–62. Raymond Picard characterizes Donneau de Visé as "toujours prêt à mettre les idées les plus stupides en phrases éloquentes" (*La Carrière de Jean Racine* [Paris: Gallimard, 1961], 292) [always ready to express the most stupid ideas in eloquent sentences]. Georges Couton reproduces the fragments of Donneau de Visé's work most directly related to the quarrel surrounding *L'Ecole des femmes* (*OC* 1:1015–49, 1094–1113).

2. Jean de La Bruyère, *Les Caractères ou les moeurs de ce siècle*, ed. Robert Garapon (Paris: Garnier, 1962), 83. The source of translations of passages from the *Caractères* is Jean de La Bruyère, *Characters*, trans. Henri van Laun (London: Oxford University Press, 1963).

3. All that remains of the "chanson" is what was probably a refrain:

> Coquille, dit-il, si belle et si grande,
> N'accommode pas mon limaçon.
> Coquille, dit-il, si belle et si grande,
> Demande un plus gros poisson.

(OC 1:1386)

> [The shell, he says, so beautful and so large,
> Does not suit my snail,
> The shell, he said, so beautiful and so large,
> Wants a bigger fish.]

See also Antoine Adam's discussion of the "chanson" (*Histoire*, 3:290–91). Curiously, despite his opposition to Molière in the quarrel over *L'Ecole des femmes*, Donneau de Visé appears to have developed, in the end, an amicable relationship with Molière, who produced a number of his plays.

4. "D'abord ce jeune étourdi peut bien, quoique imprudemment, par une démangeaison de découvrir sa bonne fortune, raconter à Arnolphe les premiers succès de son amour; mais la froideur avec laquelle ce jaloux l'écoute devrait l'empêcher d'y revenir: cependant il y revient jusques à cinq ou six fois, bien qu'Arnolphe lui fasse toujours un accueil si froid que, lorsqu'il le vient trouver dans la sixème scène du quatrième acte, il lui dit jusques à quarante vers, et s'en retourne ensuite, sans avoir tiré de lui une seule parole, ce qui le rend ridicule, aussi bien qu'Arnolphe" (*OC* 1:1028) [At first, this young scatterbrain, itching to disclose his good fortune, might indeed, although imprudently, tell Arnolphe about his early successes in love; but the chilliness with which the jealous Arnolphe hears him out ought to prevent him from bringing up the subject again. However, he does just that five or six times, even though Arnolphe greets his stories so coldly that when Horace finds him in the sixth scene of the fourth act, speaks about forty lines to him, and leaves without Arnolphe's having spoken a word, both men appear to be ridiculous].

5. Unless otherwise indicated, the source of translations of passages from *L'Ecole des femmes* is Molière, The Misanthrope, Tartuffe, *and Other Plays*, trans. Maya Slater (Oxford: Oxford University Press, 2001). Reprinted by permission of Oxford University Press.

6. As Ralph Albanese puts it, Arnolphe "brûle de se montrer supérieur à autrui, de se faire reconnaître comme unique" (*Le Dynamisme de la peur chez Molière: une analyse socio-culturelle de "Dom Juan," "Tartuffe," et "L'Ecole des femmes"* [University, Mississippi: Romance Monographs, Inc., 1976], 147) [is burning to show himself superior to others, to have himself recognized by them as unique].

7. Marcel Gutwirth, *Molière ou l'invention comique* (Paris: Minard, 1966), 93.

8. James F. Gaines, "L'Eveil des sentiments et le paradoxe de la conscience dans *L'Ecole des femmes*," *French Review* 70 (1997): 409.

9. *Molière: côté jardin, côté cour*, 82.

10. Antoine Furetière, *Dictionnaire universel*, 3 vols. (The Hague: Arnout & Reinier Lers, 1690; reprint, Geneva: Slatkine Reprints, 1970), 2:no pag.

11. "*Sot* signifie aussi un cocu, un cornard, le mari d'une femme dissoluë ou infidelle" (ibid., 3:no pag.) [*Sot* also means a cuckold, a person with horns, the husband of a dissolute or unfaithful wife].

12. From different perspectives, Marie-Odile Sweetser ("La Nature et le naturel chez Molière: le cas d'Agnès," in *Thèmes et genres littéraires aux XVIIe et XVIIIe siècles. Mélanges en l'honneur de Jacques Truchet*, ed. Nicole Ferrier Caverivière [Paris: Presses Universitaires de France, 1992], 443–49) and Max Vernet (*Molière: côté jardin, côté cour*) discuss the important function of nature and *le naturel* in the play.

13. Arnolphe's near-obsession with honor supports Serge Doubrovsky's conviction that "Arnolphe tente de prendre l'attitude du héros cornélien" ("Arnolphe ou la chute du héros," *Mercure de France* 343 [1961]: 111) [Arnolphe attempts to adopt the attitude of a hero like those of Corneille].

14. In response to Chrysalde's expression of concern about his friend's marrying and risking cuckoldry, Arnolphe pointedly suggests that all may not be well in Chrysalde's household: "Il est vrai, notre ami. Peut-être que chez vous / Vous trouvez des sujets de craindre pour chez nous" (1.1.9–10) [My friend, you're very nervous. What you say is true / In some cases—not mine. It may apply to you].

15. Translation from Molière, *One-act Comedies of Molière*, trans. Albert Bermel (Cleveland: World Publishing Company, 1962), 93.

16. See Vernet, *Molière: côté jardin, côté cour*, 131.

17. In his chapter on *L'Ecole des femmes,* Judd Hubert speaks of a tragic side to Arnolphe's suffering (*Molière and the Comedy of Intellect* [Berkeley and Los Angeles: University of California Press, 1962], 66–85).

18. Arnolphe has six monologues in the course of the play. Bernard Magné correctly reads Arnolphe as a character who dominates others by using language as his cudgel ("*L'Ecole des femmes* ou la conquête de la parole," *Revue des Sciences Humaines* 145 [1972]: 125–40).

19. To emphasize how long he has spent in this effort, Arnolphe repeats the number of years (4.7.1188, 1202). Pierre Force sees in Arnolphe's "vingt ans et plus de méditation" (4.7.1202) [twenty years and more of meditation] (Translation by author) a "point de rencontre entre Descartes et les personnages philosophes de Molière" [a ground on which Descartes and Molière's "philosophers" meet] in that both are "spectateurs plutôt qu'acteurs" (*Molière ou le prix des choses,* 40) [spectators rather than actors].

20. Ralph Albanese makes clear that Arnolphe "est avant tout soucieux de garder intacte l'unicité de son moi. Il s'aperçoit de sa singularité irréductible par rapport à autrui à tel point qu'il en vient à croire que le cocuage entraîne nécessairement, la corruption de son être: en un mot être cocu = être comme autrui" (*Le Dynamisme de la peur,* 147) [is above all concerned to keep the oneness of his self intact. He is so conscious of his irreducible singularity in relation to other people that he comes to believe that cuckoldry will necessarily bring about the dissolution of his own being. In a word, to be a cuckold = to be like others].

21. Patrick Dandrey holds that Molière's characters, "leurs désirs résultant de la contagion de ceux d'autrui . . . se trouvent souvent aspirer à des biens qui leur conviennent mal" [since their desires are infected by those of other people . . . often want things that are, in fact, bad for them]. He goes on to analyze Arnolphe's relationship with Agnès as an example of this kind of desire: "le risque de la voir prise par un autre qui l'aime et qu'elle aime aiguise l'affectivité du barbon, le convertit à la passion comme par contagion, il aspire à ce bien qu'il voit obtenu par un autre, tente d'imiter le blondin . . . et échoue lamentablement" (*Molière ou l'esthétique du ridicule* [Paris: Klincksieck, 1992], 368) [the risk of seeing her taken by another man who loves her and whom she loves sharpens the old man's affectivity, converts him to passion as if by contagion; he wants to have what he sees has been obtained by another, attempts to imitate the young beau . . . and fails deplorably].

22. *Molière ou le prix des choses,* 50.

23. Barbara Johnson, "Teaching Ignorance: *L'Ecole des femmes,*" *Yale French Studies* 63 (1982): 175.

24. Richard Goodkin, "Molière and Bakhtin: Discourse and the Dialogic in *L'Ecole des femmes,*" *Papers on French Seventeenth Century Literature* 21 (1994): 155.

25. François de La Rochefoucauld, *Oeuvres complètes,* ed. L. Martin-Chauffier (Paris: Gallimard, 1964), 412.

26. See Antoine Adam, *Histoire,* 3:284.

27. Bossuet was shocked that Molière "étale cependant au plus grand jour les avantages d'une infâme tolérance dans les maris" (*Maximes et réflexions sur la comédie,* in *Oeuvres complètes,* ed. F. Lachat [Paris: Louis Vivès, 1875], 27:27) [displays in the full light of day the advantages of a foul tolerance on the part of husbands].

28. Until 1734, all editions have Arnolphe say "Oh!" It is, however, certain that when Molière played the role of Arnolphe, the last word he spoke was "Ouf!" (*OC* 1:1281–82).

CHAPTER 3. ENEMY BROTHERS

1. Andrew McKenna shows how difference inspires laughter in *Tartuffe*: "Molière, through his characters' relations with one another, teaches us . . . to laugh when we take ourselves too seriously" ("Laughter and Difference in *Tartuffe*," in *Approaches to Teaching Molière: Tartuffe and Other Plays*, ed. James F. Gaines and Michael S. Koppisch [New York: Modern Language Association of America, 1990], 49).

2. Unless otherwise indicated, the source of translations of passages from *Le Tartuffe* is Molière, The Misanthrope, Tartuffe, *and Other Plays*, trans. Maya Slater (Oxford: Oxford University Press, 2001). Reprinted by permission of Oxford University Press.

3. Descartes speaks of "la puissance de bien juger, et distinguer le vrai d'avec le faux, qui est proprement ce qu'on nomme le bons sens ou la raison" (*Discours de la méthode*, ed. Etienne Gilson [Paris: Librairie Philosophique J. Vrin, 1947], 2) [the power to judge correctly and distinguish the true from the false, which is properly what one calls good sense or reason].

4. For Jacques Guicharnaud, the behavior of Elmire and her allies becomes the norm against which the audience makes judgments about the actions of characters in the play (*Molière: une aventure théâtrale*, 23).

5. See Judd Hubert, *Molière and the Comedy of Intellect*, 101–2.

6. Among critics who share this view, see, for example, Jacques Guicharnaud (*Molière: une aventure théâtrale*, 28) and Jacques Scherer, for whom the entire play is founded upon "la croyance à l'efficacité de la distinction du vrai et du faux" (*Structures de Tartuffe* [Paris: Société d'Edition d'Enseignement Supérieur, 1967], 101) [belief in the efficacy of the distinction between what is true and what is false].

7. Tartuffe's appetite, according to Jules Brody, reflects a more general character flaw: "What Molière denounces in Tartuffe's demeanor and behavior is an all-encompassing acquisitive appetite that makes of him the exemplary, hyperbolic enemy of the reigning social order" ("Love in *Tartuffe*, Tartuffe in Love," in *Approaches to Teaching Molière: Tartuffe and Other Plays*, 47). Larry Riggs relates Tartuffe's insatiable appetite to his speech: "Clearly, too much comes out of his mouth too fast. His 'appetite' for speaking in an imposing way is as excessive as are his other appetites. His motives are betrayed as much by his talk as by his eating habits" (*Molière and Plurality: Decomposition of the Classicist Self* [New York: Peter Lang, 1984], 176).

8. Michel Serres, *The Parasite*, trans. Lawrence R. Schehr (Baltimore: Johns Hopkins University Press, 1982), 201.

9. Ibid., 202. Michel Serres's richly suggestive essay follows in a line of readings that have emphasized Tartuffe's parasitic quality. Marcel Gutwirth reminds his readers that "In comedy, the parasite can boast an ancient pedigree" ("*Tartuffe* and the Mysteries," *PMLA* 92 [1977], 35). Among those for whom Tartuffe's parasitic nature has stood out are Henry Carrington Lancaster (*A History of French Literature in the Seventeenth Century*, 9 vols. [Baltimore: Johns Hopkins University Press; London: Humphrey Milford, Oxford University Press; Paris: Les Belles-Lettres, 1929–42], pt. 3, 2:628) and Jacques Guicharnaud (*Molière: une aventure théâtrale*, 78). Ronald Tobin calls Tartuffe a "ver parasite qui mine la maison de l'intérieur" ("Tartuffe, texte sacré," in *Mélanges Jacques Scherer* [Paris: Nizet, 1986], 379) [a parasitic worm that undermines the house from the inside].

10. Michel Serres, *The Parasite*, 185.

11. James F. Gaines, *Social Structures in Molière's Theater* (Columbus: Ohio State University Press, 1984), 199.

12. See Ralph Albanese, *Le Dynamisme de la peur*, 137.

13. Larry Riggs says the same of *L'Avare*'s Harpagon: "In his unbridled ambition and his fear of the same ambition in others, he *is* an absolutist" ("The *Régime* of Substitutions: Panoptical Gluttony in the Modern, 'Manageable' World of *L'Avare*," *Romanic Review* 88 [1998]: 558).

14. *Men and Masks*, 102. Mitchell Greenberg's quite different, psychoanalytical reading of Orgon emphasizes the character's need for something like the self-sufficiency that Lionel Gossman has in mind: Orgon's desire is "on a metaphysical level, the desire to find an integrity of being, an apprehension of the self as entire that is, in diverse ways, essential to all of Molière's (male) protagonists" (*Subjectivity and Subjugation in Seventeenth-Century Drama and Prose: The Family Romance of French Classicism* [Cambridge: Cambridge University Press, 1992], 122).

15. This in itself would not be significant were the word "maître" not used repeatedly in reference to Tartuffe.

16. See *OC* 1:1159.

17. See Michel Serres, *The Parasite*, 206.

18. Jean de La Bruyère, *Les Caractères ou les moeurs de ce siècle*, ed. Robert Garapon (Paris: Garnier, 1962), 408. The chapter and the number of the passage cited are indicated in the text.

19. *Les Caractères*, 409.

20. Erich Auerbach, "The Faux Dévot," in *Mimesis*, trans. Willard R. Trask (Princeton: Princeton University Press, 1953), 362.

21. With Auerbach's essay as a backdrop, Marc Escola compares Onuphre and Tartuffe, concluding that La Bruyère's portrait weakens the boundary between *fausse dévotion* [hypocrisy] and piety, because Onuphre must play the role with such perfection. *Tartuffe* stirred up trouble among religious fanatics, but with his portrait of Onuphre, La Bruyère was on riskier ground yet ("Vrai caractère du faux dévot: Molière, La Bruyère et Auerbach," *Poétique* 98 [1994]:181–98).

22. Patrick Dandrey speaks of an "étrange osmose" [a strange osmosis] between the two men. Tartuffe and Orgon absorb each other: "Faut-il . . . continuer à parler de complémentarité et de réciprocité à l'intérieur du couple formé par les deux compères? Cette interprétation, en fait, paraît presque grossière, et trop superficielle: quand la complémentation tourne à l'assimilation l'une à l'autre des deux parties, c'est plutôt de reflet qu'il s'agit" (*Molière ou l'esthétique du ridicule*, 383) [Should we . . . continue to speak of complementarity and reciprocity within the couple constituted by the two accomplices? In fact, this interpretation seems almost crude and too superficial: when being complementary moves toward the mutual assimilation of the two parties, what we have is reflection rather than complementarity].

23. "Orgon is as much Tartuffe's creator as Tartuffe is himself" (*Men and Masks*, 110).

24. See Tadeusz Kowzan, "*Le Tartuffe* de Molière dans la mise en scène de Roger Planchon," *La Voie de la Création Théâtrale* 6 (1978): 311.

25. The "Lettre sur la comédie de l'*Imposteur*" confirms this. Molière, it declares, "a appris d'Aristote qu'il n'est rien de plus sensible que d'être méprisé par ceux que l'on estime, et qu'ainsi c'était la dernière corde qu'il fallait faire jouer, jugeant bien que le bonhomme souffrirait plus impatiemment d'être traité de ridicule et de fat par le saint frère, que de lui voir cajoler sa femme jusqu'au bout" (*OC* 1:1164) [learned from Aristotle that nothing is more painful than being

scorned by those whom one esteems highly, and that this was, therefore, the last indignity that would have to be inflicted upon him. For the simple fellow would more patiently endure watching his wife be seduced than being treated as ridiculous and foolish by his holy brother].

26. Tadeusz Kowzan, "*Le Tartuffe* de Molière dans la mise en scène de Roger Planchon," 317.

27. Henry Carrington Lancaster (*A History of French Literature in the Seventeenth Century*, pt. 3, 2:627) and Jacques Scherer (*Structures de* Tartuffe, 118), among others, agree fundamentally with this assessment of Elmire's character.

28. *Le Dynamisme de la peur*, 125.

29. *Men and Masks*, 135.

30. "Laughter and Difference in *Tartuffe*," 54–55.

31. John Cairncross, "Impie en médecine," *Cahiers de l'Association Internationale des Etudes Françaises* 16 (1964): 36; Henry Carrington Lancaster, *A History of French Literature in the Seventeenth Century*, pt. 3, 2:630.

32. *Structures de* Tartuffe, 132.

33. This reading coincides with Andrew McKenna's brief comments on the quarrel between the lovers ("Laughter and Difference in *Tartuffe*," 56).

34. Marc Fumaroli's description in his book on La Fontaine of the publicity mongering of Louis XIV and his ministers makes it difficult to imagine how a successful writer of the period could avoid indulging in royal flattery from time to time (*Le Poète et le roi: Jean de La Fontaine et son siècle* [Paris: Editions de Fallois, 1997], 245–49).

Chapter 4. "Grand Seigneur méchant homme"

1. See Jean Rousset, *Le Mythe de Don Juan* (Paris: Armand Colin, 1978), 5–7.

2. Jean-Marie Teyssier contends that "Dom Juan et Sganarelle ne parlent pas une seule fois de la Statue du Commandeur dans les scènes qui suivent son intervention" (*Réflexions sur le "Dom Juan" de Molière* [Paris: Nizet, 1970], 13) [Dom Juan and Sganarelle do not speak even once about the statue of the Commandeur in the scenes following its appearance]. Although this is not exactly accurate (see 4.1), the Statue's appearances are passed over with less commentary from the characters than might reasonably be expected.

3. George Couton calls it a "placet" (*OC* 2:20) [petition]. Jacques Scherer (*Sur le* Dom Juan *de Molière* [Paris: Société d'Edition d'Enseignement Supérieur, 1966], 32–33) and Georges Forestier ("Langage dramatique et langage symbolique dans le *Dom Juan* de Molière," in *Molière: Dom Juan*, ed. Pierre Ronzeaud [Paris: Klincksieck, 1993], 169–70) also mention the strong link between the two plays. That *Tartuffe* and *Dom Juan* are closely related has been widely recognized by critics. The editors of the Grands Ecrivains de la France edition of Molière say that Dom Juan "devint sans peine un autre Tartuffe" [easily became another Tartuffe]; the later *Dom Juan* is to its predecessor "comme une suite, un redoublement" (Molière, *Oeuvres*, ed. Eugène Despois and Paul Mesnard, 13 vols. [Paris: Hachette, 1877–1900], 5:35) [like a continuation, an intensified repetition].

4. Georges Couton maintains that Dom Juan makes a profession of faith, like members of a religious order: "Dom Juan fait en effet 'profession' d'hypocrisie, et si l'on se rappelle le sens religieux du mot profession, qui désigne les voeux du novice entrant en religion, on se dit que Dom Juan est entré dans une manière d'anti-Église, une Église infernale dont Satan est le chef" (*OC* 2:20) [Dom Juan

makes a "profession" of hypocrisy, and if we recall the religious meaning of the word "profession," which refers to the vows of a novice entering the religious life, we see that Dom Juan has joined a kind of anti-Church, an infernal Church whose head is Satan].

5. The source of translations of passages from *Dom Juan* is Molière, *Tartuffe and Other Plays*, trans. Donald M. Frame (New York: New American Library, 1967).

6. According to Antoine Adam, Molière already takes revenge on his pious enemies with *Tartuffe* (*Histoire*, 3:333). Jacques Guicharnaud makes a strong point of the polemical nature of Dom Juan's turn to hypocrisy (*Molière: une aventure théâtrale*, 294).

7. Lionel Gossman analyzes this with typical precision: "It is because he is so absolutely free and so absolutely unique, so independent of any slavish obedience to common standards and so utterly self-sufficient—so Dom Juan would like people to think—that he cannot be captured and examined and judged as ordinary mortals are. The truth, however, is the very opposite of this. All the apparent contradictions in Dom Juan's behavior can be accounted for quite satisfactorily in the light of an obsessional preoccupation with others which he refuses to admit, since to admit it would be to deny the very image of himself that he is preoccupied to create in others" (*Men and Masks*, 42).

8. Ibid., 42.

9. "What Dom Juan makes perfectly clear is that . . . his desire for Done Elvire was a mediated one, a desire that was inspired in him by jealousy of and rivalry with the object of Elvire's devotion, in this instance, God" (ibid., 43–44). Kathryn A. Hoffmann believes that "Molière's Dom Juan is the most audacious of all the Don Juans, for his envy of the Christian god is the greatest" (*A Society of Pleasures: Interdisciplinary Readings in Pleasure and Power during the Reign of Louis XIV* [New York: St. Martin's Press, 1997], 74).

10. *Molière ou le prix des choses: morale, économie et comédie*, 182.

11. *Men and Masks*, 37.

12. Roxanne Decker Lalande comments that in *Dom Juan* "women are viewed as essentially interchangeable" (*Intruders in the Play World: The Dynamics of Gender in Molière's Comedies* [Madison: Fairleigh Dickinson University Press, 1996], 60). Jean-Marie Apostolidès remarks that "elles s'équivalent toutes" (*Le Prince sacrifié* [Paris: Editions de Minuit, 1985], 168) [one is as good as the other]. Max Vernet extends this idea: "L'équivalence des femmes est même la condition fondamentale de la séduction. . . . Tout le travail de la séduction consiste donc à réduire au même, pour pouvoir s'ennuyer, pour pouvoir repartir vers le divers" (*Molière: côté jardin, côté cour*, 285) [The equal value of all women is the fundamental condition of seduction. . . . All the work of seduction consists, therefore, in reducing everything to sameness, in order to be bored, then to be able to set out again toward difference].

13. Blaise Pascal, *Pensées et opuscules*, ed. Léon Bruschvicg (Paris: Hachette, n.d.), 390. All citations from the *Pensées* will be taken from this edition. Fragment numbers will be indicated in the text.

14. Sganarelle is present in twenty-six of the twenty-seven scenes (Guicharnaud, *Molière: une aventure théâtrale*, 183).

15. Jacques Scherer refers to Dom Juan and Sganarelle as the play's "seul couple indissoluble" (*Sur le Dom Juan de Molière*, 83) [only indissoluble couple].

16. To Jacques Guicharnaud, "il est évident que son crime consiste aussi à nous faire perdre la notion fondamentale de la distinction du vrai et du faux" (*Molière:*

une aventure théâtrale, 232) [it is clear that his crime also consists in making us lose the fundamental notion of the distinction between truth and falsehood].

17. Lionel Gossman notes that "Behind the bravura and independence of Dom Juan is in fact a slavish preoccupation with the opinions others have of him. . . . he is utterly dependent on the opinion of others for his entire existence" (*Men and Masks*, 38).

18. Ralph Albanese, "Dynamisme social et jeu individuel dans *Dom Juan*," *L'Esprit Créateur* 36 (1996): 57.

19. Adam, *Histoire*, 3:334.

20. Patrick Dandrey, *Dom Juan ou la critique de la raison comique* (Paris: Honoré Champion, 1993), 22–23.

21. *Molière: une aventure théâtrale*, 184; Ronald Tobin, Tarte à la crème. *Comedy and Gastronomy in Molière's Theater* (Columbus: Ohio State University Press, 1990), 48.

22. Michel Serres, "Apparition d'Hermès: *Dom Juan*," in *Hermès I. La Communication* (Paris: Editions de Minuit, 1968), 234–35.

23. *Men and Masks*, 48–49.

24. Patrick Dandrey discusses at some length the medical aspects of this and other scenes (*La Médecine et la maladie dans le théâtre de Molière*, 2 vols. [Paris: Klincksieck, 1998], 1:245–324).

25. *Men and Masks*, 54–55.

26. See *OC* 2:1312.

27. According to Shoshana Felman, "the Donjuanian belief in arithmetic is atheological in that it deconstructs, above all, the hierarchical value of the 'first'" (*The Literary Speech Act: Don Juan with J. L. Austin, or Seduction in Two Languages*, trans. Catherine Porter [Ithaca: Cornell University Press, 1983], 37). Dom Juan's goal, of course, is to institute a new hierarchy in which he can himself be first.

28. See Jules Brody, "*Dom Juan* and *Le Misanthrope*," 559.

29. *Oeuvres complètes*, 58.

30. Gérard Defaux characterizes Dom Juan's hypocrisy as a transformation by which "il s'est résolu à devenir Tartuffe, à jouer le jeu de la société, à se fondre dans la grisaille et l'anonymat de la grimace ambiante" (*Molière ou les métamorphoses du comique: de la comédie morale au triomphe de la folie* [Lexington: French Forum Publishers, 1980], 155) [he made up his mind to become Tartuffe, to play society's game, to blend into the gray monotone and the anonymity of the hypocritical grimace on every face].

31. Dom Juan's using Sganarelle in this fashion is a sign of the master's total degradation: "By his adoption of hypocrisy, Dom Juan increases his dependence on Sganarelle. Henceforth he is absolutely bound to his servant, for his whole being now depends on Sganarelle's recognition of it. Dom Juan is thus degraded to the level of an actor who pays the lowest persons in society to watch his performance" (*Men and Masks*, 62).

CHAPTER 5. THE WORLD TURNED UPSIDE DOWN

1. Unless otherwise indicated, the source of translations of passages from *Amphitryon* is Molière, *Amphitryon*, trans. Richard Wilbur (New York: Harcourt Brace & Company, 1995).

2. See *OC* 2:351–52.

3. Molière, *Oeuvres*, 6:313–16.

4. See *OC* 2:351.

5. *Molière ou les métamorphoses du comique*, 213.

6. Charles Daremberg and Edmond Saglio describe the role of Jupiter as the guarantor of order in the universe: "Zeus, principe de tout ordre et de toute règle, est en particulier le dieu de l'ordre social; il préside aux multiples rapports entre les hommes, à la vie de la famille et à la vie publique, à l'hospitalité, aux traités" [Zeus, the source of all order and every rule, is especially the god of social order; he presides over the multiple relations among men, family and public life, hospitality, and treaties]. Ironically, he also presides over "naissances légitimes" [legitimate births] and "protège, avec Héra, déesse des justes noces, la sainteté du lien conjugal" (*Dictionnaire des antiquités grecques et romaines*, 5 vols. [Paris: Hachette, 1881–1918], 3: pt. 1, 694) [with Hera, goddess of just weddings, protects the sanctity of the conjugal bond].

7. Paisley Livingston considers that "as Molière's career progresses the conflictual situations become more and more intricate, yet the disease is always a disruption of social mechanisms brought by rivalry" ("Comic Treatment: Molière and the Farce of Medicine," *MLN* 94 [1979]: 678).

8. Plautus has Mercury specify that these distinguishing marks will be visible only to the audience, not to members of the household (*Plautus*, trans. Paul Nixon, 5 vols. [London: William Heinemann; Cambridge: Harvard University Press, 1916–38], 1:14). My colleague Wm. Blake Tyrrell has suggested to me that the typical audience of Plautus's time required this kind of concession in order to be able to follow the action of the play. By making his gods indistinguishable from the humans they imitate, Molière engages his audience in the dilemma of his characters.

9. René Girard discusses the literary use of twins to represent mimetic desire and notes that the myth of the doubles Amphitryon and Jupiter has this advantage over stories of twins, namely, that it attributes to desire its rightful importance, whereas in tales about twins, problems of identity are more often than not caused by an accident of birth ("Comedies of Errors: Plautus—Shakespeare—Molière," in *American Criticism in the Poststructuralist Age*, ed. Ira Konigsberg [Ann Arbor: Michigan Studies in the Humanities, 1981], 77).

10. Molière, *Oeuvres complètes*, ed. Robert Jouanny, 2 vols. (Paris: Garnier, 1962), 2:1186.

11. Pierre Corneille, *Oeuvres complètes*, ed. Georges Couton, 3 vols. (Paris: Gallimard, 1980–87), 1:924. This is not the kind of meditative introversion for which Montaigne would have humankind reserve and nurture a personal "arrière-boutique" [back shop]. In Auguste's speech, desire is always—"toujours"—there, and having reached a summit, the "esprit . . . aspire à descendre."

12. The source of this translation is Paul Landis, ed., *Six Plays by Corneille and Racine* (New York: Modern Library, 1959), 79.

13. Despois and Mesnard hold that the omission would have been incomprehensible to the ancients—"La légende des deux serpents omise, la pièce, pour eux, eût été décapitée"—but "Sur notre théâtre, le point de vue s'est déplacé" (*Oeuvres*, 6:337) [Without the legend of the two serpents, the play, for them, would have been missing a crucial part. In the French play, the point of view has been shifted].

14. Jacques Scherer cites this same verse and points out that to steal Sosie's name is to steal his very being ("Dualités d'*Amphitryon*," in *Molière: Stage and Study. Essays in Honor of W. G. Moore*, ed. W. D. Howarth and Merlin Thomas [Oxford: Clarendon Press, 1973], 193).

15. *Pensées et opuscules*, 400.
16. *Men and Masks*, 13.
17. The text of Plautus reads: "[N]eque lac lactis magis est simile quam ille ego similest mei" (*Plautus*, 1:62, 63) [One drop of milk is no more like another than that I is like me].
18. Speaking of Molière's earliest works, Joseph Pineau refers to jealousy as an aspect of "ce qui ne tardera pas à s'épanouir dans les oeuvres de leur auteur" (*Le Théâtre de Molière: une dynamique de la liberté*, 12) [what will not be long in blossoming in their author's works].
19. Ronald W. Tobin offers another indication of the breakdown of order and good sense in Amphitryon's futile call for justice at play's end: "The supposition that the gods will render an eye for an eye is, of course, ironic and, in fact, refuted by the context; that is, integrity, truth, and faithfulness have no special power to attract the protection of the gods. Morality . . . disintegrates at this point" (*Tarte à la crème*, 80).

CHAPTER 6. DARK COMEDY

1. Jean-Jacques Rousseau, *Lettre à Mr. d'Alembert sur les spectacles*, ed. M. Fuchs (Lille: Giard; Geneva: Droz, 1948), 46.
2. Ibid., 47.
3. Louis Bourdaloue, "Sermon sur l'impureté" (Dimanche de la 3ᵉ semaine de Carême), in *Oeuvres complètes*, 4 vols. (Paris: Louis Vivès, 1890), 1:360–61.
4. Translations of passages from *George Dandin* are by the author.
5. Ralph Albanese, "Solipsisme et parole dans *George Dandin*," *Romance Quarterly* 27 (1980): 424.
6. *Men and Masks*, 153.
7. Ibid., 154.
8. Lionel Gossman observes that Dandin "does not seek to be recognized as a person, as George Dandin, but as Monsieur de la Dandinière, and he does not revere the Sotenvilles for what they are, he reveres only their name. In the second place, the Sotenvilles are in the same position. They are not respectors of persons" (*Men and Masks*, 153).
9. Ralph Albanese sees *George Dandin* as "un véritable drame de l'incommunicabilité" [a real drama of incommunicability] and emphasizes "l'effondrement de la communication entre les interlocuteurs et ce personnage [Dandin]" ("Solipsisme et parole dans *George Dandin*," 428) [the breaking down of communication between the character and his interlocutors].
10. As René Girard states, "La vengeance constitue donc un processus infini, interminable. Chaque fois qu'elle surgit en un point quelconque d'une communauté elle tend à s'étendre et à gagner l'ensemble du corps social. Elle risque de provoquer une véritable réaction en chaîne aux conséquences rapidement fatales dans une société de dimensions réduites. La multiplication des représailles met en jeu l'existence même de la société. C'est pourquoi la vengeance fait partout l'objet d'un interdit très strict" (*La Violence et le sacré* [Paris: Grasset, 1972], 31) [Vengeance, therefore, sets up an infinite, endless process. Each time it looms up at any spot whatsoever in a community, it tends to spread and take over the entirety of the social body. It runs the risk of inducing a veritable chain reaction with consequences that rapidly become fatal in a society of limited size. The multi-

plication of reprisals puts at stake the society's very existence. That is why vengeance is everywhere strictly prohibited].

11. It is not without interest that the victim's compliance to his fate was an imperative of sacrifice among the ancient Greeks. See Wm. Blake Tyrrell and Frieda S. Brown, *Athenian Myths and Institutions. Words in Action* (New York: Oxford University Press, 1991), 76–79.

12. See *OC* 2:1382–83.

13. *La Violence et le sacré*, 27.

CHAPTER 7. "J'AI DÉCOUVERT QUE MON PÈRE EST MON RIVAL"

1. The source of translations of passages from *L'Avare* is Molière, *Comedies*, trans. Donald M. Frame (Franklin Center, Pa.: Franklin Library, 1985). This edition was published by arrangement with Penguin Group (USA) Inc., which has kindly granted permission to use Donald Frame's translation.

2. Molière, *L'Avare*, ed. Louis Lacour (Paris: Librairie des Bibliophiles, 1876), vii.

3. *Lettre à Mr. d'Alembert sur les spectacles*, 47.

4. Georges Couton compares the two plays in his introduction to *L'Avare* (*OC* 2:508–9).

5. Patrick Dandrey reads *L'Avare* differently but also sees the great distance separating Molière from Plautus (*Molière ou l'esthétique du ridicule*, 97).

6. "Anxious about his gold, Euclio hides it outside the house. Everything he does having been witnessed, a rascally servant of the girl's assailant [Lyconides] steals it. His master informs Euclio of it, and receives from him gold, wife, and son." (Euclio's daughter Phaedria is already pregnant by Lyconides, whence the son.) Both the original text and the translation are from *Plautus*, 1:232–33.

7. The stage directions in the translation emphasize the similarity of the characters' words.

8. Barbara Piqué highlights the similarities between Harpagon and his son in the introduction to her edition of *L'Avare*: "Le contraste entre Cléante et Harpagon, en effet, ne traduit pas seulement une diversité d'âge et de mentalité: il trahit également une parenté étroite" (Molière, *L'Avare*, ed. Barbara Piqué [Genoa: Cideb Editrice, 1996], xviii) [The contrast between Cléante and Harpagon, as a matter of fact, not only conveys a difference in age and mentality. It also betrays a close relationship]. She attributes Cléante's behavior to his youth, emphasizing that "il reste avant tout un jeune homme de vingt-cinq ans" (ibid., xix) [he remains above all a young man twenty-five years old].

9. As Max Vernet writes, "La violence des paroles échangées entre Cléante et Harpagon est l'exemple le plus clair de la dissolution des liens sociaux et du caractère conflictuel de l'indifférenciation" (*Molière: côté jardin, côté cour*, 323) [The violence of the words exchanged by Cléante and Harpagon is the clearest example of the dissolution of social ties and the conflictual character of the absence of differentiation].

10. See, for example, Despois and Mesnard: "Molière, à l'exemple de Plaute, a cru qu'en cet endroit un peu d'exagération ne dépassait pas les droits de la comédie. Autrement peut-être, la scène risquait-elle d'être trop voisine du tragique" (Molière, *Oeuvres*, 7:175) [Molière, following the example of Plautus, believed that in this spot, a bit of exaggeration was not unjustified in comedy. Otherwise, perhaps, the scene might border too much on tragedy].

11. As Georges Couton puts it, "Cela pue à la fois l'argent et le cadavre" (*OC* 2:513) [That reeks of money and death at the same time].

12. The equation of murder and robbery is repeatedly made by Harpagon. It appears first in his monologue in act 4 and twice in the fifth act (5.3 and 5.5).

13. For Judd Hubert, "the dénouement is hardly convincing, nor is it meant to be." Rather than being a weakness, however, the artificiality of the ending "expresses [Molière's] fundamentally ironic attitude" ("Theme and Structure in *L'Avare*," *PMLA* 75 [1960], 32, 36).

CHAPTER 8. IMPOSSIBLE DESIRE

1. Jean-Léonor Le Gallois, sieur de Grimarest, *La Vie de M. de Molière*, ed. Georges Mongrédien (Paris: Michel Brient, 1955), 113.

2. Georges Mongrédien casts doubt on the story by pointing out a mistake in Grimarest's account: between the play's first and second performances, only two days elapsed, not five, as Grimarest says (ibid., 113). Mongrédien also thinks it improbable that members of the court would criticize the Turkish ceremony, which the king himself had suggested to Molière. The editors of the Grands Ecrivains de la France edition of Molière see the story as "une anecdote trop souvent répétée sur la foi de Grimarest, si coutumier de recueillir de douteuses légendes ou même d'en imaginer" (*Oeuvres*, 8:6–7) [too often repeated on the faith of Grimarest, who was in the habit of gathering up doubtful legends or even of inventing them].

3. *La Vie de M. de Molière*, 113.

4. Ibid.

5. Ibid., 114.

6. The source of translations of passages from *Le Bourgeois gentilhomme* is Molière, *Comedies*, trans. Donald M. Frame (Franklin Center, Pa.: Franklin Library, 1985). This edition was published by arrangement with Penguin Group (USA) Inc., which has kindly granted permission to use Donald Frame's translation.

7. Jean de La Fontaine, *Selected Fables*, trans. Christopher Wood, ed. Maya Slater (Oxford: Oxford University Press, 1995), 202. The translation is also from this edition. Marc Fumaroli cites this passage to illustrate the difference between the community in which La Fontaine circulated and felt at ease and that of the court (*Le Poète et le roi: Jean de La Fontaine et son siècle* [Paris: Editions de Fallois, 1997], 383).

8. Mongrédien's note on this comment indicates that Grimarest is mistaken here: "Cette représentation, au Palais-Royal, fut en réalité la première; elle eut lieu le 11 *mars* et non le 11 *mai* 1672. Grimarest aura mal lu la notice de l'édition 1682 ou aura été victime d'une faute d'impression" (*La Vie de M. de Molière*, 116) [This performance at the Palais-Royal was, in fact, the first; it took place on 11 *March* and not 11 *May* 1672. Grimarest must have either misread the introductory notice in the 1682 edition or fallen prey to a misprint]. Grimarest did, nonetheless, seem keen to repeat the story of the king's delayed reaction to a production and Molière's different response on this occasion.

9. *Histoire*, 3:379, 383.

10. *Molière and the Comedy of Intellect*, 219.

11. Gérard Defaux, "Rêve et réalité dans *Le Bourgeois gentilhomme*," *XVIIᵉ Siècle* 117 (1997): 19–20.

12. *Histoire*, 3:379.

13. *Molière and the Comedy of Intellect*, 218.

14. As Harold Knutson writes, "Jourdain has little genuine affection for his Marquise; she is rather a vehicle, interchangeable with any other, for the promotion of his noble self-image: gentlemen indulge in *galanteries*, so he must" (*Molière: An Archetypal Approach* [Toronto: University of Toronto Press, 1976], 111).

15. Jourdain endorses the young couple's marriage while under the spell cast by the Turkish ceremony and in the belief that Lucile is about to marry the "fils du Grand Turc" [son of the Grand Turk]. Still, his *"affectation* bears good fruit and he participates in the positive results of his actions" (Tobin, *Tarte à la crème*, 112). Harold Knutson classifies *Le Bourgeois gentilhomme* among the "heavy father" plays but remarks that "Monsieur Jourdain is notably mild as a heavy father" (*Molière: An Archetypal Approach*, 111).

16. Jules Brody, "Esthétique et société chez Molière," in *Dramaturgie et société: rapports entre l'oeuvre théâtrale, son interprétation et son public au XVIᵉ et XVIIᵉ siècles*, ed. Jean Jacquot, 2 vols. (Paris: Editions du Centre National de Recherche Scientifique, 1968), 1:311.

17. Ronald Tobin believes that the play is archetypal, albeit in a more limited way: "The theme of *affectation*—attempting to become other than what one is— finds its most natural expression, among all of Molière's plays, in the representation of the 'Would-be Gentleman.' From this point of view, *Le Bourgeois gentilhomme* is not only typical of Molière, it is virtually archetypal" (*Tarte à la crème*, 110–11). Hallam Walker adds that in comedy the individual has no hope of victory over the social group and that *Le Bourgeois gentilhomme* "seems to revolve about an idea which partakes powerfully of a basic principle of the comic genre, the principle that the social group or force is the true protagonist which inevitably triumphs" ("Strength and Style in *Le Bourgeois gentilhomme*," *French Review* 37 [1963–64]: 282).

18. The editors of the Grands Ecrivains de la France edition hold that the "marchand" [merchant] must be a "marchand d'étoffes" (*Oeuvres*, 8:115) [fabric merchant]. Georges Couton thinks that "ce pourrait être son 'pourvoyeur'" (*OC* 2:1427) [it could be his supplier].

19. *Histoire*, 3:383.

20. René Girard uses the Maître de Philosophie's violent outburst as the point of departure for a telling comparison of comedy and tragedy ("Comedies of Errors," 121–34). Andrew McKenna begins his discussion of René Girard and Jacques Derrida with Molière's philosopher (*Violence and Difference: Girard, Derrida, and Deconstruction* [Urbana: University of Illinois Press, 1992], 1–26).

21. Despois and Mesnard find the quarrel less fully integrated into the play's plot than a similar scene in *Tartuffe* (*Oeuvres* 8:141). For Robert Nicolich, this scene exemplifies the baroque in *Le Bourgeois gentilhomme* ("Classicism and Baroque in *Le Bourgeois gentilhomme*," *French Review* 45, special no. 4 [1972]: 22). Odette de Mourgues discusses the scene's balletic aspects ("*Le Bourgeois gentilhomme* as a Criticism of Society," in *Molière: Stage and Study. Essays in Honor of W. G. Moore*, ed. W. D. Howarth and Merlin Thomas [Oxford: Clarendon Press, 1972], 174). In Jacques Copeau's commentary, the scene is "un épisode gratuit. Elle n'est point nécessaire à l'action, elle ne sert pas le sujet et ne se rapporte qu'indirectement au caractère central. C'est en quoi elle peut paraître la plus faible de la pièce" (*Registres II. Molière*, ed. André Cabanis [Paris: Gallimard, 1976], 281) [a gratuitous episode. It is not necessary to the action, it does nothing for the subject, and is only indirectly related to the central character. It is for this reason that the scene can seem to be the weakest in the play]. The scene's value for Copeau lies in its recalling to the audience that the play is a *comédie-ballet*.

22. See Hubert, *Molière and the Comedy of Intellect*, 223.

23. It is not certain that Jourdain himself is taken in. There may be some irony in his response to the *garçon tailleur* who calls him "Votre Grandeur": "Ma foi, s'il va jusqu'à l'Altesse, il aura toute la bourse" [My word, if he goes as far as "Your Highness," he'll get the whole purse]. When he does not receive this ultimate honorific, Jourdain says: "Il a bien fait: je lui allais tout donner" (2.5) [A good thing he stopped; I was going to give him the whole thing].

24. André Gide, *Journal 1939–49. Souvenirs* (Paris: Gallimard, 1954), 712.

CHAPTER 9. PHILOSOPHERS AND FOOLS

1. Many critics have remarked upon the structural analogies between *Le Tartuffe* and *Les Femmes savantes*. Gérard Defaux, for example, has called the latter play "cette comédie bâtie sur le modèle de *Tartuffe*" (*Molière ou les métamorphoses du comique*, 28) [this comedy built on the model of *Tartuffe*].

2. Unless otherwise indicated, the source of translations of passages from *Les Femmes savantes* is Molière, The Misanthrope, Tartuffe, *and Other Plays*, trans. Maya Slater (Oxford: Oxford University Press, 2001). Reprinted by permission of Oxford University Press.

3. According to Despois and Mesnard, "tenir son coin" is a "terme du jeu de paume pris au figuré; un joueur, dit Littré, 'tient bien son coin, quand il sait bien soutenir et renvoyer les coups qui viennent de son côté'" (Molière, *Oeuvres*, 9:141) [a tennis term taken in the figurative sense; Littré says that a player "holds up his corner well when he knows how to take on and return the strokes that come to his side"].

4. Pierre Brisson sees this important pattern but does not develop its implications for the play: "La pièce prend ainsi l'allure d'une compétition et se déroule au coup de sifflet. Les adversaires sont répartis en deux groupes symétriques; cinq joueurs dans le camp des Précieux . . . contre cinq joueurs dans le camp des Antiprécieux. L'agressivité est la même de part et d'autre et les deux camps observent la même règle" (*Molière: sa vie dans ses oeuvres*, 19th ed. [Paris: Gallimard, 1942], 276) [The play thus takes on the aspect of a competition and unfolds as if with the blowing of a whistle. The opponents are divided into two symmetrical groups; five players in the camp of the Précieux . . . against five in the camp of the anti-Précieux. The aggressiveness is the same on each side and the two camps observe the same rules].

5. *Histoire*, 3:395.

6. Judd Hubert recognizes that "On the level of the plot, everything depends on whether Chrysale or his wife will be obeyed" (*Molière and the Comedy of Intellect*, 247).

CHAPTER 10. DOCTORS AND ACTORS

1. *Journal 1939–49. Souvenirs*, 82.

2. *Histoire*, 3:396–97.

3. *Molière ou les métamorphoses du comique*, 295. Defaux does not include *L'Avare* in this comparison.

4. Robert Garapon, *Le Dernier Molière* (Paris: Société d'Edition d'Enseigne-

ment Supérieur, 1977), 158; John Cairncross, "Impie en médecine," *Cahiers de l'Association Internationale des Etudes Françaises* 16 (1964): 279–81.

5. Partrick Dandrey, *La Médecine et la maladie dans le théâtre de Molière*, 2 vols. (Paris: Klincksieck, 1998), 2:284.

6. Despois and Mesnard describe this edition in some detail (*Oeuvres*, 9:252–53).

7. *Men and Masks*, 102.

8. Ibid., 67.

9. The source of translations of passages from *Le Malade imaginaire* is Molière, *Comedies*, trans. Donald M. Frame (Franklin Center, Pa.: Franklin Library, 1985). This edition was published by arrangement with Penguin Group (USA) Inc., which has kindly granted permission to use Donald Frame's translation.

10. Ralph Albanese addresses Argan's "insécurité fondamentale" [fundamental insecurity], which he has in common not only with Orgon but with other Molière characters as well ("*Le Malade imaginaiare* ou le jeu de la mort et du hasard," *XVIIe Siècle* 154 [1987]: 4).

11. As James F. Gaines points out, "Argan has hopelessly confused the medical and economic codes, and keeps parallel records of expenses and enemas." Gaines also observes that Argan "is sure that he can buy health just as Orgon attempted to buy salvation by extending charity to Tartuffe" (*Social Structures in Molière's Theater*, 220).

12. "Où est-ce donc que nous sommes? et quelle audace est-ce là à une coquine de servante de parler de la sorte devant son maître?" (1.5) [What are we coming to? And what kind of effrontery is that, for a slut of a maidservant to talk that way in front of her master?].

13. Patrick Dandrey makes the interesting point that Argan's madness "se complique en effet d'un paramètre absent chez tous les autres imaginaires de Molière: c'est que la lubie porte ici sur un objet très particulier . . . *le corps* du sujet désirant et délirant" (*La Médecine et la maladie dans le théâtre de Molière*, 2:286) [is indeed complicated by a parameter absent in all of Molière's other fanciful characters: the whim bears here on a quite particular object . . . *the body* of the desiring and raving subject].

14. Paisley Livingston does not ignore this point in his study of Molière's farcical depiction of medicine ("Comic Treatment: Molière and the Farce of Medicine," *MLN* 94 [1979]: 678).

15. Harold Knutson places emphasis on the presence of the scapegoat in Molière's theater (*Molière: An Archetypal Approach*, 15–16).

16. According to Despois and Mesnard, this stage direction does not appear in all editions of the play (*Oeuvres*, 9:347).

17. Ralph Albanese speaks in psychological terms of Argan's encounter with the doctors, whom he sees as mirror images of Argan ("*Le Malade imaginaire* ou le jeu de la mort et du hasard," 8).

18. *Molière: une aventure théâtrale*, 143.

19. Gérard Defaux's distinction between "la comédie morale" [moral comedy] and a later comedy of a new kind in Molière's theater seems especially pertinent to this question (*Molière ou les métamorphoses du comique*, 300).

20. *Molière: An Archetypal Approach*, 169.

21. Harold Knutson remarks upon the resemblance between Toinette's proposal and a *sparagmos* (ibid., 107).

22. *La Violence et le sacré*, 401–2.

23. Philip R. Berk, "The Therapy of Art in *Le Malade imaginaire*," *French Review* 45, special issue no. 4 (1972): 39.

24. *Pensées et opuscules*, 363.

25. Ibid.

26. Ibid., 366.

27. For Ralph Albanese, Argan's hypochrondia "est une conséquence extrême de sa peur de la maladie et de la mort" ("*Le Malade imaginaire* ou le jeu de la mort et du hasard," 3–4) [is an extreme consequence of his fear of illness and death].

28. Jean Serroy sees Purgon's fear of death as "fondamentale" ("Argan et la mort. Autopsie du malade imaginaire," in *L'Art du théâtre. Mélanges en hommage à Robert Garapon* [Paris: Presses Universitaires de France, 1992], 244) but argues that Molière, to celebrate life in his last play, makes death ridiculous.

29. See Jacques Arnavon, Le Malade imaginaire *de Molière: essai d'interprétation dramatique* (1938; reprint, Geneva: Slatkine Reprints, 1970), 26.

30. Louison plays a minor role in the play, appearing only once. Her greatest importance is to place Argan face to face with death. According to Robert Garapon, among others, Argan is not really taken in by his daughter's feigned death. Nor, however, can he stand the image of death confronting him as his daughter's body goes limp before his eyes (*Le Dernier Molière*, 183).

31. The prominence of death in *Le Malade imaginaire* prompted Gide to see a tragic element in this comedy, which he refers to as "cette farce tragique" (*Journal 1939–49. Souvenirs*, 83) [this tragic farce].

32. *Pensées et opuscules*, 354.

Works Cited

Adam, Antoine. *Histoire de la littérature française au XVIIe siècle*. 5 vols. Paris: del Duca, 1948–56.

Albanese, Ralph. *Le Dynamisme de la peur chez Molière: une analyse socio-culturelle de "Dom Juan," "Tartuffe," et "L'Ecole des femmes"*. University, Miss.: Romance Monographs, Inc., 1976.

———. "Dynamisme social et jeu individuel dans *Dom Juan*." *L'Esprit Créateur* 36 (1996): 50–62.

———. "*Le Malade imaginaire* ou le jeu de la mort et du hasard." *XVIIe Siècle* 154 (1987): 3–15.

———. "Solipsisme et parole dans *George Dandin*." *Romance Quarterly* 27 (1980): 421–34.

Apostolidès, Jean-Marie. *Le Prince sacrifié*. Paris: Editions de Minuit, 1985.

Arnavon, Jacques. *Le Malade imaginaire de Molière: essai d'interprétation dramatique*. 1938. Reprint, Geneva: Slatkine Reprints, 1970.

Auerbach, Erich. "The Faux Dévot." In *Mimesis: The Representation of Reality in Western Literature*, translated by Willard R. Trask, 359–94. Princeton: Princeton University Press, 1953.

Bénichou, Paul. *Man and Ethics: Studies in French Classicism*. Translated by Elizabeth Hughes. Garden City, N.Y.: Doubleday & Company, 1971.

———. *Morales du grand siècle*. Paris: Gallimard, 1948.

Berk, Philip R. "The Therapy of Art in *Le Malade imaginaire*." *French Review* 45, special issue no. 4 (1972): 39–48.

Bossuet, Jacques Bénigne. *Maximes et réflexions sur la comédie*. In *Oeuvres complètes*, edited by F. Lachat. Vol. 27. Paris: Louis Vivès, 1875.

Bourdaloue, Louis. "Sermon sur l'impureté" (Dimanche de la 3e semaine de Carême). In *Oeuvres complètes*. 4 vols. Paris: Louis Vivès, 1890.

Brisson, Pierre. *Molière: sa vie dans ses oeuvres*. 19th ed. Paris: Gallimard, 1942.

Brody, Jules. "*Dom Juan* and *Le Misanthrope*, or the Esthetics of Individualism in Molière." *PMLA* 84 (1969): 559–76.

———. "Esthétique et société chez Molière." In *Dramaturgie et société: rapports entre l'oeuvre théâtrale, son interprétation et son public au XVIe et XVIIe siècles*, edited by Jean Jacquot, 2 vols., 1:307–26. Paris: Editions du Centre National de la Recherche Scientifique, 1968.

———. "Love in *Tartuffe*, Tartuffe in Love." In *Approaches to Teaching Molière's Tartuffe and Other Plays*, edited by James F. Gaines and Michael S. Koppisch, 42–48. New York: Modern Language Association of America, 1995.

Cairncross, John. "Impie en médecine." *Cahiers de l'Association Internationale des Etudes Françaises* 16 (1964): 269–84.

———. *New Light on Molière*. Geneva: Droz; Paris: Minard, 1956.

Copeau, Jacques. *Registres II. Molière*. Edited by André Cabanis. Paris: Gallimard, 1976.

Corneille, Pierre. *Oeuvres complètes*. Edited by Georges Couton. 3 vols. Paris: Gallimard, 1980–87.

Dandrey, Patrick. *Dom Juan ou la critique de la raison comique*. Paris: Honoré Champion, 1993.

———. *La Médecine et la maladie dans le théâtre de Molière*. 2 vols. Paris: Klincksieck, 1998.

———. *Molière ou l'esthétique du ridicule*. Paris: Klincksieck, 1992.

Daremberg, Charles, and Edmond Saglio. *Dictionnaire des antiquités grecques et romaines*. 5 vols. Paris: Hachette, 1881–1918.

Defaux, Gérard. *Molière ou les métamorphoses du comique: de la comédie morale au triomphe de la folie*. Lexington: French Forum Publishers, 1980.

———. "Rêve et réalité dans *Le Bourgeois gentilhomme*." *XVIIe Siècle* 117 (1977): 19–33.

Descartes, René. *Discours de la méthode*. Edited by Etienne Gilson. Paris: Librairie Philosophique J. Vrin, 1947.

———. *Les Passions de l'âme*. Edited by Geneviève Rodis-Lewis. Paris: Librairie Philosophique J. Vrin, 1955.

Doubrovsky, Serge. "Arnolphe ou la chute du héros." *Mercure de France* 343 (1961): 111–18.

Escola, Marc. "Vrai caractère du faux dévot: Molière, La Bruyère et Auerbach." *Poétique* 98 (1994): 181–98.

Felman, Shoshana. *The Literary Speech Act: Don Juan with J. L. Austin, or Seduction in Two Languages*. Translated by Catherine Porter. Ithaca: Cornell University Press, 1983.

Force, Pierre. *Molière ou le prix des choses: morale, économie et comédie*. Paris: Nathan, 1994.

Forestier, Georges. "Langage dramatique et langage symbolique dans le *Dom Juan* de Molière." In *Molière: Dom Juan*, edited by Pierre Ronzeaud, 161–74. Paris: Klincksieck, 1993.

Fumaroli, Marc. *Le Poète et le roi: Jean de La Fontaine et son siècle*. Paris: Editions de Fallois, 1997.

Furetière, Antoine. *Dictionnaire universel*. 3 vols. 1690. Reprint, Geneva: Slatkine Reprints, 1970.

Gaines, James F. "L'Eveil des sentiments et le paradoxe de la conscience dans *L'Ecole des femmes*." *French Review* 70 (1997): 407–15.

———. *Social Structures in Molière's Theater*. Columbus: Ohio State University Press, 1984.

Garapon, Robert. *Le Dernier Molière*. Paris: Société d'Édition d'Enseignement Supérieur, 1977.

Gide, André. *Journal 1939–49. Souvenirs*. Paris: Gallimard, 1954.

Girard, René. "Comedies of Errors: Plautus—Shakespeare—Molière." In *American Criticism in the Poststructuralist Age*, edited by Ira Konigsberg, 66–86. Ann Arbor: Michigan Studies in the Humanities, 1981.

———. *Mensonge romantique et vérité romanesque*. Paris: Grasset, 1961.

———. *La Violence et le sacré*. Paris: Grasset, 1972.

———. "Perilous Balance: A Comic Hypothesis." In *"To Double Business Bound":
Essays on Literature, Myth, Mimesis, and Anthropology*, 121–34. Baltimore: Johns
Hopkins University Press, 1978.

Goodkin, Richard. "Molière and Bakhtin: Discourse and the Dialogic in *L'Ecole
des femmes*." *Papers on French Seventeenth Century Literature* 21 (1994): 145–56.

Gossman, Lionel. *Men and Masks*. Baltimore: Johns Hopkins University Press,
1963.

Greenberg, Mitchell. *Subjectivity and Subjugation in Seventeenth-Century Drama and
Prose: The Family Romance of French Classicism*. Cambridge: Cambridge University Press, 1992.

Grimarest, Jean-Léonor Le Gallois, sieur de. *La Vie de M. de Molière*. Edited by
Georges Mongrédien. Paris: Michel Brient, 1955.

Guicharnaud, Jacques. *Molière: une aventure théâtrale*. Paris: Gallimard, 1963.

Gutwirth, Marcel. "*Dom Garcie de Navarre* et *Le Misanthrope*: de la comédie héroïque au comique du héros." *PMLA* 83 (1968): 118–29.

———. *Molière ou l'invention comique*. Paris: Minard, 1966.

———. "*Tartuffe* and the Mysteries." *PMLA* 92 (1977): 33–40.

———. "Visages d'Alceste." *Oeuvres et critiques* 6 (1981): 77–89.

Hazard, Paul. *La Crise de la conscience européenne 1680–1715*. 3 vols. Paris: Boivin,
1935.

———. *The European Mind (1680–1715)*. Translated by J. Lewis May. London:
Hollis & Carter, 1953.

Hoffmann, Kathryn A. *A Society of Pleasures: Interdisciplinary Readings in Pleasure
and Power during the Reign of Louis XIV*. New York: St. Martin's Press, 1997.

Horowitz, Louise K. "Life in the Slow Lane: Molière's Marginal Men." *Papers on
French Seventeenth Century Literature* 16 (1989): 65–76.

Hubert, Judd D. *Molière and the Comedy of Intellect*. Berkeley and Los Angeles: University of California Press, 1962.

———. "Theme and Structure in *L'Avare*." *PMLA* 75 (1960): 31–36.

Jasinski, René. *Molière et* Le Misanthrope. Paris: Nizet, 1970.

Johnson, Barbara. "Teaching Ignorance: *L'Ecole des femmes*." *Yale French Studies* 63
(1982): 165–82.

Knutson, Harold. *Molière: An Archetypal Approach*. Toronto: University of Toronto
Press, 1976.

Kowzan, Tadeusz. "*Le Tartuffe* de Molière dans la mise en scène de Roger Planchon." *Les Voies de la création théâtrale* 6 (1978): 279–340.

La Bruyère, Jean de. *Characters*. Translated by Henri van Laun. London: Oxford
University Press, 1963.

———. *Les Caractères ou les moeurs de ce siècle*. Edited by Robert Garapon. Paris:
Garnier, 1962.

La Fontaine, Jean de. *Selected Fables*. Translated by Christopher Wood. Edited by
Maya Slater. Oxford: Oxford University Press, 1995.

Lalande, Roxanne. *Intruders in the Play World: The Dynamics of Gender in Molière's
Comedies*. Madison: Fairleigh Dickinson University Press, 1996.

Lancaster, Henry Carrington. *A History of French Literature in the Seventeenth Century*. 9 vols. Baltimore: Johns Hopkins University Press; London: Humphrey
Milford, Oxford University Press; Paris: Les Belles-Lettres, 1929–42.

Landis, Paul, ed. *Six Plays by Corneille and Racine*. New York: Modern Library, 1959.

La Rochefoucauld, François de. *Oeuvres complètes*. Edited by L. Martin-Chauffier. Paris: Gallimard, 1964.

Livingston, Paisley. "Comic Treatment: Molière and the Farce of Medicine." *MLN* 94 (1979): 676–87.

Magné, Bernard. "*L'Ecole des femmes* ou la conquête de la parole." *Revue des Sciences Humaines* 145 (1972): 125–40.

McKenna, Andrew. "Laughter and Difference in *Tartuffe*." In *Approaches to Teaching Molière's* Tartuffe *and Other Plays*, edited by James F. Gaines and Michael S. Koppisch, 49–58. New York: Modern Language Association of America, 1990.

———. *Violence and Difference: Girard, Derrida, and Deconstruction*. Urbana: University of Illinois Press, 1992.

Molière. *Amphitryon*. Translated by Richard Howard. New York: Harcourt Brace & Company, 1995.

———. *L'Avare*. Edited by Louis Lacour. Paris: Librarie des Bibliophiles, 1876.

———. *L'Avare*. Edited by Barbara Piqué. Genoa: Cideb Editrice, 1996.

———. *Comedies*. Translated by Donald M. Frame. Franklin Center, Pa.: Franklin Library, 1985.

———. *Oeuvres*. Edited by Eugène Despois and Paul Mesnard. 13 vols. Grands Ecrivains de la France. Paris: Hachette, 1873–1900.

———. *Oeuvres complètes*. Edited by Georges Couton. 2 vols. Paris: Gallimard, 1971.

———. *Oeuvres complètes*. Edited by Robert Jouanny. 2 vols. Paris: Garnier, 1962.

———. *One-act Comedies of Molière*. Translated by Albert Bermel. Cleveland: World Publishing Company, 1962.

———. *Tartuffe and Other Plays by Molière*. Translated by Donald M. Frame. New York: New American Library, 1967.

———. *The Misanthrope, Tartuffe and Other Plays*. Translated by Maya Slater. Oxford: Oxford University Press, 2001.

Mourgues, Odette de. "*Le Bourgeois gentilhomme* as a Criticism of Society." In *Molière: Stage and Study. Essays in Honor of W. G. Moore*, edited by W. D. Howarth and Merlin Thomas, 170–84. Oxford: Clarendon Press, 1972.

Nicolich, Robert N. "Classicism and Baroque in *Le Bourgeois gentilhomme*." *French Review* 45, special issue no. 4 (1972): 21–30.

Pascal, Blaise. *Pensées et opuscules*. Edited by Léon Brunschvicg. Paris: Hachette, n.d.

Picard, Raymond. *La Carrière de Jean Racine*. Paris: Gallimard, 1961.

Pineau, Joseph. *Le Théâtre de Molière: une dynamique de la liberté*. Paris: Minard, 2000.

Plautus. *Plautus*. Translated by Paul Nixon. 5 vols. London: William Heinemann; Cambridge: Harvard University Press, 1916–38.

Riggs, Larry. "Another Purloined Letter: Text, Transparency, and Transcendence in *Le Misanthrope*." *French Review* 66 (1992): 26–37.

———. "Intimations of Post-Structuralism: Subversion of the Classicist Subject in *Les Femmes savantes* and *Le Tartuffe*." *Literature, Interpretation, Theory* 2 (1990): 59–75.

————. *Molière and Plurality: Decomposition of the Classicist Self*. New York: Peter Lang, 1984.

————. "Molière, Paranoia, and the Presence of Absence." *Cahiers du Dix-Septième* 6(1992): 195–211.

————. "Reason's Text as Palimpsest: Sensuality Subverts 'Sense' in Molière's *Les femmes savantes*." *Papers on French Seventeenth Century Literature* 28 (2001): 93–103.

————. "The *Régime* of Substitutions: Panoptical Gluttony in the Modern, 'Manageable' World of *L'Avare*." *Romanic Review* 88 (1998): 557–69.

Rousseau, Jean-Jacques. *Lettre à Mr. d'Alembert sur les spectacles*. Edited by M. Fuchs. Lille: Giard; Geneva: Droz, 1948.

Rousset, Jean. *Le Mythe de Don Juan*. Paris: Armand Colin, 1978.

Scherer, Jacques. "Dualités d'*Amphitryon*." In *Molière: Stage and Study. Essays in Honor of W. G. Moore*, edited by W. D. Howarth and Merlin Thomas, 185–97. Oxford: Clarendon Press, 1973.

————. *Structures de* Tartuffe. Paris: Société d'Edition d'Enseignement Supérieur, 1966.

————. *Sur le* Dom Juan *de Molière*. Paris: Société d'Edition d'Enseignement Supérieur, 1967.

Scherer, Jacques, and Jacques Truchet, eds. *Théâtre du XVIIᵉ siècle*. 2 vols. Paris: Gallimard, 1975–86.

Serres, Michel. "Apparition d'Hermès: *Dom Juan*." In *Hermès I. La Communication*, 233–45. Paris: Éditions de Minuit, 1968.

————. *The Parasite*. Translated by Lawrence R. Schehr. Baltimore: Johns Hopkins University Press, 1982.

Serroy, Jean. "Argan et la mort. Autopsie du malade imaginaire." In *L'Art du théâtre. Mélanges en hommage à Robert Garapon*, 239–46. Paris: Presses Universitaires de France, 1992.

Sweetser, Marie-Odile. "La Nature et le naturel chez Molière: le cas d'Agnès." In *Thèmes et genres littéraires aux XVIIᵉ et XVIIIᵉ siècles. Mélanges en l'honneur de Jacques Truchet*, edited by Nicole Ferrier-Caverivière, 443–49. Paris: Presses Universitaires de France, 1992.

————. "Structure et signification du *Misanthrope*." *French Review* 49 (1976): 505–13.

————. "Théâtre du monde et monde du théâtre: *Le Misanthrope*." *Le Moliériste* 3 (1996–97): 57–71.

Teyssier, Jean-Marie. *Réflexions sur "Dom Juan" de Molière*. Paris: Nizet, 1970.

Tobin, Ronald. *Tarte à la crème. Comedy and Gastronomy in Molière's Theater*. Columbus: Ohio State University Press, 1990.

————. "Tartuffe, texte sacré." In *Mélanges Jacques Scherer*, 375–82. Paris: Nizet, 1986.

Tyrrell, Wm. Blake, and Frieda S. Brown. *Athenian Myths and Institutions. Words in Action*. New York: Oxford University Press, 1991.

Vernet, Max. *Molière: côté jardin, côté cour*. Paris: Nizet, 1991.

Walker, Hallam. "Strength and Style in *Le Bourgeois gentilhomme*." *French Review* 37 (1963–64): 282–87.

Index